In nontechnical language and in an [obj]ective spirit, Dr. Cohen here provides [ins]ight into the changing patterns of [liv]ing and thinking of three generations [of] American Jews. Beginning with Jew[ish] mass immigration in 1881, this study [ana]lyzes the major sociocultural changes [in] the life of American Jews in the last [nine] decades. These changes are mir[ror]ed in American-Jewish fiction, of [wh]ich Dr. Cohen has made an admirable [sele]ction portraying the experiences and [tran]sformations of Jews during the three [gen]erations of adjustment and integra[tion] into the American society.

The development of Jewish literature [in] America parallels and reflects the [stag]es in the adjustment process of these [gen]erations, and fiction, especially, pro[vide]s source material for sociological re[sear]ch in the areas of occupation, status, [mar]riage, family relationships, Jewish [edu]cation of youth, religion, welfare ac[tivi]ties, and leadership, the patterns of [whi]ch have noticeably changed through [urb]anization, secularization, social mo[bilit]y, and intercultural relationships.

D1085243

Such factors of social change and environmental influence have altered both the structure and the function of the American-Jewish family. The traditional East European authoritarian, patriarchal Jewish family has been replaced by the democratic, equalitarian form of family life. American patterns of dating, courting, mate choosing, and the wedding ceremony have in a measure become accepted. Intermarriage has increased, as has divorce, as traditional family stability has declined. The tendency of second-generation Jews to move into the middle class and the professions started a process of deproletarianization. Lacking a sense of group belonging and a stable set of life definitions, this alienated generation became marginal and tended to self-hatred and hatred of their people. With the rise of the third generation there is evident an increasing sense of group consciousness and a desire for group identification. Consequently, a number of literary works changed from a mood of protest and rejection to one of affirmation.

This book offers a guide and a comprehensive view of contemporary Jewry to all who are concerned with the fundamental issues of the survival of Jewish life and its destiny in America.

Sociocultural Changes in American Jewish Life as Reflected in Selected Jewish Literature

Sociocultural Changes in American Jewish Life as Reflected in Selected Jewish Literature

Bernard Cohen

Rutherford • Madison • Teaneck
Fairleigh Dickinson University Press

Associated University Presses, Inc.
Cranbury, New Jersey 08512

Library of Congress Cataloging in Publication Data

Cohen, Bernard, 1906—
    Sociocultural changes in American Jewish life as reflected in
selected Jewish literature.

    Bibliography: p.
    1. Jews in the United States—Political and social conditions.
    2. Jews in literature. I. Title.
E184.J5C59   301.451'924'073   75-146162
ISBN 0-8386-7848-3

Printed in the United States of America

To the sacred memory of my parents,
Yoel Hersh and Raisel Konopiaty,
and family,
who perished with the six million

and

to the blessed memory of our beloved grandson,
Allan Rosenfeld

Contents

Foreword

by Mordecai M. Kaplan

When some years ago I was a visiting lecturer at the University of Judaism in Los Angeles, Dr. Bernard Cohen showed me his doctoral dissertation, which dealt with the cultural and religious changes American Jewry underwent during the last nine decades, changes reflected in selected literature. I then found reason to congratulate him on his performance. All the more now, now that he has elaborated that study both in detail and depth, and through the publication of it has managed to get its message spread broadcast. Its message is that, thanks for the most part to the Jewish self-hating attitude of the intellectual elite among our Jewish writers, our Jewish masses are likely to become, at best, only marginal Jews, and at worst, drop-outs.

It should therefore be the main function of our spiritual leaders, the rabbis, educators, and social workers, to immunize the Jewish masses against the poison of Jewish self-hate and the derogation of Jewish values. Every member of a congregation should be expected to own a copy of *Sociocultural Changes in American Jewish Life,* and make it a part of his required reading. At the same time, the rabbis should deal with its subject matter in at least one out of every four sermons they preach from the pulpit.

Preface

The central theme of this study is the great change in the life of the American Jewish community in the past nine decades. This transition is traced back to the 1880s, with the first mass immigration of Jews from East European countries marking the beginning of the rise and growth of the great new center of Jewish life, the American Jewish Community of today. In consequence of major social factors operating in the modern American society, the complexion of American Jewry has been thoroughly transformed.

The object of this study is, first, to examine and analyze sociocultural changes in the major areas of life of the American Jew, and second, to find in what manner these changes are reflected in contemporary selected literary works of American Jewish writers. Concerned with the crucial issue of creative survival or assimilation of American Jews as a minority group in the general American society, this study examines the changing sociocultural patterns and tendencies of three generations of American Jews, with reference to their self-awareness, or, sense of alienation, and to the direct relevance of the new patterns to the central problem facing American Jewry: assimilation, or creative survival in the open, assimilative, American society.

This book has grown out of the author's interest, research, and study in the history, sociology, and literature of American Jewry. Originally written as a doctoral dis-

sertation for the Sociology department of the University
of Southern California, it examines and views these cultural changes within the conceptual sociological framework of the processes of urbanization, social mobility,
alienation, marginality, social interaction, culture contact,
and accommodation. The selected literature discussed
here is offered as illustrative of the growth and change
that has shaped contemporary American Jewry.

It is hoped that this book will interest those concerned
with the changing American Jewish community, particularly as the changes are reflected in contemporary Jewish
belle-lettres, and that it will also be useful to secondary
schools and adult education classes. Such a study is most
rewarding if, as the author hopes, it stimulates similar
studies of sociocultural change among other religious or
ethnic groups, as they are reflected in their respective
literatures.

I wish to express my gratitude to those scholars who
read the original manuscript and encouraged its publication, particularly my revered teacher, Professor Mordecai
M. Kaplan; Dr. Will Herberg; Dr. Simon Greenberg, Vice Chancellor of the Jewish Theological Seminary of America; the late Dr. Samuel Margoshes; Dr.
David Lieber, President of the University of Judaism;
the late Dr. Philip R. Goldstein; and my friend and col-
league, Rabbi David Cohen.

I also wish to thank Mrs. Mathilde E. Finch, Associate Editor of Associated University Presses for her
careful checking and editing of the manuscript.

Finally, I owe much to my dear wife, Ethel, without
whose encouragement, patient understanding, and cooperation throughout the years of study and work this book
could not have been completed. I hope that she and our
daughters, Liebe and Eleanor, will feel that their efforts
and sacrifices were justified.

Bernard Cohen

Acknowledgments

I wish to thank the following for their kind cooperation in preparing my manuscript for publication:

Josephine Lewine and Marcia Blend, who typed and
retyped the material. I am especially grateful to Wilma
Schneidermyer, of the English department of California
State College at Los Angeles for her kind assistance in
checking and in preparing the final draft of the manuscript for publication.

I should also like to thank the Estate of Sholem Asch
for permission to reprint selections: from *The Mother*.
Copyright 1937, Sholem Asch. Copyright renewed effec-
tive 1965, Ruth Shaffer, Moses Asch and John Asch.
All rights reserved; from *East River*. Copyright 1946,
Sholem Asch. All rights reserved; from "Uncle Moses"
and "Chaim Lederer's Return," from the book entitled
Three Novels. Copyright 1938, Sholem Asch. Copyright
renewed effective 1966, Ruth Shaffer, Moses Asch and
John Asch. All rights reserved.

I am also grateful to the following publishing houses
for permission to quote from books copyrighted by them:

The Beechurst Press, for excerpts from Charles Angoff's *Journey to the Dawn*, 1951; *The Morning Light*,
1952; and *The Sun at Noon*, 1952.

Thomas Y. Crowell Company, for excerpts from *My
Son the Lawyer* by Henry Denker. Copyright 1950 by

Henry Denker, with permission of the Publisher, Thomas Y. Crowell Company.

Harcourt Brace Jovanovich, Inc., for excerpts from Alfred Kazin's *A Walker in the City*, 1951.

Holt, Rinehart and Winston, Inc. for excerpts from Myron Brinig's *Singermann*, 1929, and *This Man is My Brother*, 1932.

The Jewish Publication Society of America, for excerpts from Ludwig Lewisohn's *The Island Within*, 1940.

The Macmillan Co., for excerpts from Morris R. Cohen, *Reflection of a Wandering Jew*, 1950.

G. P. Putnam's Sons for excerpts from Sholom Asch's *Uncle Moses*, 1938; *The Mother*, 1937; *East River*, 1945; and *Chaim Lederer's Return*, 1938.

Random House, Inc., for excerpts from Budd Schulberg's *What Makes Sammy Run?*, 1952.

Thomas Yoseloff, Publisher, for excerpts from Charles Angoff's *Between Day and Dark*, 1959; *Bitter Springs*, 1961; and *Memory of Autumn*, 1968.

Introduction

Ours is a rapidly changing world. The tempo of its transition, quickened by the rapid advance of technology and science and the dynamic complex character of our urban and industrial mode of life, has turned the past nine decades of the century into a major epoch in the development of human society. And as the life of American society in general is altered in many ways, so is the life of various religious and ethnic groups in process of change.

The Jews, a highly urbanized religious and ethnic minority group in the United States, currently estimated at about 5,869,000 people (less than three percent of our total population)[1] and in size constituting the third major religious group in the United States with its own social organization and cultural group life, have in the last eight decades undergone a profound alteration.

In examining the nature of certain major changes in the sociocultural patterns of the Jews since their mass immigration from Eastern Europe to the United States, as reflected in selected Jewish literature, the following principal areas will be considered: occupation, marriage, family relations, religious observances, Jewish education, social welfare, and community leadership.

The literary works, the source materials for this study,

---

1. Alvin Chenkin, *American Jewish Year Book,* ed. Morris Fine and Milton Himmelfarb, vol. 70 (New York: The American Jewish Committee, the Jewish Publication Society of America, 1969), p. 260.

include selected novels and short stories dealing with the life of the American Jew and were written in Yiddish, Hebrew, and English since the beginning of the mass immigration in the United States in 1881. Some deal primarily with the new problems of adjustment and the experiences of the Jewish immigrant, including the generation gap; others concern the problems of alienation and marginality particularly evident in the thought and behavior patterns of the second generation. All too often these problems expressed themselves in a restlessness leading to self-effacement and hatred of one's people. Works of modern Jewish literature that deal with the experiences and problems of Jews in America provide a deep insight into human character and an authentic record of human experiences and actions resulting from changed social situations. With their help we shall attempt to answer the following questions:

What have been the determining factors of sociocultural change in the life of the Jews in the United States?

How has the social change in American life affected the sociocultural patterns of the immigrant Jew—and those of his children, the second and third generations—in the principal areas of personal and group life?

How has this change influenced the Jew's attitude to the problems of Jewish assimilation and Jewish survival?

How is this multiform change reflected in some of the literary works, especially in prose fiction, by American-Jewish writers?

The period beginning with Jewish mass immigration in 1881 and continuing through the last two decades of the nineteenth century to this day has been one of momentous historical development and has witnessed important social and cultural occurrences in the life of the American Jew. The mass emigration of Jews from East European countries to the North American continent is but the starting point. The rise of the dynamic social movements of labor, socialism and Zionism in the United States, the annihilation of six million European Jews by the Nazis, and the rebirth of the State of Israel are other such events.

These events, and the social changes in the life style and thought of three generations of American Jews, are here viewed within the sociological framework of the processes of migration, industrialization, urbanization, secularization, culture contacts and conflict, and their resultant problems.

The Jewish literature of these periods enables its readers to gain an insight into the social and cultural processes influencing the changing patterns of life of the American Jew. The novels and short stories selected for this study are generally considered true and realistic portrayals of the changing style of Jewish life in America. They are here cited for their sociological implications.

The material for the study was obtained through an intensive examination of the literature, ancient and modern; through study of the cultural heritage, history, and social organization of the Jewish people; and through the author's close familiarity and personal identification with the problems and movements of contemporary American Jewish life.

My sources include more than sixty novels and ten short stories written by American Jews, mostly in English but some in Yiddish and Hebrew. They include historical and sociological studies of the various phases of American Jewish life—the Jewish family, education, religion, community organization, and welfare activities —as well as of the Bible, the Talmud, and Jewish Codes relating to Jewish law and patterns of Jewish living. I have also drawn on classic literary works in Hebrew and in Yiddish written since the latter part of the nineteenth century for their influence on the development of modern Jewish literature in America.

Secondary sources include studies of social change, migration, urbanization, society and literature, the changing family, and ethnic and religious minorities with their problem of survival in the open democratic American society. Commentaries on modern American literature and current developments in the American Jewish community appearing in contemporary periodicals and newspapers have also been utilized.

A few terms in this book are used in a specialized sense. They are:

Culture. The term culture as used in this study includes the behavior patterns and accomplishments that are socially acquired and transmitted. It includes language, literature, religion, folkways and mores, and social institutions.

Social Change. The changing life patterns of American Jews are here viewed as part of the general American society in transition. The phrase *social change* describes changes in group composition, such as age, occupation, mobility, status, and role, and also changes in the process of interaction, such as conflict, cooperation, culture contact, economic adjustment, and the like that characterize inter- and intra-group relations. *Cultural* change on the other hand, refers to changes in individual attitudes and values, mores, folkways, religious ritual, and language.

The data of social characteristics used in this study indicate, as one would expect, that the processes of social and cultural changes are causally connected, that factors of social change often induce cultural change.

In support of this claim Kingsley Davis points out the "close connection between social interaction and social change, for it is mainly through interaction that change comes about."[2]

Social Mobility. Robert E. Park regards social mobility as the very stuff of social change, for with change in residence come basic modifications in occupation, child rearing, religious practices and man's other activities of organized social life.[3]

Pitrim A. Sorokin points out that social mobility results in social change. Social mobility is a state of being susceptible to change. It is seen here as growing out of moving from one locality to another and leads to giving up one set of attitudes and values for another.[4]

Human Interaction. When two or more people communicate and modify each other's behavior, social interaction is taking place. Among the important types of human interaction, or processes of social change, are acculturation, assimilation, and accommodation. The last two, along with cooperation, are called conjunctive social processes.

Assimilation. This term is used in the sense of adoption by a person (or a group) of the culture of another social group, to the extent that that person (or group) loses all culturally distinct characteristics that would identify him with his own cultural or ethnic group and gives up all loyalties to his former group and its culture. Thus, in relation to Jewish group survival in American society, assimilation here denotes the abandonment of Jewish

2. Kingsley Davis, *Human Society* (New York: The Macmillan Company, 1949), p. 623.
3. Robert E. Park, *Research in the Social Sciences,* ed. Wilson Gee (New York: The Macmillan Co., 1924).
4. From Emory S. Bogardus, *Contemporary Sociology,* p. 358. Bogardus refers to Pitrim A. Sorokin, *Social Mobility* (New York: Harper and Brothers, 1927).

group life. This may well lead to the complete disappearance of all differentiating traits, so that the Jewish group will ultimately be swallowed up by the dominant group and disappear.

Accommodation. All of human life is a continual process of adjustment. Individuals within the family and within religious groups, as well as religiocultural ethnic groups within the larger community, are constantly adjusting themselves to one another. Accommodation may be looked upon as agreement to disagree.[5] When one segment of an aggregate accommodates itself to another, there need not be any insistence on uniformity of behavior.

Henry Pratt Fairfield defines accommodation as the process of "alteration of functional relations between personalities and groups so as to avoid, reduce or eliminate conflict and to promote reciprocal adjustment."[6]

In this way it is possible to have in our majority-minority relations a means of integration in the general American culture while retaining the possibility of survival. By accepting the concept of accommodation, which will be discussed in a later chapter, American Jews are enabled to integrate themselves with the larger American culture without losing their religious and cultural heritage and their important cultural patterns.

Social Institution. In this study of change in American-Jewish group life I shall use as a unit of analysis the social institutions, such as the family, the synagogue, and the school. They function to meet the human needs associated with the basic problem of the life of the group.

---

5. Marshall E. Jones, *Basic Sociological Principles* (Boston: Ginn and Company, 1949), pp. 383–84.
6. Henry Pratt Fairfield, "Accommodation," *Dictionary of Sociology* (Ames, Iowa: Littlefield, Adams and Company, 1955), p. 2.

It is through these social institutions that the cultural heritage of the group is transmitted from one generation to another.

Because of the various uses of the term "social institution," it is difficult to define it. Perhaps the best and most concise definition is the one by Sumner: "An institution is a concept plus a structure."[7] By this is meant that institutions involve not only the socially sanctioned patterns of activity to meet and regulate human needs, but also the organizational pattern for their execution.

Social Movement. Social movements, as used in sociological literature, ordinarily grow out of a condition of social unrest and widespread dissatisfaction with existing conditions. As used in this study the term refers to those movements in modern American-Jewish history which endeavor to alter conditions and patterns of existing Jewish group life. They include Zionism, colonization movements, Jewish labor, and the religious movements of reform and conservatism.

Jewish Culture. Living in the different cultures of the Diaspora, Jews have in varying degrees combined elements of the surrounding non-Jewish culture with elements that were regarded by both Jews and their neighbors as essentially Jewish. Jewish culture includes laws and regulations directing the patterns of behavior of all Jews with regard to marriage, family, education of children, business, and relations to non-Jews.

Jewish Literature. In a broader sense Jewish literature include the literary expressions of the Jewish people throughout their long history, the Bible, the Talmud, the vast post-Talmudic literature, and the literary creations

---

7. William Graham Sumner, *Folkways* (Boston: Ginn and Company, 1906), pp. 53 ff.

of Jewish life and lore until today. Here it refers to what Jews living in the United States have written about themselves and their life in any of the languages they have used, Hebrew, Yiddish, or English.

Jewish Community. As used by modern sociologists, a community may be as large as an empire or as small as a village if it is marked by a sense of sharing experiences and the feeling of a common destiny. In the words of R. M. MacIver, "It represents a degree of common living and not a complete boundary of it."[8]

"A community," according to Bogardus, "may extend to all who commune together in the fellowship of similar attitudes and values. To develop a real community of spirit, it is necessary that all the members participate and share a sense of belonging."[9]

Although in most cities today Jewish people are spatially dispersed, they nevertheless maintain a community of interests and activities. Thus *Jewish community* as used here is used in the psychosocial sense, in terms of the social interaction of the people within the group, implying the notion of "consciousness of kind" and the "we" feeling, rather than mere spatial proximity.

American Jewry. First, a definition must be given of the term *Jew,* for there are a variety of opinions on this. The term will be used here in accordance with the following quotations. Sociologist Louis Wirth states:

> It is my impression from the study of this problem that we cannot really define a Jew except to say that a Jew is a person who thinks of himself as a Jew and who is treated by other persons as if he were a Jew.[10]

8. R. MacIver, *Society* (New York: Farrar and Rinehart, 1937), p. 10.
9. Emory S. Bogardus, *Sociology* (New York: The Macmillan Co., 1943), p. 176.
10. Transcript, University of Chicago Round Table Radio Program, Jan. 28, 1940, p. 5.

Another acceptable interpretation is one given by Mordecai M. Kaplan:

A people is a group of human beings whose ancestors once lived together, and who have developed a We-feeling which is transmitted from one generation to the next. We-feeling results from living together and acting in common in the furtherance of shared interest . . . it is the "we-feeling" the sense which Jews have of mutual belongingness.[11]

---

11. Mordecai M. Kaplan, "When Will American Judaism Be Born?" *The Reconstructionist* 14 (Nov. 26, 1948) : 15.

Sociocultural Changes
in American Jewish Life
as Reflected in Selected
Jewish Literature

1

Social Change and Literature

That there is a close relationship between literature and actual human society is a view held by many literary critics and social historians.[1] Miss Ruth A. Ingles, investigating the relation between literature and social change, distinguishes between the "reflection" theory and the "control" theory.[2] According to the first, works of fiction merely reflect social changes that are already taking place. According to the second, people are socially controlled through their reading habits. The control theory maintains that literature, like art in general, has been used effectively as a means of bringing about social change through the centuries. In his discussion of art as a means of control, Edward Alsworth Ross maintains that

> the emancipation of Negro slaves or Russian serfs is hastened because a Mrs. Stowe or a Turgeniev makes them comprehended. A Dickens or Reade is formidable to social abuses because he has the power to make us yokefellows of their vic-

1. David Daiches, *Literature and Society* (London: Victor Gollancz, 1938); Grant C. Knight, *American Literature* (New York: Long and Smith, 1932); Max Lerner, *Ideas Are Weapons* (New York: Viking Press, 1932): Russell Blakenship, *American Literature as as Expression of the National Mind* (New York: Henry Holt, 1931).

2. Ruth A. Inglis, "An Objective Approach Relationship Between Fiction and Society," *American Sociological Review* (August 1938), p. 528.

27

tims. A Tolstoi or a Millet, by making the peasant understood, gives him a new social weight. Slaves, serfs, convicts,
exiles, outcasts, sufferers of every sort, gain strength the moment genius gives them a voice.[3]

He further states that

what the artist holds up to nature is not always a mirror,
sometimes it is a model; [the artist] flashes before our eyes a
Werther or a Hernani, a King Arthur or a Prince Hal, a
Gretchen or a Julie, and we troop after him as children after
the Piper of Hamelin. In this way, Calderon, a Rousseau or
a Bunyan leaves his stamp on national character.[4]

In asserting the power of literature in molding the
national character of a people, Ross quotes Max Nordau:
"whole generations of German girls and women have
formed themselves upon the model of Lauren's female
figures, as now upon the Gold Elsies and Geier Wallys of
recent fiction."[5]

In a study undertaken to ascertain the extent to which
literature itself is conditioned by society, Albert Guerard
states:

Certain it is that all the literature we talk about and write
about is a social product; the selection and manifestation of a
group and of an age, an integral part of our civilization.[6]

In an address before the American Historical Society
in 1936 on the interrelations of history and literature,
Bernard De Voto said:

Literature is affected by all social energies and is frequently
the best and sometimes the only place where their actual working can be examined. It is the most dependable guide to ethics

3. Edward Alsworth Ross, *Social Control* (New York: The Macmillan
Company, 1912), p. 260.
4. *Ibid.,* p. 267.
5. *Ibid.,* p. 267.
6. Albert Guerard, *Literature and Society* (Boston: Lothrop, Lee &
Shepherd, 1935), p. 19.

and morals, to the process of change in them, and to the implications of change.[7]

Other literary authorities deal specifically with fiction and society and find them closely related. J. Herbert Mueller, who devotes a volume to the relation of modern fiction to society, states:

> The novel is typically a representation of human experience, a comment upon life.[8]

In her preface to "What's in a Novel," Helen G. Haines says:

> In the most ephemeral and transitory fiction of the past the social historian traces emerging patterns of social change. . . . It [modern fiction] reflects the activities, the complexities, the human, social and moral problems, the satisfactions and inquietudes of the modern world with a more pervasive radiation than any other form of writing. In novels conditions were recorded, ideas transmitted, new areas of experiences opened.[9]

LITERATURE'S IMPACT ON LIFE

Modern history is replete with examples of literature as a force shaping social life. It is maintained that the novels of Charles Dickens, particularly *David Copperfield,* were instrumental in changing the entire school system of Britain. Harriet Beecher Stowe's *Uncle Tom's Cabin* made America aware of the plight of the Negro slave and affected greatly the war between the states. Upton Sinclair's novel *The Jungle* aided greatly in changing the Chicago packing houses from centers of filth and

7. Bernard DeVoto, in *Approaches to American Social History,* ed. William E. Llingelbach (New York: D. Apppleton-Century Company, Inc., 1937), p. 54.
8. Herbert J. Mueller, *Modern Fiction: A Study of Values* (New York: Funk and Wagnalls, 1937), p. xiv.
9. Helen E. Haines, *What's in a Novel* (New York: Columbia University Press, 1942), p. 3.

infection to models of cleanliness and sanitation. John Steinbeck's *Grapes of Wrath* made the people aware of the social problem connected with intra-migration. It is generally maintained that the Hebrew poem, "City of Slaughter"[10] written by the national Hebrew poet, Chaim N. Bialik, after the pogrom at Kishineff, Russia, in 1903, has been a factor of social change in recent Jewish history. As a direct result of the poem, which called for self-respect and self-defense, Jewish youth in Russia organized themselves in self-defense groups and made the pogromists pay dearly for their attacks. The poem greatly influenced the Jewish national renascence movement throughout the world and helped to arouse Jewish youth to resistance against the Nazis in Warsaw and to the forming of the Haganah movement in Palestine, which fought and won the war for the independence of Israel in 1948.

LITERATURE A VALID SOURCE FOR STUDY OF SOCIETY

The value of literature, particularly fiction, in the study of society has been recognized by leading historians and sociologists. Historian Henry Steele Commager says:

> They were not so much philosophers as reporters, and so comprehensive and accurate were their transcriptions of the contemporary scene that, if the whole documentary record of this generation should be lost, we could reconstruct it faithfully from imaginative literature.[11]

Sociologist William G. Sumner says that we gain more information about the mores of a people and about the

---

10. "The City of Slaughter," trans. Abraham M. Klein, in *Complete Poetic Works of Hayim Nahman Bialik,* vol. 1 (New York: The Histadruth Ivrith of America, Inc., 1948), pp. 129–43.

11. Henry Steele Commager, *The American Mind* (New Haven: Yale University Press, 1950), pp. 55–81.

everyday social interaction from fiction and drama than from mere historical records. Charles H. Cooley distinguishes between two sorts of knowledge: one, the development of sense contacts into knowledge of things, which he calls "spatial and material" knowledge; and second, "social" knowledge, developed from contact with the minds of other men, through communication, which sets going a process of thought and sentiment similar to theirs and enables us to get an insight into the mental states of others.

According to Cooley, human-cultural phenomena, to be comprehended, must be sympathetically felt or seen, experienced as well as observed. Literature—fiction or drama—because of its vivid and dramatic portrayal of human experiences, sentiments, attitudes, and values, tends to reveal those aspects of human and social relations which we can comprehend with sympathetic interpretation. It is this type of knowledge which Cooley defines as "social."[12] Literature can best give us that insight and has, therefore, special significance as a source of sociological study.

As Florian Znaniecki points out,

> Personal experience and observation are the ultimate bases of all knowledge, the final criteria of validity of all general concepts and laws, and undoubtedly there is as much good observation and careful description of social data involved in works of literature as in works with scientific claims.[13]

And moreover, he continues,

> many a sociological problem has already been, and many more will yet be suggested by works of art, for the literary genius often sees first the importance of facts neglected and ignored.[14]

---

12. Charles Horton Cooley, "The Roots of Social Knowledge," *American Journal of Sociology* 32 (1926–1927): 60.
13. Florian Znaniecki, *The Method of Sociology* (New York: Farrar and Rinehart, Inc., 1934), p. 195.
14. *Ibid.*, p. 197.

The validity of life histories for the study of contemporary life is stressed by Robert E. Park:

> Life histories such as immigrant biographies, of which so many have been published in recent years, illuminate the struggle and make intelligible the character of the cultural process involved. They have rather the character of confessions, intimate personal documents intended to record, not so much external events as to reveal sentiments and attitudes.

According to Pitrim A. Sorokin,[15] we may learn much about the social conditions of any particular period by studying the art products of a people. Discussing social distance in poetry, Emory S. Bogardus says that while "the poet has not necessarily used the sociological concept as such, he has presented the ideas in more expressive ways than a sociologist could do."[16]

Melvin J. Vincent observes that fiction and the drama have been concerned with nearly every phase of human experience and have dealt with almost every type of social situation.

> The social processes which shape human personalities, their groups, their institutions, their problems, are all registered in fiction and drama which is socially conscious. Fiction and drama make possible an imaginative penetration into human character and social events. When presented with consummate literary skill, this offers a more precise and deeper insight into both human character and events and their significance.[17]

The novel is especially important as source material for the study of the family. In an address to the American Society of Sociology, L. Pruette said: "There is a

15. Pitrim A. Sorokin, *Social and Cultural Dynamics* (San Francisco: The American Book Co., 1937), 1:35–101.
16. Emory S. Bogardus, "Social Distance in Poetry," *Sociology and Social Research* 36 (Sept.-Oct. 1961):40–47.
17. Melvin J. Vincent, *Social Aspects of Fiction and Drama* (Syllabus, 46V2–7), p. 1.

certain reality to a 'story' which must always be lacking in case studies or statistical tables."[18]

To the list of multiple inventions given in Ogburn's *Social Change*,[19] L. Pruette adds the novel, which

> is a product of the same condition which produced the Industrial Revolution . . . its interests are the interests of the democracy and center primarily around the activities of the family as a sociological institution.[20]

Pruette sums up his ideas on the novel by reemphasizing the point that

> the literary invention of the novel drawn as it is from the culture patterns of the time, has a greater validity as a social document that is customarily recognized and that modern novels suggest that family life of today is in an unsettled and even critical condition.[21]

---

18. *The Family* 9 (April 1928) :47.
19. William F. Ogburn, *Social Change* (New York: Houghton, Mifflin Co., 1947).
20. *The Family* 9 :50.

2

Social Change and the Development of Jewish Literature

Jewish literature, ancient as well as modern, has more than anything else portrayed the important events and experiences of life, and reflected the social habits, changes, and adjustability of the Jewish people in various times and climes.

In its broader sense, Jewish literature has a continuity of three thousand years or more. The earliest poems, the Song of Moses[1] and the Song of Deborah[2] are more than thirty-two centuries old, and the latest examples belong to the seventies of the twentieth century. The Biblical books of Ruth and Esther are short novels that portray the early life of Israel.

Living in various countries of different cultures, Jews had constantly to adjust themselves not only economically, but also linguistically, to the environment in which they happened to live. Their cultural life thus expressed itself in various forms, and in more than the one original, historic, national tongue of Hebrew. As early as the days of Ezra the Scribe (450 B.C.), the Jews were speaking Ara-

---

1. Exodus 15:1–19.
2. Judges 5:1–31.

maic, and Ezra had to interpret the Torah to the people
in their vernacular. The Gemora, that vast body of Talmudic studies which was a commentary and supplement
of the Mishnah,[3] was also written in Aramaic.

During the period of Hellenistic expansion the Jews
of Alexandria, Egypt, spoke Greek and for the first time
translated the Bible into Greek (Septuaginta). In the
eleventh and twelfth centuries, the monumental works of
Jewish philosophy, poetry, and theology were written in
Arabic. Later, at the end of the fifteenth century, after
their expulsion from Spain (1492), Jews spoke Ladino,
which evolved as a mixture of Hebrew, Spanish, and
Arabian-Turkish elements and is still being spoken today
by many of the Sephardic Jews.

THE HASKALAH MOVEMENT: STRIVING FOR CHANGE
THROUGH HEBREW LITERATURE

It was the aim of the Haskalah (Enlightenment)
movement to bring about a greater adjustment of Jews
to the culture of the modern world. Its leaders and
adherents being anti-traditionalist intellectuals were
eager to enlighten the life and thinking of their fellow
Jews, that is, to Europeanize and secularize Jewish life
and letters.[4] When the Haskalah movement first began to
penetrate and take root among the Jews of Germany in
the middle of the eighteenth century, and when the
strict religious motif that for many centuries had domi-

---

3. Mishnah literally means teaching by means of repetition, and is
the collection of Jewish oral tradition supplementing and interpreting the
laws contained in the Pentateuch. It was compiled and edited by Rabbi
Judah, the Prince of Palestine, at the close of the second century. It
forms the basis of the discussions which made up the two Talmuds—
the Jerusalem (or Palestinian) Talmud, and the Babylonian Talmud—
which were completed at the close of the fourth and fifth centuries, re-
spectively.
4. Cf. Jacob S. Raisin, *Haskalah Movement in Russia* (Philadelphia:
The Jewish Publication Society of America, 1913).

nated Jewish life and behavior began to give way to secularism, it became evident to the adherents of the Haskalah that the Hebrew language was the best medium for spreading their ideas among the Jewish people. In the first stage of the Haskalah movement, of which Moses Mendelssohn (1729-1786), regarded as its father, was the foremost figure, there was created an extensive literature of poetry, popular science, ethics, collections of fables, and works on Hebrew grammar. Two Hebrew periodicals, the *Ha-Measef* (a miscellany), founded in 1784 in Germany, and *Bikurei Haitim,* which began to appear in Vienna in 1829, reflected the striving for change. They published articles criticizing the social, economic, and cultural life of the people, and sought to undermine the influence of strict orthodox religious dogmatism. The credo of the Maskilim (followers of Haskalah) in Germany was the "rule of reason." They believed that once the old traditional folkways of the ghetto and general ignorance of secular knowledge were abolished, the way would immediately open for the transformation of Jewish life to a higher material and cultural plane.

When the Haskalah movement later began to spread among Russian Jews, it underwent a change of purpose and direction. While it still aimed at enlightenment by means of secular education and modernization of Jewish life, it laid greater stress on creating permanent Jewish values and on the need for a revival of the Hebrew language and literature as vehicles of modern learning.

In their efforts to normalize Jewish life, the Haskalah adherents proclaimed the ideal of manual labor and especially of agricultural occupation. The ideal of a changed mode of living through labor became the theme song and motif for many Hebrew poems, allegories, and stories of the period. Thus the Haskalah movement endeavored to create a modern Hebrew literature which itself proclaims the importance of the idea of change in the life of the Jewish people.

Two new Hebrew weeklies began to appear in Russia, *Ha-Melitz,* (the Advocate) in 1860 and *Ha-Zefirah* (Daybreak) in 1863, both of which were later converted into daily newspapers and greatly influenced the cultural life of Jews in Eastern Europe. The efforts of the Maskilim soon caused great strides in the direction of cultural change, evidenced in the national revival of modern Hebrew literature.

FIRST HEBREW NOVELS INFLUENCING CHANGE

The desire for cultural and economic change in the life of the people permeated the prose and the poetry of the period, which realistically portrayed and critically scrutinized the life of the people. Judah Leib Gordon (1830-1892), foremost poet of the period, depicts in his epic poems tragic episodes in Jewish life in Russia due to lack of cultural adjustment to the modern environment. The first realistic Hebrew novels expressing the motifs of the period were: *Lost in the Ways of Life* (Hatoe Bedarkei Hahayim) by Peretz Smolenskin (1842-1885), a native of White Russia, and *The Painted Vulture* (Ayit Tzovua) by Abraham Mapu (1808-1868), a native of Lithuania. These novels vividly described the life of the people, and manifested a strong desire for change in their economic and religious life. Mapu's historic novel, *The Love of Zion* (Ahavat Zion), published in 1853 and considered the first novel in modern Hebrew literature, marked a new literary style in the Hebrew language and immediately found an enthusiastic reading audience. In it the author sought to widen the Jewish horizon and to raise the average Jew in Russia above the sordidness of ghetto existence to the contemplation of his Jewish historic grandeur.

This romantic novel, set in the Biblical days of Isaiah and King Hezekiah, had a tremendous impact on Jewish youth. It assumed an importance far beyond its literary value for it "lifted Jewish morale in the 1850's above the swamp of despondency and lethargy into which it had sunk during the long and cruel reign of Nicholas II."[5]

After reading *Ahavat Zion,* the strong longing of the Jews in East Europe for a homecoming to Zion became almost unbearable and nurtured what was later to mature into the Zionist movement and was to inspire the acts of the pioneers who transformed the vision of the novel into a living reality, the rebuilt land of Israel. In this case the novel anticipated the purpose of the Zionist movements long before it was founded, and was influential in effecting a radical transformation in the life of the Jewish people.

THE SOCIAL ORIGIN OF YIDDISH LITERATURE

The term *Yiddish literature* refers to the literary writings in Yiddish produced in Eastern Europe and America in the past century. As a language and literature Yiddish is several hundred years old, and may be traced back to the sixteenth and seventeenth centuries. The Jews who migrated from the German-speaking countries into Poland and Russia brought with them the Judaeo-German dialect which later developed into Yiddish, a language consisting of old German, Hebrew, and some grammatical elements of the Slavic languages. Because of the cultural and social distance, and the isolation of Jews from the non-Jewish majority group, Yiddish developed into a distinct language and at the outbreak of the Second World War, the Yiddish-speaking group

---

5. Sol Liptzin, "News and Views" (Guest Column), *The Day Journal* (October 15, 1952), p. 1.

numbered about ten million, or about sixty percent of the Jewish population of the globe.[6]

By the end of the sixteenth century, with the urbanization of Jews in Eastern Europe and their increasing cultural contacts with peoples speaking Slavic, the "Yiddish-Teutsch" (Judeo-German) merged with the Slavonic language elements, absorbing new words and phrases, and developed a sentence structure resembling the Slavonic pattern. Thus Yiddish became distinct from both its Hebrew background and its Germanic origin, a European language in its own right.[7]

As early as the fourteenth century, poetic translations of the Bible stories and legends of Talmudic lore were rendered into Yiddish, chiefly for the women, who were not able to understand clearly the sacred literature in Hebrew. Most popular with Jewish women for the longest time, up to today, was the book *Come Forth and Behold* (Tzena u-Reenah), an ethical commentary on the Five Books of Moses, on which Jewish women were brought up and the contents of which they immensely enjoyed. Similar in moral intent were the devotional prayers in Yiddish (Tkhines) composed often by women for women.

Influence of Hassidism. The religious movement of Hassidism in the eighteenth century, which emphasized a joyous affirmation of life, reached out to Jews in all their dwellings by its use of Yiddish in prayers, songs, and parables. In the latter half of the nineteenth century, Yiddish, carried by the Jewish immigrants to North and South American countries, became a medium of communication for most Jews all over the globe.

6. *Ibid., The Flowering of Yiddish Literature* (New York and London: Thomas Yoseloff, Publisher, 1963). Also Maurice Samuel, *In Praise of Yiddish* (New York: Cowles Book Co., 1971).

7. Cassel's *Encyclopedia of World Literature* (New York: Funk and Wagnalls Company, 1954), 1:571.

For centuries the books commonly used and regarded sacred by Jews were the Prayer Book, the Bible, the Talmud, and codes of law and conduct. These were all written in Hebrew and, to a lesser degree, in Aramaic, as was the Talmud. Yiddish was regarded as the "Handmaiden," while Hebrew was the "Mistress."

With the emancipation of the Russian peasants in 1861, important social and economic changes occurred that resulted in the rise of the Russian working class and their struggle for a better and freer life. Because of this general social awakening, the Jewish masses in Russia began to feel the need of books and newspapers in their languages—Hebrew, and especially the one they knew best, Yiddish.

With the changing social scene in Russia, and the spread of secular influence among Jews, Yiddish gained in importance and recognition. With the appearance of the first Yiddish newspaper, *Kol Mevasser* (Voice of the Messenger) in 1862 in Odessa, journals and literature in both Hebrew and Yiddish began to flourish.

THE CLASSICS OF MODERN JEWISH LITERATURE
AND THEIR INFLUENCE

The first of the classic writers of modern Yiddish literature to elevate Yiddish to a literary and artistic level was Sholom Yakov Abramovitch (1835-1917), commonly known by his pen-name of Mendele Mokher Sforim (Mendele, the Bookseller). He is regarded as the master of literary, artistic prose in both Hebrew and Yiddish and is affectionately referred to as the Zeide (Grandfather) of modern Jewish literature. Strongly influenced by the Haskalah movement, and concerned with the tragic state of the Jewish masses, Mendele exposed the limitations of Jewish ghetto life in Russia.

After writing in Hebrew for a decade, Mendele turned

to Yiddish, the language most commonly used by East European Jews.

In his social satires and realistic novels Mendele expressed a new approach to the problems of Jewish group life. He regarded the people's social inequality and economic insecurity as greater evils than their old, extremely orthodox mode of living. With penetrating observation, he portrayed the social situations and life patterns of the "shtetl" (the small Jewish town) in the Russian Pale, which he renamed Kabtzansk (Paupertown), and the Jewish life in the larger city, which he called Glupsk (Simpletown). Among his important Yiddish novels worthy of mention are: *Die Takse* (The Tax); *Dos Kleine Menshele* (The Little Man), a devastating satire on currupt leadership in Jewish community life; *Die Klyatsche* (The Nag), an allegory on Jewish history; *Fishke der Krumer* (Fishke the Lame); and *Masooth Benyamin Hashlishi* (Travels of Benjamin the Third), a satirical novel about Jewish Utopian idealism.

In his realistic social satire *Die Klyatsche*,[8] Mendele portrays the social situation and daily life of Jews in the Russia of one hundred years ago. He points out that "there is no dancing before the meal. Let the nag first be given proper food and fresh air to breathe, and then try to teach her to dance." In sharp words he rebukes those leaders who "ride the nag for their own selfish purposes," and with characteristic irony he calls on his fellow Jews to face the realities of life and to find within themselves the resources to carry on.

Through his novels Mendele not only articulated the mood of his generation and the social situation of the times, but he also profoundly influenced the people's thinking and actions. Thus the legacy of the grandfather of modern Jewish literature was his realistic approach

---

8. Mendele Mocher Sforim, *The Nag* (1873), trans. Moshe Spiegel (New York: Beechhurst Press, 1955).

to the social life of the people, and his implied admonition not to permit a separation and estrangement of literature from real life and its social problems. By his artistic and exacting description of the social milieu of Jewish living, he set an example for the new generation of Hebrew and Yiddish prose writers in Europe and in the New World.

Following Mendele is the man who regards himself as "grandson" to the "Zeide," Sholom Rabinovitch (1859-1916), better known as Sholom Aleichem, most popular and beloved for his remarkable wit and humor, and often called the "Jewish Mark Twain." His first visit to America was in 1908, and in 1914 he returned again and died in New York in 1916. His characters, depicted with enormous affection and drawn from all strata of the Jewish social milieu—from Kasrilevke, the Jewish "shtetl" in Russia, to the East Side of New York—furnish inexhaustible material for the student of Jewish life and folk psychology, for his writings reveal the mind, wit, and inner life of Eastern European Jewry and give a realistic portrayal of their changing mode of living.

Sholom Aleichem portrays Kasrilevke, the typical Jewish town in Russia, in its transition, on the march, when its people leave it and migrate to new lands. In *Adventures of Mottel Peisie, the Cantor's Son,* he delineates the changes in a Jewish family as it moves from Kasrilevke to the "golden land," the adventures of the immigrants on the road, and their first steps and struggles in adjustments to a strange new environment. Through his writings, Sholom Aleichem taught a suffering people to laugh at its troubles and thus brought to them a new therapeutic power.

In his autobiography, *Fun Yarid* (From the Fair), written in New York and consisting of reminiscences of his life's experiences, Sholom Aleichem portrays as well

the life of the American Jewish family; the conflict between generations, and the weakening of Jewish traditional values. Characteristic of his moral personality is
his wish expressed in his will that he be laid at rest not
among the aristocrats or men of great wealth but "among
the poor, that their graves may shine on mine, and mine
on theirs."[9] He died on May 13, 1916; however, his
writings still bring laughter and joy to millions of people
in many lands, into whose languages his works have been
translated and often dramatized for the stage.

The third of the classic trio of modern Yiddish writers
whose influence on Jewish literature and life is profound
is Yitzhok Leibush Peretz (1851-1915). His writings
give artistic expression to the thought processes and feelings of the people. He brought to modern Jewish literature the "storm and stress" of his age, the thunder and
lightning of the rising social movements. A strong advocate of social justice, Peretz espoused the cause of democracy and of the Jewish labor movement. His writings
radiate sympathy and love for the poor and humble, for
those who demand so little from life and are denied
even that.

In his very popular short story, *Bonstsche the Silent,*
Peretz depicts the degrading effects of poverty upon the
human soul. Bontsche, the typical meek sufferer, bears
all insults and injustices in grave silence, without uttering
a complaint. After a wretched and miserable life on
earth, Bontsche goes up to heaven. Since life on earth
has taught him to expect nothing, he expects nothing in
heaven, either. Even when the angels turn out to honor
him he remains mute and bewildered, and when the pre-
siding judge tells him that he can have whatever reward
he desires for his humble life on earth, the only request

9. Cf. Maurice Samuel, *The World of Sholom Aleichem* (New York:
Schocken Books, 1965), p. 330. Also, Marie Waife-Goldberg, *My Father
Sholom Aleichem* (New York: Simon & Schuster, 1968).

Bontsche makes—to the confusion and embarrassment of the court—is that he be given every morning "a hot roll with fresh butter."

Peretz's awareness of the continuous change taking place in the Jewish family—the generation gap—is illustrated in his sketch, "Four Generations—Four Wills," which portrays the gap and transformation of culture patterns from one generation to the next.[10]

Especially aware of the new tendencies and social forces that were effecting radical changes in the cultural life of the Jewish people and threatening its group life with gradual disintegration, Peretz was looking for those spiritual and cultural elements that would preserve the cohesion and ensure the continuity of creative Jewish group life and culture. The creative continuity of Jewish life and culture amidst general social change is the idea especially stressed in his drama *The Golden Chain (Die Goldene Keit)*.

A proponent of progressive ideas and favoring changes in Jewish life, Peretz was particularly contemptuous of those who, in the name of social progress, would abandon the idea of Jewish creative survival and have the Jews disappear among the nations without a trace. He was opposed to that kind of assimilation of either the rich or the revolutionary working class. In his famous essay "Hope and Fear," which he wrote in 1906 at the height of the revolutionary movement in Russia, Peretz warned that the oppressed may become oppressors and expressed his fear that a victorious proletariat might become an oppressor and establish a dictatorship which would eradicate everything proud and creative in the human spirit. He concludes this remarkable essay with the words: "My heart is with you in your struggle—and

10. Sol Liptzin, *Y. L. Peretz* (New York: Yiddish Scientific Institute—Yivo, 1947), pp. 266–74.

yet, I fear you. . . . I hope for your victory, but fear and dread it."

Timely and relevant to the attitude of some of our contemporary American-Jewish writers and intellectuals is also the message by Peretz written about six decades ago:

> What does our literature lack? I am not for confining ourselves in a spiritual ghetto. We should get out of the ghetto, and with our own spirit, with our own spiritual treasure, and exchange: to give and take, but not to beg.[11]

Some of the foremost Jewish novelists—Sholem Asch, David Pinski, Abraham Reisen, Menachem Boreisha, and Joseph Opatoshu—were as literary aspirants encouraged and profoundly influenced by Peretz while residing in Warsaw, Poland. They later immigrated to the United States and created important novels of American Jewish life, some of which are considered and analyzed in subsequent chapters of this study.

Appreciation of Peretz's influence on Jewish literature was expressed in 1952, forty years after his death and on the one hundredth anniversary of his birth, when a street on the lower East Side of New York, between Houston and First Streets, was named "Peretz Square."[12]

The world of Mendele, Sholem Aleichem, and Peretz —the life lived by the Jews of the Eastern European countries—was utterly annihilated during the Second World War by Nazi German cruelty and later by the brutal Communist intolerance in Russia. However, the life of European Jews as portrayed, mirrored, and enshrined in the fiction, poetry, and drama of the three great classic Jewish writers is of enduring value and significance to the American Jew of today.

---

11. *Ibid.*, p. 378.
12. *Ibid.*

3

Factors of Change in the Life
of American Jews

MIGRATION

Migration has been defined as "the physical transition of an individual or a group from one society to another."[1] As such, migration effects a radical social and cultural change in the life of the migrating individual or group.

Sociologists and historians agree that migrations play an important role in human history. The words of Franz Oppenheimer, that "all world history is essentially the history of the movement of masses of people,"[2] may be applied especially to the historic experience of the Jewish people, who for the past thirty-five centuries have crossed every continent and every ocean. The uncertainty of life for the Jew during the dark ages made him a nomad, and has earned for him the epithet "Wandering Jew."[3] Migration has thus become a basic element in the history of the Jewish people, and a determining factor in their social and cultural development and mode of living.

1. T. S. N. Eisenstadt, *The Absorption of Immigrants* (Glencoe, Ill.: The Free Press, 1955), p. 1.
2. Quoted by Jacob Lestchinsky in *Yivo Annual of Jewish Social Science* (New York: 1954) 9:377.
3. Louis Wirth, *The Ghetto* (Chicago: The University of Chicago Press, 1929), p. 13.

A brief review of the historical background of Jewish immigration into the United States may help to explain the factors and processes affecting their adjustment and the changing patterns of life in the new environment.

MAIN WAVES OF JEWISH IMMIGRATION

The history of Jewish immigration to the United States is generally divided into three main waves:

The first Jews who came to the shores of America were of Spanish and Portuguese origin (Sephardim). In the year 1654 a group of twenty-three Jewish refugees from Brazil arrived on the *St. Charles* in the harbor of New Amsterdam. They spoke Ladino, a mixture of Spanish and Hebrew, among themselves; they engaged in foreign trade, were well-to-do, and adhered to orthodoxy in their religious ritual. Due to their early arrival, they held a position of leadership until they were outnumbered later, in the middle of the nineteenth century, by the influx of Jews from Germany and its neighboring states.

In 1790 there were about 2,500 Jews in the United States, who formed one "middle class."[4] In 1840 the Jewish population was estimated at 15,000 persons.[5] Although by this time the Spanish-Portuguese Jews had already been reduced to a minority among the Jewish population, they still considered themselves the aristocracy of American Jewry because of their longer residence in the country, their smaller number, and their higher social status. They tended to remain aloof from their poorer and more humble brethren, the later arrivals from Central and Eastern Europe, and moved in the

---

4. Jacob Reader Marcus, *Early American Jewry* (Philadelphia: The Jewish Publication Society, 1951), 2:413.
5. Charles B. Sherman, *The Jewish People: Past and Present* (New York: Centrale Yiddishe Cultur Oraganizatzie, 1948), 2:218.

direction of greater assimilation into the American environment.

The second period of Jewish immigration took place in the years between 1815 and 1880, usually referred to as the major period of German-Jewish immigration into the United States of America. Those years marked a period of expansion in American history, the period of the covered wagon, the steam locomotive, and the "gold rush." Differing radically from the Sephardim in several respects, the German-Jewish immigrants, by their industry, ability, and courage overcame poverty and developed thriving businesses. They settled in the cities along the Atlantic seaboard, became successful in business, and later played an important role in American social and financial history.[6] Some, as peddlers with packs on their shoulders, followed the covered wagon, while the more adventurous pushed out with the other pioneers into the thinly settled districts in the south and middle west, and across the desert and mountains to the Pacific coast.

The rate of increase of the Jewish population during the second "wave" of immigration is revealed by the following figures:

1820	Estimated population		5,000
1850	"	"	50,000
1860	"	"	150,000
1880	"	"	275,000[7]

Thus in the last twenty years represented (1860-1880), the Jewish population increased by immigration almost twofold.

By 1881 four-fifths of the quarter million Jews in America were of German origin. Possessing great or-

6. Stephan Birmingham, *Our Crowd* (New York and London: Harper and Row, 1967).
7. Jacob Lestschinsky, *The Jewish People—Past and Present* (New York: Jewish Encyclopedia Handbook, Inc., 1955), pp. 56, 57.

ganizational skill, these German-Jewish immigrants founded many of the early Jewish charitable institutions: orphanages, hospitals, homes for the aged; and institutions which later have attained national recognition, such as Mt. Sinai Hospital and the Young Men's Hebrew Association of New York City. Along with their economic success came social prestige and leadership in charity institutions and in communal work. Although in the early years of their settlement the majority of them were formally orthodox in their religious life and rituals, they later changed to Reform Judaism.

Toward the end of the nineteenth century, when the boundaries of the United States had become stabilized and the country's rapid industrialization took place, the need for labor increased. America then welcomed the hungry and oppressed masses of immigrants who flocked from all corners of the globe into this country. This favorable attitude toward new immigrants was fittingly expressed by Emma Lazarus in her famous sonnet, "The New Colossus," which is engraved on the base of the Statue of Liberty in New York Harbor:

Mother of Exiles, from her beacon-hand
Glows world-wide welcome. . . .
"Keep, ancient lands, your storied
Pomp!" cried she with silent lips.
Give me your tired, your poor,
Your huddled masses, yearning to breathe free,
The wretched refuse of your teeming shore.
Send these, the homeless, tempest-tossed to me,
I lift my lamp beside the golden door.[8]

The radical change which was to alter the complexion of Jewish life in America came with the next, the third

---

8. Emma Lazarus, "The New Colossus," in *A Second Treasury of the Familiar* (New York: The Macmillan Co., 1950), p. 111.

wave of immigration, which included Jewish immigrants from Russia, Poland, Roumania, and sections of the Austro-Hungarian Empire. They fled from the pogroms and miserable economic conditions of their native countries. When Czar Alexander the Third ascended the throne in 1881 and inaugurated a definite anti-Jewish policy, encouraging anti-Jewish pogroms as an outlet for the growing popular discontent with the Government, the great exodus of Jews from Russia began.

The conditions in Czarist Russia in the latter part of the nineteenth century are vividly pictured in the autobiographic novel, *The Rise of David Levinsky,* by Abraham Cahan.

> Thousands of Jewish families were left homeless. Of still greater moment was the moral effect which the atrocities produced on the whole Jewish population of Russia. Over five million people were suddenly made to realize their birthplace was not their home. (A feeling which the great Russian revolution has suddenly changed). Then it was that the cry "To America!" was raised. It spread like wild fire, even over those parts of the "Pale of Settlement" which lay outside the riot zone.[9]

The enormity of this new third wave of Jewish immigration, which completely overshadowed the quarter million Jews of both Sephardim and German origin, is told by Oscar I. Janowsky:

> Between 1880 and 1920, American Jewry was completely transformed. In 1880, they numbered about 250,000, approximately one half of one per cent of the total population. . . . In 1920, about 3,500,000 of the 106,000,000 inhabitants of the United States were Jews—nearly 3½ percent of the population.[10]

---

9. Abraham Cahan, *The Rise of David Levinsky* (New York: Harper & Bros., 1917), pp. 60–61.
10. Oscar I. Janowsky, *The JWB Survey* (New York: The Dial Press, 1948), p. 239.

According to Jacob Lestchinsky, Jewish immigration from Eastern Europe at this time constituted nearly one third of the total East European immigration (see Table I), and nearly two thirds of all Jewish immigrants came to the United States during the thirty years from 1891 to 1920, a period which witnessed the largest general immigration from Eastern and Southern Europe (see Table II).

TABLE I* JEWISH IMMIGRATION FROM EASTERN EUROPE 1820–1952

Period	Number of immigrants	Percent of total East European immigration
1820–1870	150,000	5.2
1871–1890	250,000	8.8
1891–1920	1,850,000	64.9
1921–1952	600,000	21.1

* Source: Jacob Lestchinsky, in *Yivo Annual of Jewish Social Science,* edited by Koppel S. Pinson, vol. 9 (New York: Yivo, 1954), p. 377.

TABLE II* GROWTH OF JEWISH POPULATION IN THE UNITED STATES 1820–1953

Year	Number of Jews	Percent of total population in the United States	Percent of Jewish people in the world
1820	5,000	0.05	0.16
1850	50,000	0.21	0.06
1880	275,000	0.55	3.44
1900	1,100,000	1.45	10.00
1925	3,800,000	3.25	27.14
1945	4,700,000	3.35	44.80
1955	5,100,000	3.25	44.00

* Source: Jacob Lestchinsky, "The Jewish People Past and Present," *Jewish Encyclopedia Handbook, Inc.,* 1955, 4:56.

EFFECTS OF MIGRATION, URBANIZATION,
AND SECULARIZATION

This significant social change in American Jewry is largely the effect of immigration and its related social processes of urbanization and secularization. Referring to the new era of industrialization and urbanization in the United States, Van Wyck Brooks says:

> In the decade preceding 1890 the growth of the great cities had gradually changed the character of the country and the people and the tone of the rising civilization was less and less rural and agricultural and more and more industrial and urban.[11]

The character of most of the Jewish population was transformed from that of the small east European town to that of a large American Metropolitan city. It is estimated that about 85 percent of the Jewish population in the United States are now settled in cities of more than one hundred thousand inhabitants. The great immigration created in New York a Jewish community of approximately two million persons; the same is almost true of Chicago and of Philadelphia. This change becomes more obvious when one remembers that, while about sixty years ago almost 86 percent of world Jewry lived in backward agricultural countries, today about 90 percent of the Jewish population lives in industrialized and urbanized lands.[12]

The great impact of such change on one's life is given much consideration in the important sociological studies by W. I. Thomas and F. Znaniecki.[13] Discussing urbanism, Louis Wirth points out that instead of the close

---

11. Van Wyck Brooks, *The Confident Years, 1885–1915* (New York: E. P. Dutton & Co., 1952), p. 120.
12. *Hadoar*, November 5, 1954, p. 9. (Hebrew Weekly published by Hadoar Association, Inc., New York, N.Y.).
13. W. I. Thomas and Florian Znaniecki, *The Polish Peasant in Europe and America* (New York: Alfred A. Knopf, Inc., 1927).

personal contacts typical of the small community, relationships in the city tend to be "impersonal, superficial, transitory, and segmental."[14] Urbanization tends, among other things, to weaken the group's control of the individual. This is because, living in a larger metropolitan center, one can easily evade communal responsibility, while in the smaller community, where there is greater social control or group pressure, it becomes more difficult to evade these responsibilities.[15]

The rapid progress in technology and science has also brought about a change in the thinking of man, which has resulted in secular tendencies and in weakened and changed religious beliefs and practices. In sum, these sociological factors of migration, urbanization, and secularization brought about greater social interaction and culture contact between the different religious and ethnic minority groups, which in turn strongly affected their thinking and patterns of behavior.

14. In "Urbanism as a Way of Life," *American Journal of Sociology* (July 1938), pp. 1–24.
15. Arthur Rupin, *The Jewish Fate and Faith* (London: Macmillan and Company, Ltd., 1940), p. 42.

4

Generations and Stages in the Life and Literature of American Jews

PERIODS AND STAGES

It is worthwhile to view the development of American Jewish literature in terms of historic periods which parallel and reflect respective stages in the adjustment process and the historical development of three generations of American Jews.

First Period (1880-1905). During the first period, the years from 1880 to 1905, the largest portion of the Jewish population in the United States came from East European countries. The new environment, and altered social conditions brought about by the continuing urbanization and secularization of American society, marked a radical transformation in the life of the East European Jewish immigrants.

The prose and lyric poetry of this period well expressed the mood of the times. The difficulties of the immigrant and his family in their economic and cultural adjustment, their experiences as working men or as peddlers, their longing for their old home-town, and their protest and bitterness against the exploitation of the sweatshop system are the dominant themes and motifs in the literary writings of those days. Best known among the writers of this period were: Joseph Bovshover (1873-1915) David Edelstadt (1866-1892), Morris Vinchevsky (1856-1933), and Morris Rosenfeld (1862-1923).

Second Period (1905-1920). The second period in the development of American Jewish literature, particularly of its prose, began about 1905 and continued through the First World War and up to 1920. The penury of the Jewish masses in Russia, the failure of the Russian revolution, and the new wave of pogroms in 1904 increased the stream of new arrivals, which included a new element of political immigrants, communal leaders, literati, and others of the more educated class.

During these years a new type of Jewish writer emerged, foremost of which were Leon Kobrin, Z. Libin, Sholem Asch, Joseph Opatoshu, David Pinsky, Sholem Aleichem, H. Leivick, David Ignatev, and Isaac Raboy. These writers of the immigrant generation depicted in Yiddish the life of the Jewish immigrant in novels, short stories, and dramas.

In the second decade of the present century, however, books began to appear in English—autobiographical novels such as *The Promised Land* by Mary Antin, *Hungry Hearts* by Anzia Yezierka, *The Rise of David Levinsky* by Abraham Cahan, *Fannie Herself* by Edna Ferber, and others to which reference will be made later. These novels described the experiences and style of life of the immigrant generation.

Third Period (1920-1939). In the early 1920s the growth of the American Jewish population was affected by the stopping of immigration into the United States. Nevertheless, there was an increase in the number of children of immigrants who began to grow up and were called the second generation. From 1920 to 1939, much of the prose fiction written by American Jews in English dealt with Jewish experiences and problems resulting from the depression and anti-Jewish discrimination. They reflect the anxieties and insecurities of the alienated second generation, the issues and problems of alienation, disharmony between generations, intermarriage, assimilation, and group survival. A number of these writers reflected radicalism in their works and rejection of their religious and historic Jewish heritage.

Fourth Period (1939-1955). In the period from 1939 to 1955, roughly the era of the new third generation, one discerns a change in the literary writings of some Jewish writers—an increased sense of group consciousness and a desire for group identification. Some novelists of this period were keenly aware of the problem of Jewish group survival and were grappling with the vexing problem of integration into the general American society while ensuring the continuity of Jewish group life.

EXPERIENCES AND ADJUSTMENT PROBLEMS OF THE
JEWISH IMMIGRANT GENERATION

The experiences and problems of the emigrant were difficult and complex, from the day of leaving his old home until his arrival in the new land. The exchange of the "shtetl" in East Europe for the city of the New World; the crossing of the ocean and then, after arrival in America, the difficulties in earning a living; and the often unhappy problems of spiritual adaptation in the new strange land are all portrayed by humorist Sholom Rabinowitz, popularly known by his pen name, Sholem Aleichem. In *Adventures of Mottel Peisy, the Cantor's*

Son,[1] the last book written by him while in this country, Sholem Aleichem describes his personal experiences as an emigrant. First he portrays the family's emigration from the native "shtetl" at the turn of the century, their long trip from Europe to America, and finally their arrival and first years in the new homeland. Their motives for leaving their native home are to escape pogroms and persecution, poverty, and compulsory service in the Czar's armies. He tells that an earlier emigrant from Kasrilovka had written back home that America is a free country, "everyone is having a terrible time and is making a living." Hence, America becomes their goal.

Pinney, a friend of Mottel's brother Eli, who pretends to be an authority on American history and on the meaning of freedom, remarks as follows to an official of the Emigrant Committee in Lemberg[2] from whom he seeks aid in getting to the United States:

> We are traveling to America not only because of the draft, but in the name of independence and civilization and also because we were stifled not only with respect to lack of progress but even for lack of air, as the writer Turgeniev says. Secondly, because there arose the Jewish problem, pogroms, the constitution, et cetera, as Buckle says in the "History of Civilization."[3]

When the group of emigrants finally sailed into New York harbor, Pinney, overcome by his deep feeling for history, knelt on the deck, bowed his head and said, "How do you do, Columbus! Greetings to you, land of the free—golden, happy land!"[4]

The feeling of joy that overwhelmed the immigrant

---

1. Sholem Aleichem, *Adventures of Mottle Peisy, the Cantor's Son,* trans. Tamara Kohana (New York: Henry Schuman, 1953), p. 105.
2. A city in Galicia then under the Austro-Hungarian imperial regime.
3. Sholem Aleichem, p. 140.
4. *Ibid.,* p. 222.

on arrival in the land of the free is pictured by Mary Antin, a Russian Jewish girl who came to the United States in 1893 at the age of twelve. Glowing with enthusiasm for the free land and its democratic institutions, she describes her first impressions and experiences in the New World:

> I was at a most impressionable age when I was transplanted to the new soil. . . . The emigration became of the most vital importance to me personally. All the processes of uprooting, transportation, replanting, acclimatization, and development took place in my own soul. I felt the pang, the fear, the wonder, and the joy of it.[5]

Abraham Cahan says of the recently arrived immigrants:

> When David Levinsky arrived in the New World he felt like newly born. He tells of his first impression of America. When the discoverers of America say land at last they fell on their knees and a hymn of thanksgiving burst from their souls. The scene, which is one of the most thrilling in history, repeats itself in the heart of every immigrant as he comes in sight of the American shores. I am at a loss to convey the peculiar state of mind that experience created in me.
>
> The immigrant's arrival in his new home is like a second birth to him. Imagine a new born babe in possession of a fully-developed intellect. Would it ever forget its entry into the world? Neither does the immigrant ever forget entry into a country which is, to him, a new world in the profoundest sense of the term and in which he expects to pass the rest of his life.[6]

STRUGGLE FOR ECONOMIC AND CULTURAL ADJUSTMENT

The Jewish immigrants from Eastern Europe, though happy on their arrival in the land of freedom and equal-

---

5. Mary Antin, *The Promised Land* (Boston and New York: Houghton Mifflin Company, 1912), p. xiv.
6. Abraham Cahan, *The Rise of David Levinsky* (New York: Harper and Brothers, 1917), p. 86.

ity, soon discovered the price for these blessings was high. The struggle for a bare livelihood sapped their vitality, and left neither time nor energy to enjoy the favors of the "Golden Land." Torn from their former home attachments, from traditional family life and customs, deprived of moral support in the new environment, the immigrants faced a mode of life which appeared to them confusing and perplexing.

Economic adjustment to the new situation was the chief problem of this first generation of immigrants. They were mainly concerned with the grim facts of bare existence.

Harry Rogoff describes conditions in those days thus:

> Those were the palmy days of the tenement house and the sweat shop, of the boarder and the cadet, of the white plague and of lung blocks. It was then that the tailor labored a day and a half to complete one day's task, for which he was paid two dollars in wages. It was a time when the East Side was a byword all over the country, a synonym for human degradation and suffering.[7]

Indeed, the experiences, travails, and first impressions of the Jewish immigrant, and his struggle to adjust to the new environment, constitute a "history of alienation and its consequences."[8] These experiences are depicted in the realistic novels of Abraham Cahan, Mary Antin, Leon Kobrin,[9] Sholem Aleichem, Sholem Asch,[10] Joseph Opatoshu,[11] Charles Angoff[12] and others.

7. Harry Rogoff, *An East Side Epic* (New York: The Vanguard Press, 1930), p. 3.
8. Oscar Handlin, *The Uprooted*. An Atlantic Monthly Press Book (Boston: Little, Brown and Co., 1951), p. 5.
9. *Ore die Bord* (in Yiddish) (New York: Forward Association, 1918).
10. "Uncle Moses" (New York: G. P. Putman's Sons, 1958) and "Chaim Lederer's Return" (New York: G. P. Putnam's Sons, 1938). See Acknowledgments.
11. *Di Tenzerin* (The Dancer) (Wilno: Farlag fun B. Klazkin, 1938), *Lyncherei* (Wilno: Wilner Farlag B. Klazkin, 1927), and *Hebrew* (Wilno: Farlag B. Klazkin, 1920).
12. *Journey to the Dawn* (New York: The Beechhurst Press, 1951), *The Morning Light* (New York: The Beechhurst Press, 1953), *The Sun*

Occupational Change. Jewish immigrants were mainly proletarian, and consisted mostly of wage earners in shops and factories. However, most of them, largely unskilled workers, former small tradesmen, soon drifted as laborers into light manufacturing, particularly into the then-expanding clothing industries. Out of their efforts toward economic adjustment emerged a new class of workers employed mainly in the needle trade.

In 1900, three out of every five Russian Jews were engaged in manufacturing, almost all as workers. More than half of the workers—that is, more than one third of the Russian Jews—were employed in a single industry, the manufacture of clothing. The East European Jewish peddler, observes Nathan Glazer,[13] formed only a very small part of the huge number of East European Jewish immigrants, most of whom became workers in light industry in the rapidly growing cities. Looking for an opportunity to go into business for himself, the immigrant found that the clothing trade offered the possibility of making a living wage, from which he could save enough money to bring over his family and also "be his own boss."

In Sholem Aleichem's *Adventures of Mottel Peisy, the Cantor's Son,* Eli and Pinney and their wives, after arriving in New York, find it very hard to adjust and to eke out a livelihood. They try several approaches. First Pinney works in a garment sweat shop, but he cannot keep his own jacket sleeves out of the sewing machine he operates. Later they buy and operate a tiny candy store and newsstand. Because the business at their stand is not large enough to support a family of seven, they started

at Noon (New York: The Beechhurst Press, 1955), *Between Day and Dark* (New York and London: Thomas Yoseloff, Publisher, 1959), *Bitter Springs* (New York and London: Thomas Yoseloff, Publisher, 1961), and *Memory of Autumn* (New York and London: Thomas Yoseloff, Publisher, 1968).
  13. *American Judaism* (Chicago: University of Chicago Press, 1957).

looking around for a bigger business. "In America," says Mottel, "nobody stays in one place. In America everybody advances."[14]

During the years 1881 to 1905, most of the Jewish immigrants took to tailoring. Because of the extensive division of labor they could learn this trade in a relatively short time. Also the clothing industry was advantageous because it was almost the only one in which there were a considerable number of Jewish employers. Hence Jewish immigrants found it easier to get jobs there. And, because of the concentration of the clothing industry in large cities, these people clustered in the same cities. About one-half lived in New York and other large groups lived in Philadelphia, Boston, and Chicago.[15]

Some Jewish immigrants preferred to remain in New York and in the few larger cities for religious reasons, for they did not wish to risk going to a smaller town where there might not be a synagogue, a religious school for their children, or Kosher meat, or where they might have to work on the Sabbath.[16]

From the "Shtetl" to the American Metropolitan City. The effect of the sharp contrast between life in the old home town and in the New World, and the sudden change from the life of poverty in the East European semi-rural "shtetl" to the large industrialized American city life of plenty and wealth is vividly pictured in the description of David's home town in *The Rise of David Levinsky.*

Antomir, which then boasted eighty thousand inhabitants, was a town in which a few thousand rubles was considered

---

14. Sholem Aleichem, p. 9.
15. Oscar Handlin, *The American People in the Twentieth Century* (Cambridge: Harvard University Press, 1954), pp. 1, 72.
16. Judith Greenfeld, "Jews in the Clothing Industry," *Yivo Annual of Jewish Social Science* 2, 3 (New York, 1947–48):203.

wealth, as we were among the humblest and poorest in it. The bulk of the population lived on less than 50 copeks (twenty-five cents) a day, and that was difficult to earn. A hunk of rye bread and a bit of herring or cheese constituted a meal. A quarter of a copeck (an eighth of a cent) was a coin with which one purchased a few crumbs of pot-cheese or some boiled water for tea. Rubbers were worn by people "of means" only. I never saw any in the district in which my mother and I had our home. A white starched collar was an attribute of "aristocracy." Children had to nag their mothers for a piece of bread.[17]

The impact and shock of the change in environment upon the immigrant can be better understood when one recalls that in the European townlets from which most Jewish immigrants came, there was a feeling of community kinship, of each person's being part of one large family, being regarded as an indissoluble link in the community chain and interacted with as a human being.[18] In the city mode of life, the individual man is often alone, isolated; what contacts with people he has are impersonal and not durable, and he is no more than a mere number.

In the novel *The Old Bunch,* author Meyer Levin tells of the mother, Mrs. Greenstein, a first-generation immigrant, that

> Twenty-two years of this life had passed, and yet it was a strange life to her. First one lit gas and then one turned on electric lights, but still the only real life, the only safe life, was under the glow of the oil lamp, those first sixteen years back home.[19]

Filled with a keen longing for their old folkways, the immigrants, in order to recreate their former mode of living and their old institutions in the New World, or-

17. Abraham Cahan, pp. 6–7.
18. Pitrim Sorokin and C. C. Zimmerman, *Principles of Rural-Urban Sociology* (New York: H. Holt and Co., 1929), pp. 56–57.
19. (New York: Citadel Press, 1942), p. 14.

ganized "landsmanschaften" societies and congregations, which they named after their home towns in the Ukraine, Poland, Roumania, or Austro-Hungary. This nostalgic feeling for home town and this consciousness of kind explain the natural desire of many immigrants to seek work among their own friends, their "landsleit" (townsmen) and the tendency to pursue the same occupations. For example, in *The Rise of David Levinsky,* David says:

> Everything bearing the name of my native place touched a tender spot in my heart. It was enough for a cloakmaker to ask me for a job with the Antomir accent to be favorably recommended to one of my foremen. A number of the men who received special consideration and were kept working in my shop in the slack seasons, when my force was greatly reduced, were fellow-townspeople of mine. This had been going on for several years . . . till gradually an Antomir atmosphere had been established in my shop, and something like a family spirit of which I was proud.[20]

Shift to Working Class and Loss of Status. According to Judith Greenfeld, of the 66,500 workers in the New York clothing industry in the middle nineties, 75 percent were Jews;[21] of the fifteen thousand cloakmakers in 1900, twelve thousand were Jewish.[22] An account of the shift to working-class occupations by the East European Jewish immigrants in their pioneer period is given by B. Hoffman.

> Among those who became cloak operators were former Yeshivah students, store clerks, insurance agents, semi-intellectuals, teachers, storekeepers, traders, etc., an element individualistic, undisciplined, but rather capable, agile, impatient. All

20. Cahan, p. 378.
21. Greenfeld, p. 203.
22. United States Factory Inspector Report, 1897, p. 45.

these men, who in the old country had been strangers to physical labor, here harnessed themselves to a machine which rushed the life out of them.[23]

In his old home town the immigrant had a certain status and a recognized role in the group. When he came to America and had to adjust himself, changing his dress, language, ideals, and interests, it meant loss of status. Upon his arrival after leaving Castle Garden, David Levinsky meets a cloak contractor who has come in order to exploit the newly arrived immigrant for cheap labor. He soon learns of the entirely different conditions which turn "things upside down, transforming an immigrant shoemaker into a man of substance, while a former man of leisure was forced to work in a factory here."[24]

David then thought that if his revered teacher and friend "Reb Sender were here, he, too, might have to go peddling. Poor Reb Sender! The very image of him with a basket on his arm broke my heart. America did seem to be the most cruel place on earth."[25]

In *The Promised Land*, Mary Antin tells that after their arrival in America, the family were almost in the same material circumstances in Boston as in Russian Polotzk. They moved into the same squalid quarters of the city where other immigrant groups lived. Her father's training as a Hebrew scholar, which would give him special prestige and status in Russia was not much help to him here in America. It gave him no advantage over his competitors in selling kerosene and potatoes, or in serving as night watchman in the slums of Harrison Avenue.[26]

In *Uncle Moses*, Sholem Asch portrays the son of a

23. B. Hoffman, *Fifty Years of the Cloakmakers Union* (New York: Elias Laub Publishing Co., 1948), p. 194.
24. Cahan, p. 95.
25. *Ibid.*, p. 97.
26. Antin, p. 195.

poor barley grinder, who as a young man of military age left his home town of Kusmin, Poland, and came over to this country on a cattle boat with two Russian rubles in his pocket. Moses succeeds in business and becomes the wealthy owner of a large men's-wear business in the Bowery. He first brings over his family from Kusmin, and then his fellow townsmen, and provides them with employment in his tailoring establishment. Half of Kusmin are soon working for him; among them are the leading Jews in his home town, working as tailors and pressers in his shop. He regards himself as their benefactor and leader, but underpays them. The once highly respected Reb Chaim Moses and other synagogue dignitaries in the old home town now slave in Uncle Moses' sweatshop. Men of learning and lineage are made the servants of erstwhile paupers.

How the changed social situation affects the personality of the immigrant is illustrated in Berl and many other townsmen of Moses. As Berl takes up his books and puts them away in a corner, he turns to his brother Aaron with a smile:

> Do you know, Aaron, back home I used to live my life during the day. Together with other people, when we were all awake. Here I live my real life at night, when everyone else is asleep. For what am I by day? Nothing at all, a poor machine operator, working on aprons, sitting there with Italian Christian girls. But at night, when everyone is asleep—see, then I am Berl again, reciting my page of Talmudic commentaries, reading what this or that great scholar has to say, just as I used to do at home. Then I feel as though I were back home in the House of Prayer, studying. America is a topsy-turvy world, after all. Here one lives at night, and is dead during the day.[27]

More than anyone else, Aaron regretfully notices the transformation of his older brother, Berl. As Aaron

27. Sholem Asch, "Uncle Moses" (New York: G. P. Putnam and Sons, 1938), p. 21. See Acknowledgments.

looks steadily at his brother, he notices for the first time how Berl has aged during the short time he has lived in America. He is an old man now, gray-haired and stoop-shouldered. And it has not been very long since this old man was Berl the sage of Kusmin, with a black beard, glowing red cheeks, and shining black eyes. Berl the sage, who had a voice in all community affairs, a merchant of the old school, a Hasid, follower of the Gerer Rabbi, well-read in the Talmud—could this be the same Berl? Aaron feels as if he has two brothers: Berl the Talmudic scholar, who was the village spokesman, and Berl the workman, old, stoop-shouldered, pathetic, broken-down Jew here in New York.

Berl himself, aware of the radical change, says to his brother Aaron:

> You keep staring at me, and yet you don't recognize me any more, do you? . . . The old Berl is dead. I have been born anew here, I can't remember the old Berl myself. This one is an entirely different person.[28]

DISILLUSIONMENT, FRUSTRATION, AND REEMIGRATION

Disillusionment and frustration were experienced especially by the older, more religious Jews, as well as by the intellectual and professional people to whom the occupational change to a hard proletarian existence, the loss of status, and lack of the old-home spiritual atmosphere were most trying.

In *The Mother*, Sholem Asch portrays an immigrant Jewish family, the Zlotniks, brought over to America by their oldest son. The arrival in the new country turned out to be very different from what Anshel had anticipated. Anshel, the father, who had been a Reader of Scriptures in his home town, reluctantly takes a job in a shirt factory to support his family.

---

28. *Ibid.,* p. 27.

"I thought that maybe you had found a place for me as Reader of Scriptures in some big, important synagogue," said the father finally.

"Reading Scripture is no 'Business' in America—one has no use for that here in America."

"So you expect your father to turn tailor in his old age?" asked mother.

"To be a tailor is no disgrace here. Many respected Jews are tailors here, even rabbis. In this country that is not considered a disgrace."

"Then what you mean is—I am to be a tailor—that is what you want, my son? A tailor it must be, is that it?" father asked.[29]

Anshel and his wife, feeling uprooted, try to adjust themselves to the new and strange life in order to earn a livelihood. They feel lonely and frustrated.

All week long, while Anshel is sitting at work, and hears the humming of the machines in his ears, he feels cut off from his former life. . . .

"Of what are you thinking, Anshel?" Sarah Rifke recalls him from his reverie, as she puts the plate of steaming noodle soup in front of him.

"Tomorrow the weekly portion will be read is the synagogue," says Anshel, half to himself.

Sarah Rifke goes into a reverie herself. A lump rises in her throat.

"This is a topsy-turvey world, that's all, how can you help that? The ignoramuses have the upper hand here," says Sarah Rifke, as though she were making a personal apology.

Anshel says no more; but after he has finished his meat, and before he says the prayers he takes up his little Bible, and turns the pages, as it seems, quite casually. Then he begins to recite the weekly portion, at first merely humming to himself, then louder and louder, then with a flood of melody, with tenderness.[30]

The son further says to his father:

29. Sholem Asch, *The Mother,* trans. Elsa Krauch (New York: G. P. Putman and Sons, 1937), p. 93. See Acknowledgments.
30. *Ibid.,* p. 93.

"For all I care, you can be a rabbi! But one thing I must tell you, father. Here, everyone looks out for himself. The matter concerns *your* wife and *your* children, not mine. I have done enough for you now. I haven't even finished payments on the steamship tickets, and the next payment will be due soon. The next payment on the furniture, too. And the little ones will have to begin to go to school, or someone will be after us about it. . . . I really think that it would be best for me to move away from here. Then you would be forced to shift for yourself.[31]

A direct expression of this disillusionment was the frequent reemigration. In 1882, one of the first years of the mass immigration, 29 percent of the immigrants returned to Europe.[32] A similar situation is depicted in *Uncle Moses.* Uncle Berl and Uncle Moses, overwhelmed by a feeling of inadequacy in the new environment, and of longing for their old homes, are unable to adapt themselves to the new conditions and sail for Europe—back to their native town in Poland where they wish to spend their last years. But their children, born or raised in the New World, come down to the boat to bid them farewell and cannot understand why their older folk long so much for the old country.

Ideological Differentiation. The cultural impact of the new environment on the East European Jewish immigrants was profound. Accompanying the shift in their social-economic structure, there was also a change in their cultural life and in their form of expression. These East European Jewish immigrants were raised and rooted in the religious traditions of Judaism. They saw too sharp a contrast to Jewish tradition in the new Reform version of Judaism, which was organized and led by German Jews, and experienced a feeling of social distance be-

---

31. *Ibid.*
32. Solomon F. Bloom, "The Saga of America's Russian Jews," *Commentary* (February 1946), p. 5.

tween themselves and the German Jews. Among the
East European immigrants were many of Russian revolutionary background, many who had been influenced by
the Haskalah (Enlightenment) movement, and many
who were adherents of new secular ideologies. Those
among them who were religiously minded endeavored to
strengthen traditional religious life by establishing synagogues and schools; others, the secularists, devoted their
energies to the creation of a modern Jewish literature,
a Yiddish press, and also a Yiddish theater.

Because the changed social situation of the immigrant
often meant uprooting, exploitation, breakdown of religious tradition, and family conflicts, many immigrant
wage workers, in protest against the social order, joined
the socialist and labor movements and helped to organize
the important trade unions, such as the International
Ladies' Garment Workers Union and the Amalgamated
Clothing Workers.

The organizations and institutions that the immigrants
created in the process of adjustment were, in the words
of William Carlson Smith, "not outright transplantations
from the homeland but [grew] up in response to the
need in a new situation."[33]

THE YIDDISH PRESS A FACTOR
IN THE IMMIGRANT'S ADJUSTMENT

In the opinion of noted sociologists, the foreign-
language press, because of its ability to reach millions
of immigrants, helped the immigrant to orient himself
in the American environment, and aided in his adjustment to the new conditions. Robert E. Park states:

The immigrant press is interesting mainly from the light which

---

33. William Carlson Smith, *Americans in the Making* (New York:
D. Appleton-Century Co., 1939), p. 187.

its history and its contents throw upon the inner life of immigrant peoples and their efforts to adjust themselves to the new cultural environment.[34]

The Yiddish press, it is generally recognized, has been performing a vital and most useful function for the Jewish immigrant in accelerating his process of Americanization, for it has constantly aimed to inculcate in its readers sentiments of esteem for and appreciation of their newly adopted land.

The history of the Jewish press in the United States goes back to the year 1823, when a periodical, *The Jew,* appeared in New York between 1823 and 1825. In 1843 *The Occident,* edited by Isaac Lesser, began to appear and continued until 1868. Also, other periodicals in English, and some in German, were at that time edited and published by Jewish immigrants from Germany. Like the synagogue, the religious school, the landmanschaft, and the benevolent association, the Yiddish press was to the Jewish immigrants an expression of their will to transplant their cultural heritage into American soil and to continue their group life.

The different publications and newspapers that have appeared at different times expressed the ideals and attitudes of their respective readers. In the last decades of the nineteenth century, with the increased immigration from Eastern Europe, Jewish immigrants were of differing ideological backgrounds. Those who in their new home remained loyal to their religious traditions and cultural patterns, created and patronized the orthodox, conservative press in Yiddish—the *Yiddishe Gazetten, Dos Yiddische Tagenblat,* and *Morgen Journal.*

The first Hebrew-Yiddish weekly on the American continent, *Die Yiddishe Zeitung,* founded and edited by

34. *The Immigrant Press and Its Control* (New York, London: Harper and Brothers, 1922), p. 292.

I. K. Buchner,[35] began to appear on March 1, 1870. A more permanent newspaper, *The Yiddishe Gazetten,* was founded in 1874 by K. Zevi Sarahson, and was read by the middle-class immigrants, merchants, peddlers, and small business men. It later developed into the first Yiddish daily, *Dos Yiddische Tageblat.*

Others among those immigrants who comprised some of the intelligentsia were "Maskilim," Yiddishists, socialists, and labor-Zionists ("Poale Zion"), with their secular interpretation of Judaism. They carried on cultural programs of secular activities in Yiddish, and were interested in the organized labor and socialist movement. The first socialist Yiddish paper, *Die Naie Zeit,* appeared in 1885, and with the growth of the labor movement, socialist and anarchist groups arose who published their own weeklies.[36]

Ideological differences led to the founding, in 1897, of the daily *Forward,* which was to become the largest foreign-language newspaper in America and acquire the widest circulation of any Yiddish daily. The Labor-Zionists and Yiddishists rallied around the *Varheit,* founded in 1905 by Louis E. Miller, and in 1914 the *Tag* (The Day) was founded, which, in the 1950s, merged with the Jewish *Morning Journal.*

By devoting an unusually large proportion of its space to more literary reading material, the Yiddish press reflects and promotes Jewish cultural life and is a potent force in Jewish group survival.

Discussing the literary contents of the Yiddish immigrant press, Robert E. Park says:

> In an analysis of the contents of seventeen New York daily
> newspapers, of which five were published in English, three in

---

35. Moshe Starkman, *The Pioneer Woman* (New York: Pioneer Women Organization, 1953), p. 9.
36. Elias Schulman, *Geschichte Funder Yiddisher Literature in America, 1800–1870.* (New York: Biderman, 1943).

German, five in Italian, and four in Yiddish, students in sociology under Professor Tenney of Columbia University, found that the Yiddish newspapers ranked highest in the amount of space devoted to cultural news (52%).[37]

Park further states that

no other foreign language press has succeeded in reflecting so much of the intimate life of the people which it represents, or reacted so powerfully upon the opinion, thought, and aspiration of the public for which it exists.[38]

In his study of the role of the Yiddish press, Mordecai Soltes concludes that

in helping the immigrant masses in their efforts of adjusting themselves to the new environmental conditions, the Yiddish press was a factor not only in Americanizing them but also in preserving their ethnic cultural group life.[39]

THE YIDDISH PRESS A FACTOR IN THE DEVELOPMENT OF AMERICAN YIDDISH LITERATURE

For decades, fiction and poetry, and essays on economy, popular science, and sociology were first published in the Yiddish press and periodicals, and later were collected and published separately in book form. Thus it was in the Jewish periodical press that the literary products of the Jewish immigrant on American soil have had their origin. Here it may be pertinent to add a word about the literary quality of the Yiddish press as appraised by the late American-Jewish thinker, Morris

37. Park, p. 89.
38. Quoted from W. P. Shriver, "Immigrant Forces," in Dr. Mordecai Soltes, *The Yiddish Press, An Americanizing Agency* (New York: Teachers College, Columbia University, 1925), p. 22.
39. Mordecai Soltes, quoting M. Starkman, "Di Yiddishe Press," in the *Jewish Annual* 10 (New York: Jewish Book Council of America, 1951) :116.

Raphael Cohen, former chairman of the Philosophy Department of New York City College:

> I am glad to testify that I owe a good deal of my education to it. It taught me to look at world news from a cosmopolitan instead of a local or a provincial point of view, and it taught me to interpret politics realistically, instead of being misled by empty phrases.
>
> As I look back on the Yiddish and the English press in the last decade of the nineteenth century, I cannot help feeling that the former did more for the education of its readers than the latter. Having no army of reporters to dig up sensational news, the Jewish press necessarily paid more attention to things of enduring interest. It tried to give its readers something of permanence and substantial value. . . .
>
> The Jewish press can therefore look back upon its work of the last fifty years with pride. It has prepared millions of Jewish people to take a worthy part in American civilization while also promoting the natural self-respect to which Jews are entitled because of their character and history.[40]

Worthy of note is the evident influence which the Yiddish press still wields among the vast masses of American Jews. Referring to a mass meeting on November 15, 1955, when thousands of Jewish people converged upon Madison Square Garden to protest Communist arming of Arab States and to voice their solidarity with the people of Israel, Samuel Margoshes, in his English column of the Yiddish daily, *The Day,* says:

> The fact is that the vast Yiddish press audience was brought together almost exclusively by the Yiddish press. . . . The Yiddish newspapers were about the only media used in reaching the public for the Madison Square Garden meeting. . . . The tremendous attendance confirmed the strong hold which the Yiddish press still has upon the Jewish public.[41]

---

40. Morris Raphael Cohen, *Reflections of a Wandering Jew* (Glencoe, Ill.: The Free Press, 1950), pp. 31-32, 33.
41. (November 18, 1955), p. 1.

Also noteworthy is the fact that the "Bintel Brief" (letter to the editor), a popular feature in the Yiddish daily *Forward,* was used by William I. Thomas as source material for his sociological study of Jewish attitudes and behavior patterns.[42] Thomas viewed these letters addressed to the editor as attempts of Jewish immigrants, during a period of transition and crisis, to find new definitions of the situation.

In summarizing the achievements of the Yiddish Press, Abraham G. Duker says:

> The Yiddish press westernized and modernized the Jewish immigrants. It taught them how to live with their neighbors and with their own children. It helped them in the Americanization. It exerted a potent influence in spreading democratic ideals in the Jewish community. It served as the basis for trade union, social and ideological organizations. It acted as the mainspring for the Zionist and other survivalist movements. It became a rallying center for fund-raising for Jewish causes. It functioned as a spokesman for the Jewish community before the general American public, particularly on political matters. Its services in helping to bring about the establishment of the State of Israel were most important. The press generally proved to be the most successful whenever it was independent and dared to speak up vigorously.[43]

---

42. M. Bressler, "Jewish Behavior Pattern as Exemplified in Wm. I. Thomas's *Unfinished Study of the 'Bintel Brief'*" (Ph.D. dissertation, University of Pennsylvania, 1952).
43. Abraham G. Duker, *The Day* (December 25, 1949), p. 12.

5
Culture Patterns Through
Three Generations

From the beginning of mass immigration of Jews from East Europe, i.e., from 1881 to date, American Jews, as a highly urbanized ethnic group, have undergone a radical transformation. One can easily discern the cultural patterns changing from generation to generation in the adjustment process of the Jew to modern life.

A gradual continual transformation takes place in the lives of untold numbers of Jews in all strata of life, changing from one generation to the next in the process of acculturation.

WIDENING DISTANCE BETWEEN GENERATIONS

In a sketch called *Four Generations—Four Wills,* Y.L. Peretz,[1] the "father" of modern Yiddish literature, gives the texts of the last wills and testaments of the heads of four successive generations of a Jewish family.

The first will is by the father, a strictly pious scholar, living in a tiny Polish village. The second is by the son, a scrupulously observant Jewish merchant of scholarly tastes. The third generation is represented by a prosper-

---

1. Y. L. Peretz, *Four Generations—Four Wills,* trans. and ed. Sol Liptzin (New York: Yivo, 1947), pp. 266–74.

75

ous business man, a "Maskil" (a man of "enlightened views"), active in the Zionist movement and in communal affairs. The fourth will is that of a young man who is writing in a Paris hotel room before committing suicide because his life had neither roots nor fruits, neither tradition nor ideals.

Apt illustrations of the changing American Jewish family, of the widening generation gap, and of the related problem of Jewish cultural survival, are given in *The Generations of Noah Edon* by David Pinski[2] and in the novels of Myron Brinig, *Singermann,*[3] and its sequel, *This Man Is My Brother.*[4]

David Pinski, who came to America at the turn of the century, has closely observed the painful experiences of the Jewish immigrant in the new American environment and vividly portrays the changes in the mode of living, the attitudes, and the values of three generations of an American Jewish family.

When pious Noah Edon and his good wife, Marah, came to America with their three young sons in the eighteen-eighties from the small village of Brishnitz, Lithuania, they were full of hope for a new and freer life. They opened a crockery store in America, "which is New York." While struggling to earn a livelihood, they tried to continue their traditional Jewish, religious, mode of life as much as possible. Moses, the oldest of the three sons, marries a wholesaler's daughter and eventually becomes one of America's richest merchants. "I am business," he says. The second son, Oscar, becomes a successful lawyer; Charles, who had desired to be a writer, becomes a physician. As time goes on, the sons become more estranged from their parents and their mode of life. They do not attend the synagogue on the

---

2. English translation. (New York: The MacCarlough Co., 1931).
3. (New York: Farrar and Rinehart, 1929).
4. (New York: Farrar and Rinehart, 1932).

Sabbath; there is no difference in their homes between a Friday evening and any other evening. They do not care to give their children a religious education, but send them to the finest secular private schools and colleges, where they will be trained to be "ladies" and "gentlemen" of perfect manners.

The grandchildren, the third generation, are completely estranged from the religious and cultural traditions of the grandfather. Although Grandpa Noah himself does not feel strange and uprooted here in the new land, he does feel that the generation born and reared here is without roots. He feels it most forcibly on his jubilee night.

> There was his whole family assembled! There they were, every one so festive looking, his own flesh and blood; and yet so diverse, strange and distant. *His* grandfather's family had been so much more homogeneous. There had bben a bond which held them closer together.
> He found the explanation in his religion, in his Judaism and piety, which was no longer his children's. Grandpa Noah's great concern was that a chain was broken, a chain of pious, believing Jews. He remained hanging on a link in the old chain, which stretched back somewhere in the obscurity of the past generations, but the new links of the chain, his sons and grandchildren had broken off—and the chain was no more.[5]

The changing mode of living in the process of their adjustment and the contrast and widening rift between the immigrant parents—the first generation—and their children—the second generation—also find artistic expression in Myron Brinig's two novels mentioned above. The Singermann family, which migrated from Roumania at the beginning of the century, settled first in Minneapolis and was close knit. For years Moses and his boys peddled vegetables in the streets of Minneapolis until they moved to the crude mining town of Silver Bow,

5. Pinski, p. 203.

Montana, which was then developing. Here Moses Sing-ermann opens a store, works hard, and prospers. He and his wife, Rebecca, cling to their faith and to their Jewish traditions, while their children, raised in the western states of America, are influenced by modern attitudes. Their behavior estranges them from their parents and theirs parents' mode of living. Moses and Rebecca are aware of their children's beliefs and are concerned about their loyalty to their ancestral faith. Moses discusses with his wife the candidates in the Presidential election campaign, the widespread crime in the country, the money-madness, the loss of identity:

> Who is an educated man in this country? . . . The man with plenty of money, he is an educated man. He speaks, and right away the papers print every word he says. But a poor man, if he is educated, nobody knows it. Every day there is another murder. Always people are being killed. In Roumania, you never hear from such things.
> It is because this country is yet young and people don't know what they want. . . . It is like they got a fever, a great excite-ment in their hearts. Everybody wants money, always more money. It is because they have this fever, they lose their minds, their religion. Myself, when I am in the store, I forget every-thing, but sell, sell, sell. I forget I am a Jew. I forget the syna-gogue. I forget the dances in Roumania. It is like a fever is burning me up. And so I holler on the children and throw shoes at their heads. Sometimes, I am sorry we come to America. I ask myself, what kind of men will my children be and their children after them? They will not be Jews, this much I know. How can they know what it is to be a Jew in a city like this where so much is cheap, where so much passes like the wind? I am afraid my children will be married to Gentiles and my grandchildren will believe in nothing.[6]

Social Mobility. The process of social mobility began with the transition of the American cloak business from

---

6. Brinig, *Singermann,* pp. 46–47.

the control of German Jews to Jews from East European countries. The newly arrived Jewish immigrants from Russia, Galicia, and Roumania, who began as sweatshop workers, became contractors and manufacturers, and later gained ascendancy over their German-Jewish employers in the ownership of the cloak industry. The development of the American clothing trade, and the resultant occupational change and social mobility are vividly shown by Abraham Cahan.

His David Levinsky, who took a job in the garment industry only as a means of working his way through college, is insulted by his employer, Jeff Manheim. He then decides to take away his employer's designer and go into business for himself, and he finally attains financial success:

> The German manufacturers were the pioneers of the industry in America. It was a new industry; in fact, scarcely twenty years old. Formerly, and as late as the seventies, women's cloaks and jackets were little known in the United States. . . . The industry progressed, the new-born great Russian immigration—a child of the massacres of 1881 and 1882—bringing the needed army of tailors for it. There was big money in the cloak business, and it would have been unnatural if some of these tailors had not, sooner or later, begun to think of going into business on their own hook. At first it was a hard struggle. The American business world was slow to appreciate the commercial possibilities which these newcomers represented, but it learned them in course of time.[7]

Social Distance and Generation Conflict. The changed environment and efforts toward economic adjustment weakened the family, creating not only generation conflict among the poor immigrants but also among those who attained financial success and whose parents be-

7. Abraham Cahan, *The Rise of David Levinsky* (New York: Harper and Bros., 1917), pp. 201–2.

longed to the radical socialist class. Social distance and
conflict between parents and children could also be found
in wealthy immigrant families.

In "Chaim Lederer's Return,"[8] Sholem Asch portrays
a poor Jewish immigrant who, after attaining financial
success, wishes to retire to devote his time to intellectual
pursuits and ideals. But he is not understood by his family. In his earlier years, while occupied with providing
for his wife and children, he gave little time to them,
and they had consequently become estranged.

When old Lederer reflects in his retirement upon his
life and the years gone by, he finds that he was more
content when he lived with his family on the East Side
and had only two rooms and a kitchenette on the third
floor. He realizes that there is little of common interest
that can now keep his family together. There is a distance between him, the father, and his children; their
interests are far apart. His son Morris, representing the
second generation of the American-Jewish immigrant,
has married into a Jewish family who immigrated from
Germany, and has become an active member in the Reform Jewish Temple. It is characteristic of middle-class
American Jews, the newly rich, that in their striving to
climb socially they try to imitate those who are more
Americanized, usually the German-Jewish families.

Chaim, who has retired too soon from business, finds
himself bored. His son Morris, like most of the middle-
class Jews, aspires to improve his business and his social
status, and can not forgive his father for being a
"nihilist." His son Moses belongs to a Temple and to
several philanthropic organizations. Old Lederer, on the
other hand, regards himself as a radical, for which his
children can not forgive him. They resent his East-Side
habits. The atmosphere in the home lacks the warmth of

8. Sholem Asch, "Chaim Lederer's Return," in *Three Novels*, trans.
Elsa Krauch (New York: G. P. Putnam's Sons, 1938). See Acknowledgments.

the Jewish home where the customs of the Sabbath and the holy days are observed. Chaim has neither religion nor any other strong emotion that could draw his family together.

Morris has social aspirations and wishes to see his sister Stella marry into the eminently suitable Nuerenberger family, but they are frustrated by his father's attitude. When he hears his father remark jokingly about the German Jews, he breaks forth tempestuously:

> Yes, like my Germans! That's right! Not like the family that father has brought up. What did we have at home? What did father give us except our poor crust of bread, which every father brings home to his children? We had to go away from home when we were nothing but little youngsters, we had to go to visit neighbors in order to see how other families live, to see how children gather round their parents for the Sabbath celebration or for one of the solemn holidays. We never heard father bless the wine, nor knew what the Seder ceremony was. We never went to the synagogue at all. We had nothing at all like that. If we had not looked after ourselves, if we had not visited the homes of other people and seen how other people lived, we would have grown up as nihilists, without a home, or a family, we would have been just poor Russians, like father. We wouldn't have had any ambition, any idea of family life. We would have had nothing at all, just as father has nothing at all. I'm grateful to my Germans, yes, I am; I'm grateful from the bottom of my heart that they took me into their home, took me off the streets, and that they accepted me into their circle, into their family. They gave me a family circle, too, a real family with traditions, beauty, piety, and everything. I owe them everything I have: my respectability, my ambitions, my desire to get ahead—everything, everything: and father jokes about these Germans.[9]

Old Lederer feels that he belongs to no one; he is a stranger, lonely and forsaken in his own home. To find peace and purpose in life, he decides that he must return to the role of a working man.

---

9. *Ibid.*, pp. 79–80.

THE CHANGING SECOND GENERATION

The second stage in the development of American Jewish life covers the period from 1905 to 1920. During these years, marking the high point of East European Jewish immigration into the United States, there emerged a new generation born or reared on American soil. There also appeared in this period a new group of writers, whose works in Yiddish, Hebrew, and English portray the life of the American Jew in process of transition.

The social setting of the period is characterized by the following historic events: the economic crisis following the Russo-Japanese War (1904-05); the failure of the Russian Revolution in 1905; and the pogroms in Kishineff, Gomel, and other Russian cities. These conditions brought about a new mass flight of Jews from Russia, when thousands of immigrants, fleeced of their last savings, arrived penniless in the Atlantic ports of Europe. Pierre Van Passen tells how in his youth he visited the waterfront at Rotterdam, Holland,

> where thousands of Russian Jews were waiting to board ships for the great unknown . . . lying or sitting on their bales and sacks of baggage. . . . There was an air of hopeless impotence about their movements; a dumb, defeatist resignation, almost inhuman.[10]

The profound impact of the pogroms upon the Jews in Russia was that they realized that the Jewish population was doomed.[11] With the new immigration wave a number of the upper strata of Russian Jews came over, the well-to-do and the intelligentsia.

---

10. Pierre Van Passen, *Days of Our Years* (New York: Hillman, Curl, Inc., 1939), p. 26.
11. Mark Wischnitzer, *To Dwell in Safety* (Philadelphia: The Jewish Publication Society of America, 1948), p. 101.

Occupational Change. With the emergence of the second generation, a marked occupational change can be observed. There began a gradual shift in occupation, from shopwork to business, and, later, to the professions. The average American Jew of the second generation in the urban, industrialized cities of New York, Chicago, and Philadelphia was no longer the pushcart peddler or factory worker. Among the Jews in Chicago, says Louis Wirth, "the modern business-man on Halstead Street represents the ideal of the sons of the pushcart owners on Maxwell Street.[12] The sons of the former pushcart owners, or small store keepers operate fashionable shops in more affluent neighborhoods or have become lawyers, doctors, and other kinds of professionals."[13]

Trend Toward the Middle Class and Professions. A new process of "deproletarianization" started when young American Jews began to move into the ranks of the middle classes and the professions. Citing data from a survey of fourteen representative American cities, Nathan Glazer[14] observes that Jews, far more than non-Jews, are engaged in middle-class occupations rather than in manual labor. Examining the data from this survey, Glazer states:

> The proportion of Jews in the non-manual occupations (that is, of those working in the professions, as proprietors, managers, and officials, and as clerks and salesmen) ranged from 75 to 96 per cent. For the American population as a whole, the proportion engaged in this kind of work was about 38 per cent of the gainfully employed in 1950.[15]

12. *The Ghetto* (Chicago: University of Chicago Press, 1928), p. 232.
13. *Ibid.,* p. 235.
14. "Social Characteristics of American Jews," *American Jewish Year Book,* Vol. 56, Morris Fine, ed. Prepared by the American Jewish Committee, New York. (Philadelphia: The Jewish Publication Society of America, 1955), pp. 3–41.
15. *Ibid.,* p. 35.

The fourteen cities surveyed showed, according to Glazer, that 15 percent of the Jews gainfully employed were in the professions, compared with about 8 percent of the general American population. One of the reasons for this comparatively high proportion of Jews in professions is the social values of the frustrated immigrant parents. Immigrant Jewish parents strongly desire to have in the family a lawyer, a doctor, or some other professional, an attainment which they regard as a symbol of social success and achieved status.

In *My Son the Lawyer*,[16] Henry Denker depicts the son who became a lawyer only to satisfy the ambition of a strong-willed mother, who was unhappy about her husband's manual job and obsessed by the ambition to have her son become a lawyer.

> "Davelleh, Davelleh, what did I work for all my life? To have one little bit of enjoyment, to have one little bit of 'nachas' from you. I should have a son who is a professional man. When I go to 'schule' I shouldn't have to hide my face when Mrs. Levine talks about her son, the lawyer. Or Mrs. Tekulsky talks about her son, the doctor. Doctor! He's only in second-year medical school. It would be bad I should talk about my son, the lawyer? Is that wrong?"

The dialogue continues:

> "I'll do what you say. I'll be what you want." The tears stopped. She raised her wet face. She smiled at him. "You're such a good boy, Dave, such a good boy. From you I expect the best. And you wouldn't disappoint me. You couldn't. You're too good."[17]

In order to achieve that supposed glamour and social success for her son, Mrs. Brown sacrificed the happiness of her whole family. For this, she worked, planned, and

16. (New York: Thomas Y. Crowell Co., 1950.)
17. *Ibid.*, pp. 7-9.

dreamed. To satisfy his mother's wish, David gives up his own hope of becoming a writer. But when he involves himself in an illegal act as he desperately seeks money to pay for an operation for his critically ill mother, he is disbarred. His mother dies without ever knowing that the money her son was able to pay for her comfort and medical care came not as the fruit of his success in law, but as the price of his disgrace. She feels that all her sacrifices for him have been vindicated, and she triumphs when, close to her death, she proudly boasts to the nurses of her successful son, the lawyer.

> "And you shouldn't feel sorry for me. I don't want anybody to feel sorry for me. So we didn't have the best. Sometimes we froze. Sometimes we sweated. Good times we had. And bad times we had. But in the end it was all right, no? Look," she said, and she raised her hand slightly, pointing to them. "Who has more? A daughter, a teacher. A Son, a lawyer. Who has more?" . . .
> "I'm only glad I lived to see it. That's enough for me. The rest I know. You'll be a big man. You'll have a big office. Secretaries. Other men working for you. You'll be another Max Steuer. I know it, Dave. I'm telling you this because I know it." . . . "Please, Ma . . . don't talk now." . . . "Don't talk!" she echoed. "Who has a better right to talk? Who could have such 'nachas,' such satisfaction from children? The world gets better all the time. All the time," she echoed herself. "You only live for the children. When the children are all right, then it's time to die."[18]

Desire for Education. Related to the shift to better-paid professions and more skilled middle-class occupations is the great regard Jews have for higher education. It is the traditional Jewish attitude toward education which explains why Jews have a relatively larger number of college and university students than other ethnic groups:

> If the sons and daughters of needle-workers, peddlers, and

---

18. *Ibid.,* pp. 273–74.

petty merchants from Eastern Europe swarmed to the universities and professional schools, they were reacting naturally to a new freedom and an ancient yearning.[19]

Glazer points out that even those immigrant Jews who could not rise out of the working class largely retained middle-class habits and ways of thinking. He finds the origin of middle-class values present among American Jews in their religion and historic culture. Citing the thesis of Max Weber that the middle-class virtues originated in the religious outlook of Calvinism, he says:

> There is no question that Judaism emphasizes the traits that businessmen and intellectuals require, and has done so since at least 1,500 years before Calvinism. We can trace Jewish Puritanism at least as far back as the triumph of the Maccabees over the Hellenized Jews and of the Pharisees over the Sadducees. The strong emphasis on learning and study can be traced that far back, too. The Jewish habits of foresight, care, moderation, probably arose early during the two thousand years that Jews have lived primarily as strangers among other peoples. Other features of Jewish religion and culture tended to strengthen the complex of habits leading to success in trade and the professions.[20]

Even when the Jews in Czarist Russia were prevented from engaging in middle-class pursuits toward the close of the nineteenth century, they retained middle-class habits and values. The East European Jews who arrived as immigrants in the United States from 1881 to 1924

> were the sons or the grandsons of merchants and scholars, even though the merchants had only their wits for capital, and the scholars' wits were devoted to feats of memory. This background meant that the Jewish workers could almost immediately turn their minds to ways and means of improving themselves that were quite beyond the imagination of their fellow workers. Business and education were, for the Jews, not a re-

---

19. Glazer, in *American Jewish Year Book* 56:28.
20. *Ibid.*, p. 31.

mote and almost foreign possibility, but a near and familiar one.[21]

In the social situation in which the Jew then found himself he aspired to be proprietor of his own business in order to become independent of the dubious good will of a person who might be prejudiced against Jews.

David Levinsky, Cahan's young immigrant boy, goes despite his foreign accent into a business of his own, and his products are as good as those of longer-established American firms, and are cheaper.[22] He is proud of his financial success, though lonely and full of regret for being forced by environmental circumstances to give up his desire to go to college and turn from the pursuit of knowledge to the pursuit of money. He meditates with pride on the contribution his needle trade has made to American life:

> Foreigners ourselves, and mostly unable to speak English, we had Americanized the system of providing clothes for the American woman of moderate or humble means. The ingenuity and unyielding tenacity of our managers, foremen, and operatives had introduced a thousand and one devices for making by machine garments that used to be considered possible only as the product of handwork. This—added to a vastly increased division of labor, the invention, at our instance, of all sorts of machinery for the manufacture of trimmings, and the enormous scale upon which production was carried on by us— had the effect of cheapening the better class of garments prodigiously. We had done away with prohibitive prices and greatly improved the popular taste. Indeed, the Russian Jew had made the average American girl a "tailor made" girl.[23]

Change Reflected in American Hebrew Fiction. The theme of adjustment experiences and changing culture patterns of the immigrant and of the second-generation

---

21. Cahan, *The Rise of David Levinsky,* pp. 390–91.
22. *Ibid.,* p. 443.
23. *Ibid.,* p. 32.

Jews appears also in a number of novels and short stories written in modern Hebrew. Novels written in Hebrew and dealing with Jewish life in American are *Yechiel Ha-Hagri* (Yechiel the Immigrant) and *Ad Mashber* (Until the Crisis) by Simon Halkin[24] and *B'ein Dor* (A Lost Generation) by Reuben Wallenrod.[25]

In *Yechiel the Immigrant,* written in 1913, Halkin depicts the bewilderment and confusion which the young Jewish immigrant experiences in the hustle-bustle of life in New York. Yechiel tries to withdraw to a spiritual life by joining a Kabalist, engrossed in mystic thought and studies. He becomes involved in love of two girls, and ultimately feels lost. In *Ad Mashber,* Halkin presents the new generation of American Jewish immigrants who are interested in educational pursuits but are caught in a net of emotional and ideological conflicts. In this work there appears the emerging intellectual, the more integrated American Jew, who represents a synthesis of Americanism and Judaism as complementing and supplementing one another.

In *B'ein Dor,* Wallenrod delineates the American Jewish scene in the period between the two World Wars. He portrays the profound changes the new environment has brought into the life of the immigrants who came after the First World War, whose life became mechanized, emptied of things spiritual—a life of gross materialism, worthless and "generationless."

In another Hebrew novel, *Ki Panah Yom* (The Day's Decline)[26]—a characteristic title taken from the closing prayer of the Day of Atonement, a prayer for mercy "for the day is drawing to a close"—the same author bares the realities of American Jewish life in the person

---

24. Simon Halkin, *Yechiel Ha-Hagri* (New York: Hebrew Publishing Co., 1913) ; *Ad Mashber* (New York: Hebrew Publishing Co., 1929).
25. Reuben Wallenrod, *B'ein Dor* (Tel Aviv: Am Oved Publishing Co., 1954).
26. *Ibid., Ki Panah Yom* (Jerusalem: Bialik Institute, 1953).

of Mr. Halpern, owner of a mountain resort, and in the guests who come to his resort in search of pleasure.

In his collection of short stories, *Bein Homot New York* (Among the Walls of New York),[27] Wallenrod depicts differences in outlook and interests between parents and children. The stories "A Farewell Night" and "In a Country Hotel" tell of Yudel, a farmer of the Catskills, who typifies a generation of idealists who came to America hoping to become farmers and to build their lives on a productive, honest foundation, but instead became hotel keepers, catering to immigrant guests and their children who are in the process of forgetting their Yiddish and speak a poor English.

---

27. *Ibid., Bein Homot New York* (Jerusalem: Bialik Institute, 1953).

6

The Second Generation:
Alienation and Marginality

The dilemma of man in modern society, it is generally recognized, is his alienation from his group and from himself. Referring to feelings of estrangement from commonly accepted institutional values, alienation is associated with current social and cultural changes, such as industrialization and urbanization. Sociologists and social psychologists maintain that personality and morals are, to a large degree, a matter of group experience and identity. They are aware of the psychological problem created by the change from a simple community to a more complex, urban society, although they may use different terms such as "anomie" (Durkheim), "primary group" relations (Cooley), or "Gemeinschaft" and "Gesellschaft" (Community and Society) (Tonnies). The change from the "simple" to the "complex" urban society marks "the destruction of the cozy nest, the kinship group, in which men once lived out their lives and in which spontaneous personal relations were possible, and is at the root of the experience of alienation."[1]

Worthy of note on this matter of alienation and group identity is the reference made by Erik H. Erikson to

1. Nathan Glazer, "The Alienation of Modern Man," *Commentary* 3, (April 1947) :379.

Zigmund Freud in his study of "The Problem of Ego Identity." In discussing the concept of identity in its psychosocial connotation, Erikson tells that "Freud used it only once in a more than *incidental* way, and then with a psycho-social connotation. It was when he [Freud] tried to formulate his link to Judaism, that he spoke of an 'inner identity' which was not based on race or religion, but on a common freedom from prejudice which narrows the use of the intellect. Here the term *identity* points to an individual's link with the unique history of his people. The term identity expresses such mutual relations and refers to a maintenance of our inner solidarity with a group's ideals and identity."[2]

One can readily note a sharp contrast between the first and second generation of American Jews in this experience of adjusting to the new American environment. To be sure, the children of the Jewish immigrants born or reared in America had to struggle like their immigrant parents for an economic foothold and were often subject to social and economic discrimination; there was, however, a difference in the nature of the difficulties encountered and in their adjustment, because their problems became mainly psychological or spiritual—what could be called the problem of alienation.

The immigrant parents had a sense of "at homeness" and security within their group's cultural life, in their families, within their home-town societies, their synagogues and their Yiddish newspapers and theaters. All of these supported a feeling of belonging, of self-acceptance, and also a sense of continuity of their Jewish heritage. Such ties with the past, however, offered little comfort for their children, reared mostly in the American urban environment and faced with a more difficult adjustment to the new social situation. As children of immigrant parents they were in a most uncomfortable position, for

2. (Glencoe, Ill.: The Free Press, 1960), pp. 37, 38.

"whereas in the schoolroom they were too foreign, at home they were too American. . . . How to inhabit two worlds at the same time was the problem of the second generation."[3]

MARGINALITY AND CHANGING SENSE OF MORAL VALUES

Those of the second generation, finding themselves between two worlds, are marginal men. As such they present a subject of great interest to sociologists and social psychologists.[4] Their problems are especially evident in family situations and are often the cause of delinquency, personality maladjustment, generation conflict, and disintegration of the home.[5]

Knowing less than their parents about their religious traditions and cultural heritage, the children of the Jewish immigrants could not be expected to care much about their observance, and were rather anxious to depart from the life pattern of their parents and enter the mainstream of American life, which often resulted in a break with their parents. This is well illustrated in the novel *Singermann,* mentioned above, in which Myron Brinig describes Moses and Rebecca, immigrants from Roumania, as they see their children deviating from the ways of their fathers. Their eldest son, Joseph, shepherded by Daisy Korner, a crisp lady of "set phrases and interminable lusts" who drooled with Christian Science, was the first to drop out of the Singermann orbit. When once Yom Kippur happened to fall on Saturday, a pay day in Silver Bow, Jews, sincere in their beliefs, were willing to sacrifice profits for the sake of their religion, and

---

3. Marcus Hansen, "The Problem of the Third Generation Immigrant," *Commentary* 14 (1952) :492.
4. Everett V. Stonequist, *The Marginal Man—A Study in Personality and Culture Conflict* (New York: Charles Scribner and Sons, 1937).
5. Robert E. Park, "Human Migration and the Marginal Man," *American Journal of Sociology* 33 (May 1928) :881–93.

Moses, much as he loved his store, and "greatly as he looked forward to these golden pay days, did not for a moment tolerate the thought of keeping his store open for business."[6] But Joseph, who opened a rival store across the street from his father's, desecrated Yom Kippur (the Day of Atonement) by doing business as usual on that Holy Day.

> his father's store had the sign "Closed acc't Holidays," hanging behind the door. How deserted the place looked, how cold! And here, on the other side of the street, everything was light and business. Joseph's was the only store open in the block, and he was profiting at the expense of his father and younger brothers. All these customers thronging the aisles of Joseph's, their pockets jingling with money, their fingers eagerly caressing the merchandise! And on the Day of Atonement, the day that Singermanns for generations past had set aside for the worship of the one God, the true God. . . .[7]

In their efforts to take root, the first generation of the Singermanns dies, and members of the second are indeed alienated from the faith of their fathers. Joseph, the oldest son, is lost in the shuffle, riding the wave of empty success, enduring the domination of Daisy, now his wife, who is a Hollywood fan. Rachel, Moses' only daughter, falls in love with a Russian barber, a bigamist, who later disappears. David is in love with a Gentile, Maxine, a bad woman, and marries her. Louis, the hopeless dreamer of the family, often gets drunk. Sol is interested in prize fighting. Harry, the promising intellectual of the family, with artistic sense, is a homosexual, who ends his life by drowning in the ocean off the Florida coast. The youngest, Michael, studies and becomes a novelist.

A profound cultural change is also evident in the difference between the immigrant and his children in their

---

6. Myron Brinig, *Singermann* (New York: Farrar and Rinehart, 1929), p. 73.
7. *Ibid.*, pp. 76–79.

moral approach to life and their sensitivity to human suffering.

In a Yiddish short story, *Lynching,* Joseph Opatoshu describes a scene which reveals a difference in attitude and sense of moral values of the immigrant father and his son. The people of the village are assembled around Mc-Patrick's saloon and Levy's hardware store waiting for Bukert. McLure, who has himself seduced the 14-year-old Negro girl Regina, is now looking for Bukert with a loaded gun, for Bukert has raped McLure's daughter in revenge for his sister Regina.

> Old Mr. Levy searched for his 20-year-old son Harry. He found him in the saloon and got him out.
> "You will not go with them," said the father.
> "I will go," insisted the son.
> The father insisted. "I tell you no! A Jew should not mix in."
> "And it will happen to my sister," argued the son, angrily.
> "Why think that it may happen? It will not happen. No! But if we allow a drunkard like McLure to take the law in his own hands, I assure you, today he will lynch a Negro and tomorrow a Jew. Do you know what they are going to do? They are going to lynch the Negro!

When the village shoemaker asks Harry where his father is, he answers:

> "Don't you know my old man—he is crazy. Today I had an argument with him. He threatens to leave us all in Burk and settle in New York among the Jews. According to him, we should lynch the entire village and not the Negro. How do you like that?"
> "What do you think?" said the shoemaker philosophically. "To burn a Negro, one must have a heart."
> "You are a 'greenhorn' just like my old man," Harry said, laughing in his face.[8]

---

8. J. Opatoshu, *Lincherei* (Vilno: Wilner Farlag fun B. Klezkin, 1927), pp. 21–35.

This change in moral sensitivity is also depicted by I. J. Schwartz in *Kentucky*. The father, Joseph, who settled in Kentucky and whose relationship with the Negroes was friendly, has a son Jacob, who is less sensitive to human suffering and watches the mob lynching with indifference.[9]

Lack of Sense of Kinship. Another cultural change in the second generation is the weakening of the family, and the sense of kinship which was so strong among the immigrant townsmen. In the "Uncle Moses" of Sholem Asch, one finds that the townsmen of the old Polish townlet of Kusmin were held together for only a short time by their master and benefactor, Uncle Moses. Social factors soon began to undermine the Kusmin family from within. The children born in America belonged to a different world; they did not know Kusmin, the home town of their parents.

When these young people came down to the boat to bid farewell to two old Jews who were sailing back home to spend their last years in Kusmin, Uncle Berl called aside his only son, Charlie, who was a young child when he brought him to America, and said to him:

> I've only one thing to ask of you. To be quite frank with you, I wish things might have been quite different—but that can't be helped now. Promise me one thing, just this one— promise me, give me your hand! Tell me that you will do this one thing for me. When you have word that everything is over, pray a Kadish, the prayer for the dead, for me. Promise me that, my son![10]

The people standing on the deck to bid farewell to the two old men saw and knew what Berl was asking his son, and all were thinking about their own children.

9. I. J. Schwartz, *Kentucky* (New York: Verlag M. N. Meise, 1925).
10. Sholem Asch, "Uncle Moses" (New York: G. P. Putnam's Sons, 1938), p. 71. See Acknowledgments.

"All of them were thinking how alienated their children had become since the family had moved to this new country." They realized the cultural distance between themselves and their children.

GENERATION CONFLICT AND FAMILY BREAKDOWN

In *The Generations of Noah Edon* by David Pinski, referred to above, Noah is a first-generation Jewish immigrant whose children typify the generation conflict and subsequent family breakdown. They experience adultery, suicide, divorce, public disgrace, and personality disintegration and the house of Noah Edon finally collapses and ends in despair. Old father Noah wonders how it had come about:

> He had brought up his sons to be pious, but as soon as they had grown up, they had cast off their father's Judaism like a garment which they had outgrown. Charles, out of a principle, Murray, because religion was no business for him. Oscar attended a synagogue occasionally, for political reasons. Better if he didn't!
> And the grandchildren, the steps to his tall old age, grew up like heathen. Every Sabbath he kept on talking to them of Jews and Judaism, and God. But made no impression on them.[11]

In *This Man Is My Brother,* Brinig's second novel about the Singermann family, one sees how in the twenty years that have elapsed, from 1911 to 1931, everything is changed. When Michael Singermann returns after twenty years of being away in the East, he finds that the whole family had "undergone the ripening transmutations of time." The children and grandchildren of old Moses Singermann have achieved wealth and a solid position in the community. They have, however, lost their

---

11. David Pinski, *The Generations of Noah Edon* (New York: The Macaulay Company, 1931), pp. 203–4.

religious loyalties, and this, with the loss of their group consciousness, has made them feel rootless and psychologically insecure. Nina, Louis's daughter, allows herself to be dazzled by a football hero and seduced; Sylvia, Rachel's daughter, after a long struggle with her parents, marries a Gentile boy, Tim. Ralph, Rachel's son, alone is grappling with the Jewish problem; he develops a persecution complex and goes insane, but is finally cured.[12]

Alienation and Self-Hatred. The "alienated, marginal men" of the second generation, who shed their ancestral background lacking a sense of group belonging and having no stable, continuous set of life definitions, often find themselves in an intolerable position. Their marginality finds expression in a sense of rootlessness, of an inferiority complex, which at times leads them even to self-hatred and hatred of their own people.[13]

In *Wasteland,* Joe Sinclair portrays Jake Brown, an alienated young American Jew, son of a Russian Jewish immigrant, who is ashamed of his family and of being a Jew, and changes his name to John. He makes every effort to deny and to evade his Jewish identity. Jake, as a "marginal" man who finds no rest and has no emotional security, typifies a large number of second-generation American Jewish youth who are suspended psychologically between their ethnic inheritance and the uncertain, problematical future, in neither of which can they find rest and feel at home. Jake feels alone and at times his back aches. At his sister Deborah's suggestion, he sees a psychiatrist, who encourages him to talk of his past and his experiences. By listening to Jake's talk, one comes to

12. Myron Brinig, *This Man Is My Brother* (New York: Farrar and Rinehart, 1932), pp. 187, 248.
13. Will Herberg, *Protestant, Catholic, Jew* (Garden City, New York: Doubleday Company, Inc., 1955), p. 31.

know of his drab home life, economic difficulties, and the deep chasm between the cultural interests of parents and children. He lacks identity, and at the age of thirty-five is still unintegrated and obsessed with a sense of waste.[14]

Jake especially dislikes the "old ways" of his father and regards "my mother and father, my brothers, me, my sisters, as living in a wasteland, devoid of growth, all dry, all dead."[15] When the psychiatrist asks him:

> "do you ever think of the Jews of the world when you think of enlisting? The suffering, the way they're murdered and tortured?"

Jake answers:

> "No, I don't know. No, I never think of them." Jake winced back into the chair, watched the doctor miserably. "Why should I think about the Jews of the world? I'm an American. Why should I have to call myself a Jew all the time?" He blew out smoke, tapped the cigarette harshly against the ashtray on the desk.[16]

Only after a number of lengthy visits with the psychiatrist does Jake begin to realize that Judaism and Jewish group life are infinitely larger than the caricatures in his own family. By taking his Jewishness for granted, he finally gets rid of his Jewish self-hate and regains his sense of belonging, which puts an end to his alienation and "wasteland."

REJECTION OF GROUP IDENTITY AND PATHOLOGY OF THE MARGINAL JEW

Of significance in this connection is the psychosociological observation by Kurt Lewin that

14. Joe Sinclair, *Wasteland* (New York: Harper and Brothers, 1946), p. 6.
15. *Ibid.,* p. 78.
16. *Ibid.,* p. 14.

self-hatred among Jews is a phenomenon which has been observed ever since the emancipation of the Jews. Novels like that of Ludwig Lewisohn, *The Island Within* (1928) which pictures the New York Jew in the 1920's and those of Arthur Schnitzler, who deals with the problem of the Austrian Jew in the period of 1900, are striking in the similarity of the problems which they show to exist.[17]

He goes on to point out that

in an underprivileged group there are a number of persons ashamed of their membership and in the case of the Jew he will try to move as far away from things Jewish as the outside majority will permit. He will stay on this barrier and be in constant frustration. Actually he will be more frustrated than those members of the minority group who keep psychologically well inside the group.[18]

A vivid portrayal of the psychosocial situation and mood of some of the second generation is found in Lewisohn's novel, *The Island Within*. The author describes Arthur's visit with his sister Hazel and her husband, Eli, in Boston. Hazel, who was psychically injured when just a child by being made to feel inferior, strongly rejects her Judaism. She stands by, watching her young daughter in their Boston neighborhood experience anti-Jewish attitudes. Hazel lives in misery, not a Gentile but living in a Gentile community and still unable to identify herself as a Jew.

She had so shattering and crushing and tragic a Jewish inferiority complex that she could not sustain her life psychically at all without nursing a strong sense of superiority to someone, without despising someone. And the only people whom she dared despise were her own people. When her brother Arthur gently asked Hazel why she felt as she did, she said:

---

17. Kurt Lewin, *Resolving Social Conflict* (New York: Harper and Brothers, 1948), p. 186.
18. *Ibid.*, p. 193.

"I don't like Jews; I want to bring my child up as an American. All that doesn't mean anything to me."[19]

That this psychosociological phenomenon is not uncommon among Jews is attested by some of the keenest observers of contemporary Jewish life. Sociologist and historian Salo Baron asserts:

There are in all Western Jewish communities innumerable Jews whom I have frequently ventured to style the "inverted Marranos"; they appear to act outwardly as Jews; they are recognized as Jews by themselves and their environment. But they deeply resent this fact which, for one reason or another, they cannot alter. Such inverted Marranos, hating their Jewish heritage and involuntary allegiance, usually become self-haters of a pathological kind. They not only destroy their own peace of mind; they are a menace to the equilibrium of the general as well as Jewish society around them.[20]

A vivid illustration of true pathological self-disgust of the marginal Jew which leads, at times, to self-destruction is given in *The Island Within* in the depiction of Victor Goldman, a brilliant young architect who committed suicide. When Goldman's friend, Arthur, rushed to the Goldman home and talked to his brother, Joe, about the cause of Victor's death, Joe said:

"From his infancy on he was made to feel from the very air about him that to be happy and successful and acceptable in the world he must be something that he wasn't, something that he didn't even clearly grasp or understand, namely, an Anglo-American gentleman. Well, he had no gift for mimicry. He was confused. He was maddened. He shouted. He began to hate himself and his own kind. You said yourself it was self-disgust."[21]

19. Ludwig Lewisohn, *The Island Within* (New York: Harper and Brothers, The Modern Library, 1940), pp. 270–71.
20. Quoted by Milton Steinberg, *A Partisan Guide to the Jewish Problem* (New York: Bobbs, Merrill Co., 1945), p. 115.
21. Lewisohn, p. 301.

To return to Kurt Lewin, who has more to say about self-hatred in Jews and others. He remarks that

> Jewish self-hatred is a phenomenon which has its parallel in many underprivileged groups. One of the better known and most extreme cases of self-hatred can be found among American Negroes. . . .
> The self-hatred of the Jew may be directed against the Jews as a group, against a particular fraction of the Jews, or against his own family, or against himself. It may be directed against Jewish institutions, Jewish mannerisms, Jewish language or Jewish ideals.[22]

This "disease of the psyche to which some American Jews have fallen victim," says Milton Steinberg, "is because of their status as members of a minority group."[23] He sums up the situation succinctly in these words:

> A sense of being unwanted, a feeling of insecurity, special penalties, exposure to hostile propaganda, together with the absence of an inner life calculated to regenerate self-respect—these are the forces that have played uninterruptedly upon the Jew for over a century. . . .
> For many modern Jews these preservative forces are no longer operative. Having abandoned their religious tradition, ignorant of the Jewish past, unedified by its present, uninspired by aspirations for its future, they have nothing on which to sustain self-esteem. Jewishness to them is simply a disability. They have lost the secret of that spiritual prophylactic which enabled their fathers to preserve their wholeness.[24]

NOVELS OF SOCIAL PROTEST AND SELF-CONTEMPT

The dominating themes of many novels by writers of the second generation of American Jews in the late 1920s and 1930s, years of depression and rising social preju-

---

22. Lewin, p. 186.
23. *A Partisan Guide to the Jewish Problem* (New York: Bobbs, Merrill Co., 1945), p. 126.
24. *Ibid.*, pp. 110–20.

dice, are alienation and social protest. Frustrated by economic conditions and the blind fury of spreading anti-Semitism, most of the writers of that period harped on the themes of exploitation and anti-Jewish discrimination. Typical of these novels, which are classed as "proletarian" or "social protest," are Michael Gold's *Jews Without Money* (1930) and Isidor Schneider's *From the Kingdom of Necessity*. In the former, a collection of related sketches of New York's East Side, Gold furiously castigates America, which is "rich and fat because it has eaten the tragedy of millions of immigrants." For class-conscious, Communist Gold, there is no Jewish problem; there is only class struggle. He sees only that "the Jewish bankers are Fascists,—Jewish workers are radicals." Gold tells of the many immigrants who, unlike David in Cahan's *The Rise of David Levinsky*, did not rise from the poverty and filth of the East Side Ghetto, of the brutalized slum living and sweatshops which caused girls to become prostitutes and boys to become gangsters; of the religious and social hatreds of conflicting nationalities living in crowded tenement houses. Gold, as his title promises, tells of Jews without money, of crushed lives and blighted hopes.

In this group of second- and third-generation American Jewish writers who were overwhelmed by a sense of frustration and rootlessness and dominated by a feeling of inferiority may also be included Albert Halper (*Union Square, The Foundry,* and *The Shute*) and Henry Roth (*Call It Sleep*).

Pertinent to this discussion is the observation of Kurt Lewin in *Resolving Social Conflict:*

We know from experimental psychology and psychopathology that such frustration leads to an all-around state of high tension with a general tendency to aggression. This aggression should logically be directed against the majority, which is what hinders the minority member from leaving his group. However, the majority has, in the eyes of these persons, higher status and besides, the majority is much too powerful to be attacked. Experiments have shown that under these conditions, aggression is likely to be turned against one's own group or one's self.[25]

Novelists filled with protest and self-contempt often picture Jews as aggressors facing a hostile world. Sammy, in Budd Schulberg's *What Makes Sammy Run,* stops at nothing in his business transactions. An even more negative attitude of Jewish self-hatred is manifested in Jerome Weidman's *I Can Get It For You Wholesale* and *What's In It For Me?,* and in Norman Katov's novel, *Eagle at My Eye.*

Harry Bogan, the main character in *I Can Get It For You Wholesale,* is a typical characterization of the insecure Jew who becomes self-hating, and in whom some critics see a "misbegotten" creation, a lack of ease and assurance, a pathological reaction to the fury of Hitler.[26] Similar negativism to Jewish life and similar types of Jews are presented in *Remember Me to God* by Myron S. Kaufman, in *The Enemy Camp* by Jerome Weidman, and in the novel *Haunch, Paunch and Jowl* by Samuel B. Ornitz, which reflects the author's negative attitude to Judaism and to Jewish survival and his advocating of intermarriage.

Two more recent novels, Philip Roth's *Goodbye Columbus* (1959) and *Portnoy's Complaint* (1969), not only portray negative Jewish characters and an unfavorable image of today's American Jew, but are also extreme examples of the author's pathological contempt of Jewish values and of the Jewish people.

---

25. New York: Harper & Brothers, 1948, p. 193.
26. Marie Syrkin, "The Cultural Scene. Literary Expression," in *The American Jew,* ed. Oscar I. Janowsky (New York and London: Harper and Brothers, Publishers, 1942), p. 104.

7

The Jewish Family in a
Changing Society

SOCIAL CHANGE AND ITS IMPACT ON THE FAMILY

Social change is especially marked upon the family, which is a primary influence in molding the individual's personality and in transmitting the group's cultural heritage from the older to the younger generation.

Ogburn and Nimkoff, in a study made some years ago, observed that the Industrial Revolution, based upon technological inventions, caused the rise of cities, which represent a cluster of factors such as occupation, density, and new ideologies; and that these in turn effect changes in the structure and functions of the family. The population density of the city causes a transfer of certain functions from the family to the government and a diminution of authority in the family.[1] Scientific discoveries have also affected the thinking of man, and his religious beliefs and practices, resulting in the loss of traditional family functions and in changed attitudes and behavior patterns in family relationships. The same factors that affect customs and culture patterns of man in

---

1. William F. Ogburn and M. F. Nimkoff, *Technology and the Changing Family* (Boston, New York: Houghton, Mifflin Co., 1955), p. 257.

general also affect the traditions and culture patterns of the Jewish family.

The essential role of the family in Jewish life throughout the long history of the Jewish people was primary in creating and molding the individual Jew as a "group-conscious" being and in preserving group solidarity. Noted Jewish historians and sociologists maintain that the Jewish community, although without a government of its own and existing in a variety of social environments, has survived and maintained its own identity because religion and tradition have been rooted in and transmitted through the family.[2] On this matter Emory S. Bogardus is most explicit:

> Without a homeland of their own and forced to maintain themselves within other nations, often surrounded by hostile races, their family organization and their religious loyalty have been their salvation. Let their family life break down and their religion be discarded and they as a people will probably disappear.[3]

"As no other factor," asserts Samuel S. Cohon, "pure and tender family ties helped to preserve the Jewish people and to keep them on a healthy and moral plane."[4]

Indeed, just as the family in Jewish life was largely the matrix of the institutions of education, religion, and style of life, it was also the institution upon which depended the group's survival. Changes in the structure and function of the Jewish family had a profound impact upon the life of the entire group, on its social institutions, and on its continuity and survival as a distinct, unique group.

---

2. David R. Mace, *Hebrew Marriage* (New York: Philosophical Library, 1953).
3. Emory S. Bogardus, *Sociology* (New York: The Macmillan Company, 1954), p. 62.
4. In *Judaism: A Way of Life* (Cincinnati: The Union of American Hebrew Congregations, 1948), p. 166.

THE JEWISH FAMILY IN SOCIOHISTORICAL PERSPECTIVE

A study of the basic principles upon which the Jewish family traditionally rested shows that the Jewish marriage ritual and the forms of family relationships have constantly undergone modification to accommodate to changing circumstances of place and time.

Yet, in the almost four thousand years of recorded Jewish history, the family has occupied a most important place in Jewish law and literature. In the Pentateuch, in the Book of Ruth, and in other books of the Bible there are numerous references to the Biblical Jewish family. In the Talmud,[5] five large treatises are devoted to the problems of marriage and the family: Kidushin (on betrothal), Ketuboth (on marriage obligations), Yebemoth (on prohibited marriages and Levirates), Sota (on the woman suspected of adultery), and Gittin (on divorce).

The early Hebrew family was authoritarian, emphasizing monogamy and male dominance. The form of family, which was "adopted by the Christian Church in the later Roman Empire," according to social historian Harry Elmer Barnes, "was primarily a heritage from the Hebrews; and one of the chief contributions of the Hebrews to the history of the family," he continues, "was their sanctification of monogamy and the introduction of strong patriarchal tendencies."[6]

In Talmudic times, although polygamy was permitted, it was rarely practiced. Unna states that none of the rabbis of Mishnah and the Talmud ever lived in polygamy, and that the decree of Rebbenu Gersham in the eleventh century was really nothing but the sanction of a

---

5. Called the *Oral Law,* which consists of the interpretation by the Jewish Rabbis of the *Torah,* or Mosaic Law.
6. *Society in Transition,* 2nd ed. (New York: Prentice-Hall, Inc., 1952), p. 281.

long-existing condition.[7] According to George Foot Moore, the great mass of the Jewish people during the medieval period lived in circumstances which precluded polygamy. No doubt Moore's assertion that "the Rabbinical institution of the marriage contract, the Ketubah, operated not only as a check upon the freedom of divorce but upon plural marriages"[8] is accurate.

The Goal of Marriage. The founding of a family through marriage has been regarded in Judaism as a religious duty and as of the highest social significance. The Hebrew term for marriage is "Kiddushin," meaning sanctification. Man's fundamental obligation traditionally has been to fulfill the first Biblical commandment, "Be fruitful and multiply."[9] Through marriage, man becomes complete, begets children, and himself grows in character. The Talmud views the blessing of children as man's renewal and immortality, and among those regarded as dead, they include "[him] who has no children."[10] Only he who had founded a house in Israel was worthy to be considered a full-fledged member of the community; only she who had become a mother in Israel had realized her destiny.[11] For the Rabbis of the Talmud, children were the noblest fulfillment of married life and God's greatest blessing. It is man's duty to continue the life of the species by bringing children into the world and raising them properly. Abraham passionately

7. Rabbi Gersham ben Yehudah (d. 1040) called M'oor Hagolah (The Light of the Diaspora) decreed excommunication for a man who committed bigamy, or had divorced his wife against her will. His decree became the law of Jewry, first in Europe, then gradually all over the globe.

8. George Foot Moore, *Judaism,* vol. 2 (Cambridge: Harvard University Press, 1927), p. 122.

9. Genesis 1:28.

10. Abodah Zarah 5b; Nedarim 64b.

11. Israel Cohen, *Jewish Life in Modern Time* (New York: Dodd Mead and Company, 1914), p. 40.

cried to God, "What cans't thou give me as long as I walk childless?"[12]

There was, however, a second function in marriage— that of companionship. In the Biblical narrative, Eve is created as a helpmeet for Adam. "It is not good that man should be alone: I will make a helpmeet for him."[13] Marriage was not regarded as a compromise with the weakness of the flesh; thus Judaism has a positive, not an ascetic, attitude toward sex.

The modern sociological view that sex exists not only for the propagation of the race, but also for the increase of human happiness[14] was endorsed by the rabbis of the Talmud, who state that weak, old, and sterile persons should marry, even if there is no possibility of having children.[15] Thus companionship in itself is recognized as a legitimate end of marriage. Far from enjoining abstention from legitimate cohabitation, Jewish law orders both man and wife to respect each other's conjugal rights. However, it sanctions sexual relations only between husband and wife, and chastity of both the man and the woman before marriage and matrimonial fidelity on both sides are emphasized as values. Irregular sex relations unsettle the foundations of the family and of the social order, defile the wellsprings of life, and reduce their victims to the status of slaves serving as mere tools of lust.[16]

Role and Status of the Hebrew Wife. Although the status of the wife in the Jewish family never approached that of her husband, she was highly respected and

12. Genesis 2:19.
13. *Ibid.*
14. Harry Elmer Barnes, *Sex in Civilization,* p. 385. Quoted by Robert Gordis, *Judaism for the Modern Age* (New York: Farrar, Strauss and Cudahy, 1955), p. 251.
15. Eben Haezer 23:5.
16. Cohon, *Judaism,* p. 164.

greatly influential within the family. Her crowning achievement was motherhood. In Biblical times, if the wife was childless, she had sufficient authority to employ another woman to provide her vicarious motherhood.[17] While the family was patriarchal, the wife was called "Akeret Ha-Baiyth," the mistress of the house, playing a most important role in the family organization, and much of the family activity centered around her. Her status and numerous activities are vividly described in the last chapter of Proverbs. Here the Bible pays her the compliment "her price is above rubies" for "she looketh well to the ways of her household and eateth not the bread of idleness."[18]

The husband's authority over his wife and children rests upon tradition rather than force.[19] As the more dominant partner in the family, the husband was exhorted to treat his wife with respect, tenderness, and sympathetic understanding. Even in times when the woman occupied a lower status in law and in the religious ritual than the man, she was the equal of man and highly esteemed in the Jewish home, as is evidenced in the following Talmudic sayings: "One who loves his wife as himself and honors her more than himself . . . concerning him does Scripture say: And then shalt thou know that there is peace in thy tent";[20] "Man should be ever mindful of the honor of his wife more than circumstances permit";[21] "Marriage is made in Heaven";[22] and "God dwells in a pure and loving home."[23]

The Jewish mother is recognized and appreciated for her role as homemaker, filling her home with warmth,

---

17. Genesis 30:3.
18. Proverbs 31:10, 27.
19. Arthur Ruppin, *The Jews in the Modern World* (New York: The Macmillan Company, 1934), p. 277.
20. Yebamoth, p. 62b.
21. Hulin, p. 84b.
22. Tractate Shabbath, pp. 22a, b.
23. Tractate Kidushin, p. 71.

110 *Sociocultural Changes in American Jewish Life*

devotion, and love. She is affectionately called the "Yiddishe Mamma," who, in poverty and amidst many tensions, held the family together, gave the children emotional security, and inspired and prepared her sons to become doctors, lawyers, and teachers in order to have an easier and more secure life than their fathers.

Modern Jewish mothers, too, deserve the praise due a devoted homemaker for her family. A recent novel by Philip Roth, *"Portnoy's Complaint,"* presents a caricature of the Jewish mother and accuses her of being overprotective and too demanding, of being one whose love and warmth smother. Though it was a best seller, the novel, full of verbal vulgarity, gives a distorted picture of the Jewish mother. This novel is described by some as "fiction of pathological Jewishness," for what the protagonist is really complaining about "is nothing less than Jewishness itself, which in the form of mother and father have afflicted him with guilt, repression, caution, hatred of non-Jews and some perversion too painful to mention."[24]

Fine portrayals of the typical Jewish mother are presented by Sholem Asch in *The Mother*,[25] Henry Denker in "My Son, the Lawyer,"[26] in the recent works by Sam Levenson, *Everything but Money*,[27] by Harry Golden in *Es Es Mein Kind*,[28] and by Charles Angoff.[29] The "Alte Bobbe" in Angoff's novels of the Polonsky

24. Sylvia Rothschild, "Jewish Mothers Strike Back," quoted by Samuel Spiegler in *Journal of Jewish Communal Service* 46 (Fall 1969):104–5.
25. Sholem Asch, *The Mother* (New York: Putnam's Sons, 1937). See Acknowledgments.
26. Henry Denker, *My Son the Lawyer* (New York: Thomas Y. Crowell Co., 1950).
27. Sam Levenson, *Everything But Money* (New York: Simon and Shuster, 1966).
28. Harry Golden, *Es, Es, Mein Kind* (New York: Putnam's Sons, 1966).
29. Charles Angoff, *Journey to the Dawn* (New York: The Beechhurst Press, 1951), and *The Morning Light* (New York: The Beechhurst Press, 1953).

family is the matriarch who wields moral authority and whose wisdom and wit are a source of inspiration and comfort to her children and grandchildren. Aunt Chashel, too, is possessed of the lofty, humane ideals of equality and of social justice.

Protection of Wife. The Ketubah, an ancient Hebrew document, was instituted by the Rabbis of the Talmud for the purpose of protecting the wife. It is read at the wedding ceremony as a memorandum of the obligations the husband assumes toward his wife at the time of marriage. It requires that every man secure to his betrothed before marriage a dowry to be paid in case of his death or of her divorce without just cause. This prevented many a plural marriage.[30] The Ketubah was to serve as a deterrent to divorce and was necessary to prevent hasty action by the husband to terminate the marriage.[31] The divorced woman was protected by this marriage contract, which provided a financial settlement for her maintenance.[32]

The Changing Jewish Family. The Jewish family, through the centuries, has been marked by filial reverence and family solidarity. Along with the great care and attention given the children, strong emphasis was laid upon the proper relation of children to parents: "Honor thy father and thy mother; that thy days may be long upon the land which the Lord thy God giveth thee."[33]

In the Old World, and sometimes in the New, the term used for the Jewish family is the Hebrew word *Mishpacha,* meaning an extended group of grandparents, uncles, aunts, and cousins, as well as father, mother, and

30. Moore, p. 122.
31. Ketuboth 11a.
32. Gittin 90b.
33. Exodus 20:12.

children. All were regarded as family and would come together at family celebrations such as weddings, "brith" (circumcision ceremony, when the baby boy was eight days old), and Bar Mitzvahs. These celebrations reinforced the cohesiveness, identification, and solidarity of the family; provided, to a certain extent, personal, social, and economic security; and made separation and divorce difficult and rare.

Children showed their parents profound respect and provided for their sustenance when in need. Within the family each member displayed respect and devotion toward the other members, which contributed greatly to the cohesiveness, stability and solidarity of the Jewish people.

Of special significance in cementing family ties and home stability was observing the Sabbath, the holidays, and the special anniversaries within the family group, as well as the preparation of special dishes for the Sabbath, holidays, and special occasions. Following the Friday evening and the Sabbath meals, all would join in the singing of hymns and grace at the table.

Says Israel Abrahams:

> The influence of the family relations has been one of the strongest religious and social forces, making for sobriety and purity, and forming an intimate bond between the individual and the community.[34]

Even during the Middle Ages, the Jewish home was, in the words of Heinrich Heine, turned into

> a haven of rest from the storms that raged round the very gates of the ghettos, nay, a fairy palace in which the bespotted objects of the mobs' derision threw off their garb of shame and

---

34. Israel Abrahams, *Jewish Life in the Middle Ages* (London, 1896), p. 113, as quoted in James Hastings, ed., "The Jewish Family," *Encyclopedia of Religion and Ethics* vol. 5:741.

resumed the royal attire of free men. The home was the place where the Jew was at his best. In the home he was himself.[35]

CHANGING SOCIOCULTURAL PATTERNS

Courtship and Marriage. In Jewish tradition young people were encouraged to marry at the age of eighteen. Marriage arrangements were primarily the responsibility of the heads of the two extended families concerned. The Shadchon (marriage broker) was a "go-between" for the families, assisting them in the arrangement of proper matches for their children. Marriage was not a "love-affair," but rather was contracted on the basis of the qualities of the respective families, usually known as "yichess" (pedigree), and the scholastic attainment of the groom. Sometimes the couple hardly knew each other until the wedding day. The bride took the prescribed ritual bath on the day preceding the marriage. Both bride and groom fasted on their wedding day in expiation of their sins. Many of these patterns of marriage and family life have, given modern environmental conditions, considerably modified the role of the Shadchon along with other customs connected with marriage. The selection of a mate among Jews now follows the general pattern, and is believed in most cases to be a result of "falling in love." Although in the past romantic love was not very popular among Jews, family life was known to be stable, and divorce, though permitted under Jewish religious law, was a rare occurrence, which, however, is not the case today. The same factors of change that are operating in the American family in general, are operating and affecting the modern Jewish family. The modern Jewish home is no longer the epitome of filial reverence, of unity and solidarity; marriage among Jews, as among non-Jewish neighbors, is showing stress and

---

35. Cited by Abrahams in *ibid.,* p. 742.

strain; problems of mobility, the generation gap, drugs, sex, and broken relationships also attend their families. All of these conditions and experiences are reflected in contemporary American Jewish prose fiction.

Changing Size of the Jewish Family. The same factors that have caused a reduced birth rate in the general population are operative within the Jewish family as well. Birth control is generally practiced, and consequently modern American Jewish families are smaller than they were a generation ago. A study of over 10,600 Jewish families published by John S. Billings as long ago as 1889 revealed that the birth rate among Jewish women was only 70 percent of that of the general population and that parents who had been born in the United States had fewer children than those born abroad. The trend continues. Demographic research studies on fertility patterns have reported that Jews in the United States and Canada now show the smallest family size of all religious groups.

It is pointed out that Jewish women generally marry at a later age than non-Jewish women and plan to have smaller families. Nathan Goldberg's study shows that 80 percent of the Jewish respondents approved the use of contraceptives, as against 55 percent of the Protestant and 39 percent of the Roman Catholic of the same age range.[36]

Albert Gordon, in his study of the Jewish community of Minneapolis, finds that

> around 1910 there were many Jewish families with five to ten children, and few childless families . . . in 1945 the median

---

36. Nathan Goldberg, "Demographic Characteristics of American Jews," in *Jews in the Modern World,* vol. 2, ed. Jacob Fried (New York: Twayne Publishers, Inc., 1962), p. 688.

size of the Jewish family was found to be 3.82 and families with two children or even only one, are common.[37]

Factors of Decline in Home Stability. One could easily notice a decline of stability in immigrant Jewish homes even at the beginning of their acculturation process in the new American environment. In *The Promised Land,* Mary Antin tells us:

> In Polotzk we had been trained and watched, our days had been regulated, our conduct prescribed. In America, suddenly, we were let loose on the street. Why? Because my father having renounced his faith, and my mother being uncertain of hers, they had no particular creed to hold us to. The conception of a system of ethics independent of religion could not at once enter as an active principle in their life; so that they could give a child no reason why to be truthful or kind. And as with religion, so it fared with other branches of our domestic education. Chaos took the place of system; uncertainty, inconsistency undermined discipline. My parents knew only that they desired us to be like American children; and seeing how their neighbors gave their children boundless liberty, they turned us also loose, never doubting but that the American way was the best way. In public deportment, in etiquette, in all matters of social intercourse, they had no standards to go by, seeing that America was not Polotzk. In their bewilderment and uncertainty they needs must trust us children to learn from such models as the tenements offered. More than this, they must step down from their throne of parental authority, and take the law from their children's mouths; for they had no other means of finding out what was good American form.[38]

Such situations resulted in:

> laxity of domestic organization, that inversion of normal relations which makes for friction, and which sometimes ends in

---

37. Albert Gordon, *Jews in Transition* (Minneapolis: University of Minnesota Press, 1949), p. 194.
38. (Boston and New York: Houghton Mifflin Company, 1912), pp. 270–271.

Sociocultural Changes in American Jewish Life

breaking up a family that was formerly united and happy.[39]

A vivid description of the home life of the Jewish immigrant in the early years of this century is given in the Yiddish novel *Ore the Bord* by Leon Kobrin. Ore, an immigrant from Russia, a peddler, suddenly becomes rich in the real estate boom in Brownsville, New York, during the year 1903-4. He finds himself spiritually lost in the affluent environment; the stability of his home is broken by the disharmony between his mother and his young wife, Rachel, and by the weakening of his own parental authority. Thus a cold spiritless mood of monotony and materialism comes to take the place of the warm, spiritual atmosphere of family life in Ore's old home town.[40]

Changing Family Relationships. Changes in environment and in the social situation bring about changes in the relationships within the family, for they affect the family rituals, mores, and attitudes. When the old relationship between husband and wife tends to weaken, difficulties between parents and children arise.

The tension and changed relationships within the American Jewish family, the difference in outlook and sense of values of the learned, spiritually minded immigrant father, and the practical, often dominating mother, and between parents and children, are depicted in the novels on Jewish immigrant life in the first decades of the twentieth century.

Husband-Wife Relationship in Contemporary Fiction. The gradual weakening in the Jewish immigrant family of the old close-knit family relationship which existed in the old country is depicted in *A Journey to Dawn*, by

39. *Ibid.,* p. 271.
40. Leon Kobrin, *Ore the Bord* (New York: Forward, 1918).

Charles Angoff. Moshe, the new immigrant just brought over by his brother-in-law, Mottel, is upset when he witnesses a quarrel between Mottel and his wife, Bassel. This offends his ideal of the husband-wife relationship and reveals to him astonishingly the reality of family life of many Jewish immigrants in the New World:

> It was over going to a show that Mottel and Bassel had planned to attend. When the evening came Mottel was a bit depressed and did not particularly care to go, and then at the table, toward the end of the meal, Bassel burst out, as if she could not contain herself any longer,
> "No nonsense out of you, Mottel. If you think you are not going to the show, you will most definitely have to change your mind. I didn't get all dressed up for nothing. Do you hear me?" she shrieked.
> She continued to berate her man with a fury that has been pent up over ten years of slaving away day and night in the little ice-cream parlor they own.[41]

In *Sun at Noon* Angoff treats of the gradual disintegration of the Polonsky-Weinberg family of Boston in the years following World War I. The son, David, is disturbed by the changes that have taken place in his family, particularly the changing relationship between his mother and father:

> His father was completely absorbed with making a living, neglecting the little necessities of his wife more and more until little quarrels became prevalent. . . . Nechame [his mother] . . . had long thought of this tragedy that had befallen them, she had long wondered how it had happened, and she had long felt that nothing really could be done about it. It was one of the dreadful prices they had to pay for being in America.[42]

In "Uncle Moses," by Sholem Asch, one notes the strong effect that the new American environment has had on Genendel, Berl's wife, and the tense husband-wife re-

---

41. P. 88.
42. (New York: Beechhurst Press, 1955), p. 70.

lationship it has caused. The effect on her is very different from that on Berl. While he has become an old man with a stooped back, Genendel has grown younger. Instead of reading the old woman's Yiddish book with its stories of the Bible, Talmud, and Jewish folklore, which had constituted her only mental fare in Europe, she now reads the Yiddish newspapers and is interested in everything that goes on in the world. She often goes with her children to the Jewish theater and has kept up with the fashions. One also notes a marked change in her attitude toward her husband. His old habits of study and piety, which in their old home had filled her with pride, mean very little to her now in America. Because the machine has transformed Berl into a "stooped old man," she has lost all respect for him. When Genendel says, "Now put up your things and make room for the children's breakfast; it's time for them to eat," Berl says humbly, "Yes, yes, in a minute."[43]

Within Berl's family, each has become estranged from the other. Berl does not quite understand what has happened to his wife since she has come to America, but he has accustomed himself to it. For the last twelve years he has lived a solitary and lonely life within the very midst of his family. He confides in no one. Not only have his children become estranged from him before his very eyes, but his own wife, with whom he has begotten children and with whom he has devoted his entire lifetime, has likewise become a stranger.

Since Berl does not eat the same food as the rest of the family, on the night of the Sabbath he visits a friend who lives in the Jewish section of town and sells Kosher butter and cheese. He knows Berl as a pious, honest Jew. Only here, within this friendship, can Berl regain his sense of identity.

43. Sholem Asch, "Uncle Moses" (New York: G. P. Putnam, 1938), p. 21. See Acknowledgments.

Generation Gap. The situation arising from the chasm between the generation of the Jewish immigrant and that of his American-reared children is shown poignantly in the Yiddish drama *Shmates* (Rags) by H. Leivick.

Mordecai Maze, the protagonist, is a proud, scholarly, religious Jew who does not conform to the shallow, spiritless mode of living of his fellow-immigrants. In his home town in Europe he had been a recognized and respected leader, but in America he feels uneasy, uprooted. He is given the job of sorting rags in the shop of his rich son-in-law. In his own house, where he has always been the dominating figure, he becomes a stranger; he cannot even communicate effectively with his American children. Maze still recalls his former status and spends his free time studying the Talmud. He even refuses an easy job offered him by his daughter's father-in-law. The social environment in the new world remains so alien to him, that he and his children belong to two different worlds.[44]

In *East River* by Sholem Asch, Deborah, the wife of Moshe Wolf, is more practical and adapts herself more easily to conditions in the new world. She favors her son, Irving, the successful businessman, while the father, Moshe Wolf, an idealist with spiritual values and high ideals, refuses to accept support from his son.[45]

Changing Attitude Toward Divorce. Divorce was recognized in Jewish law. The Mosaic law states that "if a wife finds no favor in her husband's eyes because of some uncleanness in her then let him write her a bill of divorcement and give it in her hand and send her out of his house."[46] In patriarchal times the husband could divorce his wife whenever he chose to do so.

However, strong opposition to the unrestrained right

44. H. Leivick, *Shmates* (Wilno: Farlag B. Klezkin, 1928).
45. Sholem Asch, *East River* (New York: G. P. Putnam's Sons, 1938).
See Acknowledgments.
46. Deuteronomy 24:1, 2.

of the husband to divorce his wife was voiced by the prophets Hosea and Malachi, and under the combined influence of social, economic, and religious factors, the practice of divorce was restricted. The rabbis of the Talmudic period discouraged divorce and sought to prevent the arbitrary abuse of it. They recognized the validity of divorce only when it offered the only alternative, *i.e.*, when marital relations became hopeless, and after every effort had been made to reconcile the husband and wife. The schools of the early Tannaim of the first century, Hillel and Shammai,[47] differed in their opinions as to what constituted sufficient grounds for divorce. The school of Shammai interpreted the Biblical text, which allows a man to "send his wife away if she find no favor in his eyes because he hath found some unseemly thing in her,"[48] to mean a man may not divorce his wife unless he discovered her to be unfaithful to him.[49] The school of Hillel, on the other hand, considered inattention to matters of household, or general incompatibility of character, sufficient grounds for divorce. They interpreted the term "unseemly thing" to mean anything in the woman, however trivial, which offended her husband, even if "she burned his food."[50]

Although Jewish law followed the school of Hillel and divorce could easily be obtained, it was regarded in the Talmud as the greatest domestic tragedy, and deep-seated aversion to it was expressed in the rabbinic dictum that "the altar of God sheds tears over a man who divorces the wife of his youth."[51]

In Biblical and Talmudic times, the husband had the

---

47. Gittin (divorce) 90b.
48. Deuteronomy 24:1.
49. Gittin 9b. This interpretation is in agreement with the statement of law in Matthew 19:9.
50. Gittin 9, 10.
51. Gittin 90b.

right to divorce his wife even against her will, but after
the tenth century it was established that no man could
divorce his wife without her consent. The decree of
Rabenu Gershom threatened with excommunication the
man who would separate from his wife without her agreement.[52] Thus, throughout the centuries, divorce, though
allowed, was a rare phenomenon among Jews. But recently, under the impact of new factors of change affecting the stability of the home, the divorce rate among
Jews has increased considerably. The changed attitude
toward divorce is shown in Gordon's study of the Jewish
community of Minneapolis, Table III.

Table III*
Marriages and Divorces of the Jewish Population Compared to
the General Population of Hennepin County

Year	Number of Marriages	Number of Divorces	Number of Jewish Marriages	Number of Jewish Divorces	Ratio of Marriages To One Divorce For General Population	Ratio of Marriages To One Divorce For Jewish Population
1890	1765	125	13	1	14.1	13.
1900	2160	230	24	0	9.4	24.
1910	3447	401	74	5	8.6	14.8
1920	6381	652	182	10	9.8	18.2
1930	4562	1045	131	19	4.4	6.8
1940	5375	1166	112	16	4.6	7.1
1945	6785	2040	114	23	3.3	4.9

* Source: Albert I. Gordon, *Jews in Transition* (Minneapolis: University of Minnesota Press, 1949; London: Oxford University Press,
1949), p. 201.

The problem of *Agunah* (the deserted wife) intensi-

---

52. Rabbi Gershom ben Yehudah (d. 1040), called M'oor Hagolah
(The Light of the Diaspora), decreed excommunication for a man who
committed bigamy or divorced his wife against her will. His decree
became the law of Jewry, first in Europe, then gradually all over
the globe.

fied with the increased emigration of Jews from their home countries. As a result of the mass immigration and social mobility, deeply rooted loyalties were dissolved, traditional standards were abandoned, and new temptations were encountered. Cases increased where the husband forgot his wife back home and married again. Many of the immigrants would leave large Eastern communities and move to the South or West, and a considerable number of "deserted wives" remained behind. Without a Jewish *Get* (divorce) the wife could not remarry and was thus doomed to perpetual loneliness.

With the increased immigration in the first quarter of the twentieth century, the number of deserted wives continually increased. Their husbands, moved by malice or greed, refused, unless there was a monetary inducement, to issue a *Get*. Such women faced either spending the rest of their lives in loneliness or defying Jewish law and remarrying without a *Get*.

This situation, which has led to tragic results, finally moved the Rabbinical Assembly of America, representing the Conservative wing in American Jewry, to accept a plan worked out by Talmudic scholar, Saul Liberman. He introduced a new clause in the Ketubah, representing a private agreement between the bride and groom which was to be entered upon prior to their marriage.[53]

The Agunah Problem in the Modern Novel. The problem of *Agunah* is treated by Michael Blankfort in *The Strong Hand*.[54] Leo Bordick, a young American Rabbi, a chaplain during World War II, falls in love with Katy Waterman, a famous magazine photographer and sophisticated career girl. At first she recoils from him

---

53. Ben Zion Bokser, "The Ketubah" (reprint), *The Jewish Frontier* (December 1954), p. 7.
54. Michael Blankfort, *The Strong Hand* (Boston: Little, Brown and Co., 1955).

and hastily marries an airman, who is later reported missing in action over China and is presumed dead. Orthodox Jewish law requires actual proof of a husband's death before it will permit his widow to remarry. In the novel this proof cannot be obtained. After the war Katy and Leo meet again in New York, and she realizes that it was he whom she really loved all along. As they begin to plan for their future, they face the problem of *Agunah,* for, according to the "strong hand" of Jewish law, Katy is an *agunah* (tied) until her husband's death can be definitely established. Leo and Katy consult with authorities on Jewish law, and when the many efforts to find proof of her husband's death and get permission to remarry fail, the problem cannot be resolved. Heartbroken, Leo Bordick gives up his beloved. At the end he has also given up his pulpit and is devoting his time to the study of the Law. Some day, he says, he may find the courage "to change what needs to be changed—to pour the good old wine into new bottles." In his efforts to remain true to the traditional Jewish laws, he finally realizes that change is essential for Judaism to survive in the modern age.

Intermarriage. One of the most significant changes in Jewish family life, indicating the assimilatory tendencies in the American Jewish community, is manifested in the increased rate of intermarriage of Jew and Gentile. While among Jews of the immigrant generation intermarriage was a rarity, it increased considerably in the second and third generations. This resulted from the increased social interaction and closer culture-contact between the various religious and ethnic groups in the free society of the New World. Intermarriage is of special concern to the Jewish community for it involves the problem of survival of Jews in America as a religious and ethnic group.

Throughout the ages, Jews have opposed marriage outside their faith, and endogamy (marrying within one's own group) has been one of the principal methods of keeping the people together during the centuries of wandering and persecution.[55]

Views on Intermarriage. The importance of the subject is fully reflected in the following observations by contemporary sociologists and leaders of American Jewry. Arthur Ruppin states:

> The restriction of marriage to co-religionists formed the strongest bond between the Jews until far into the nineteenth century, making them into a homogeneous unit, able to show a unique power of resistance against the assimilating forces of Christianity and Islam. Even Jews who have become indifferent to their religion often remain averse to marrying outside their community; this is perhaps the last remnant of their national consciousness. They feel that, although they have dropped the Jewish ritual, they will remain Jews so long as they and their children intermarry with Jews, and that only a mixed marriage would finally separate them from their people. Indeed intermarriage, as soon as it occurs on a large scale marks the end of Judaism.[56]

Louis Finkelstein, Chancellor of the Jewish Theological Seminary of America, points out that

> because of the special place that the home occupies in Judaism as a center of religious life and worship, almost co-ordinate with the synagogue itself, Judaism holds it essential that both parties to a Jewish marriage be members of the Jewish faith. There is, of course, no objection to marriage with a sincere convert to Judaism. But it is not possible for the home to function in a manner prescribed by Jewish law unless both husband and wife are of the Jewish faith.[57]

55. Mabel A. Elliott and Frances E. Merrill, *Social Disorganization,* 3d ed. (New York: Harper and Brothers, 1950), p. 623.
56. Arthur Ruppin, *The Jewish Fate and Future* (New York: The Macmillan Company, 1940), p. 106.
57. Louis Finkelstein, *The Jews, Their History, Culture and Religion,* vol. 2 (New York: Harper and Brothers, Publishers, 1950), p. 1329.

Of significance, too, is the statement on intermarriage by Mordecai M. Kaplan:

> It is certain that if nothing is done to prevent the tendency to intermarriage, Judaism can barely survive another century and even if it survives it will have become hopelessly devitalized.[58]

Most leaders of Reform Judaism, too, disapprove of mixed marriages. Harry Joshua Stern, Rabbi of Temple Emanuel, Montreal, Canada, says:

> Reform Judaism opposed mixed marriages because it realizes that the Jewish minority must be safe-guarded. For, both in mixed marriages and even in intermarriages, the continuation of Jewish group life is in danger, for the offspring of such are most often lost to Judaism.[59]

In his study of the Minneapolis Jewish community, Albert Gordon reports that the early Jewish residents in Minneapolis regarded intermarriage as a calamity, and parents sat "shiva" (they observed the traditional seven-day period of mourning as if the child had died) for they were distraught and ashamed to face their friends.[60]

However, this attitude of Jewish parents has somewhat changed. Recent sociological research in Lakeville, a typical affluent midwestern suburb, showed that although Jewish parents are still anxious about Jewish survival and are therefore opposed to the intermarriage of their children, they nevertheless prefer their children's romantic and happy intermarriage, with love, to a loveless marriage within their own group.[61]

58. Mordecai M. Kaplan, *Judaism as a Civilization* (New York: The Macmillan Co., 1934), p. 417.
59. Harry Joshua Stern, *Martyrdom and Miracle* (New York: Bloch Publishing Co., 1950), p. 237.
60. Gordon, pp. 206–8.
61. Marshall Sklare and Joseph Greenblum, *Jewish Identity on the Suburban Frontier: A Study of Group Survival in the Open Society*, vol. 1 (New York: The Lakeville Studies, Basic Books, 1967).

Rate of Intermarriage. It is difficult to determine the number of Jewish-Gentile marriages in the United States, but we gain some notion of the intermarriage rate from gathered local studies. The rates are thought to be higher in places where there are no large numbers of Jews. Meyer F. Nimkoff, citing Julius Drachsler's study of intermarriage, says that in New York City in 1920 less than 2 percent of Jews married outside their faith, but the rate for second-generation Jews was seven times that of the first generation.[62] Various studies by psychologists and sociologists view intermarriage as a social problem, one that poses a possible threat to marital happiness. They show that a marriage of people of different religious and cultural backgrounds is more likely to lead to marital difficulties and to divorce than an unmixed marriage.[63]

The assimilatory tendencies that threaten the continuity of Jewish group life in the open American society are the subject of recent studies on Jewish intermarriage by sociologists Erich Rosenthal and Marshall Sklare on the Washington, D.C., community. Rosenthal's study, which provides the first useful data since Drachsler's study, more than four decades ago, found the rate of intermarriage to be 13.3 percent, with the inference that other Jewish communities of the same size (50,000 to 100,000) have a similar level of intermarriage. The study broke down the rate of intermarrying Jewish men by generations: 1.4 percent for the foreign-born; 10.2 percent for the first generation of American-born; 17.9 percent for the second generation. The rate for the college-educated members of the last group was a startling 37 percent.[64]

62. Meyer F. Nimkoff, *Marriage and the Family* (New York: Houghton Mifflin Co., 1947), p. 869.
63. Martin H. Newmeyer, *Social Problems and the Changing Society* (New York, London, Toronto: D. Van Nostrand Co., Inc., 1953), p. 187.
64. Erich Rosenthal, "Studies of Jewish Intermarriage in the United

This study finally revealed that the children of at least 70 percent of mixed families are lost to the Jewish group. The data also showed that Jewish education of the third generation contributed significantly to lowering the intermarriage rate. This confirms the belief that Jewish religious education—at least in the third generation—"does serve to check intermarriage."

In his recent article on intermarriage, published in the 1970 edition of the American Jewish Year Book, Arnold Schwarts, research analyst with the American Jewish Committee, states that marriages between Jews and non-Jews, estimated at between 10 and 15 percent of all marriages involving a Jewish partner, are likely to increase in coming years.

In Sklare's and Greenblum's recent study of Lakeville (fictitious name of a Midwestern suburban community), and also in Sklare's study "Intermarriage and Jewish Survival," the rate of intermarriage is shown to have increased in the last ten years since their investigation in 1957-1958. The study also reveals changed attitudes of the parents and an emerging pattern of "accommodation to the inevitable." Most of Lakeville today, says Sklare, are agreed that under no circumstances must they set up a situation that will "alienate them from their children, not even under the provocation of an intermarriage."[65]

This emerging pattern of accommodation to intermarriage on the part of parents and the increasing number of Reform rabbis officiating at mixed marriages, Sklare concludes, have ominous implications for the continuity of Jewish group life and strike at the very nature of Jewish identity in America. The increasing evidence of intermarriage and mixed marriages, coupled with the

States," *American Jewish Year Book* vol. 64 (New York: The American Jewish Committee; Philadelphia: The Jewish Publication Society of America, 1963), pp. 3–32.

65. Sklare and Greenblum, *Jewish Identity on the Suburban Frontier*, p. 320.

fact that the Jewish birthrate has remained stable in the last 40 years while that of the total American population has been rising, has aroused attention and grave concern in Jewish circles.

There is, however, one optimistic aspect in the fact that a growing number of Gentiles who marry Jews convert to Judaism, and, like most converts, tend to be stricter than their mates. In Los Angeles, for instance, the University of Judaism (Conservative) and the Hebrew Union College (Reform) conduct classes of instruction for converts. Some Jewish leaders feel that conversions might eventually offset losses.

Pertinent at this point is the observation that there is a growing awareness of new tendencies relating to the Jewish family, that there is also a tendency to improve and to strengthen the ethnic community so that it will offer a healthy milieu for social participation and for the development of personality.[66]

INTERMARRIAGE IN NOVELS

That there has been a considerable change in the attitude of Jews to intermarriage is pointed out by Albert Gordon. In most cases when intermarriage cannot be prevented, the members of the Jewish family make an effort to secure a formal conversion of the non-Jew to Judaism. This takes place only when the non-Jew voluntarily desires it and has taken a course in the study of Judaism. According to Gordon, nearly all who intermarry remain within the Jewish group, and "there is a growing tendency to accept such persons [Gentiles] without prejudice in the synagogues and in other Jewish organizations."[67]

66. Bessie Bloom Wessel, "Ethnic Family Patterns: The American Jewish Family," *The American Journal of Sociology* 53 (May 1948): 439–42.

67. Gordon, pp. 206–7.

Among the outstanding American Jewish novels dealing with the theme of Jewish-Gentile intermarriage are those by Sholem Asch and Ludwig Lewisohn.

In *East River,* Asch describes how the pious, observant, orthodox Moshe Wolfe, upon learning that his son, Irving, has married a Gentile girl, Mary, sat on a low bench as though in mourning for one dead in his own household. He had made the symbolical rent of mourning in his own coat and in the dress which his wife, Deborah, wore. As he sat on the mourning bench, he recited the prescribed and moving verses from Lamentations, in the traditional chant: "How doth the city sit solitary. . . ."

> Deborah complained bitterly. "You mourn as though our son were dead in reality. . . . God forbid it. . . ."
> But Moshe Wolf made no answer. He sat on the bench, swaying over the open prayer book. "She weepeth sore in the night, and her tears are on her cheeks. . . .[68]

This deeply ingrained attitude, motivated by concern for the continued existence of the Jewish people, was true of the religious and the nonreligious Jew alike.

Though Moshe Wolf showed no interest in Mary or her child, he opposed his son's separation from his wife, but felt himself torn by the inner struggle. The thought tortured him—that his own grandchild, the issue of his son's loins, the child who should have been destined to carry on the generations-long chain of Jewishness—was a Christian, a Catholic!

> My grandchild is a Christian! I have lost my place in Israel. The ancient chain has been broken. My grandchild will begin a new line of Christian generations, who will not know my God. They will be the enemies of my people. They will be pogromists against the Jews![69]

---

68. Sholem Asch, *East River* (New York: G. P. Putnam's Sons, 1946), p. 216. See Acknowledgments.
69. *Ibid.,* p. 354.

In *The Island Within,* written in the late 1920s, Ludwig Lewisohn tells of a Jewish family that moved from a Polish ghetto first to Germany, then to America, where it rose to financial success, and of the efforts of Arthur Levy, an honest young American Jew, to adjust to a Christian-Protestant civilization. On the canvas of this novel are painted four generations. The first is that of orthodox Jews living in Poland. Their children, the second generation, lived in Germany and became fairly prosperous. One son became an apostate and a great figure in the German Empire, but he was a sick soul at the last, realizing that he has given up his heritage for a mess of pottage. Jacob, another son, came to America, where he lived as a middle-class German-American Jew. He ate non-kosher food, kept his business open on Saturday, and did not attend the synagogue. It is Jacob's son, Arthur Levy, the offspring of the third generation, who is Mr. Lewisohn's peculiar concern. He is the young Jew, branded by name and feature, trying to forget on the street and at college that he is any different from his Protestant-American friends. Arthur's best friends are Gentiles, but they do not invite him to their homes. After graduating from college Arthur becomes a psychiatrist, an expert on the source of others' sensitiveness. He meets prejudice in his work in the state institution for the insane, and in a thousand little snubs and exclusions elsewhere. He sees Jews, sensitive about their Jewishness, revenging themselves by despising other Jews.

It is Arthur's experience in married life that finally brings to a crisis the problem of his relationship with his own heritage. Arthur and Elizabeth Knight do not get on too well. Arthur loves the traditional Jewish home and the Jewish conception of a home, both of which Elizabeth hates. Engrossed in her work as a writer, Elizabeth refuses to settle down to domestic responsibilities. Arthur feels a sense of void; he wants to set up

a home and to be rooted. "Elizabeth doesn't need that
security," he observes; "she belongs somewhere, and, in
fact, everywhere."

After they visit his parents' home and have dinner
with them, Arthur feels utterly dispirited:

> Elizabeth was friendly and even cordial. No fault could be
> found with her. But she was cordial as with people of whom
> she wanted to make friends. . . . Elizabeth was charming in
> a way that seemed to Arthur's mother unbearably casual and
> detached. . . . Intellectually he [Arthur] was entirely on
> Elizabeth's side. No fault could be found with her. She had,
> in all sincerity, done her best. On the other hand, there tugged
> and gnawed at him the profound sense of his parents' grief. He
> felt this so strongly that he rebelled against its irrational causes.
> Why did one have to be so sentimental about family matters?
> Why did one have at a first meeting of this kind to melt? What
> function did this immense Jewish sense of family solidarity
> have in modern life? Of course, Elizabeth couldn't even com-
> prehend what had been expected of her. . . . And all the
> while below these thoughts he knew how happy he would have
> been, how instinctively and completely happy, if his wife could
> have assumed the part of a Jewish daughter and he could have
> come out of his father's house on that day with the conviction
> that the bonds of solidarity and love had been strengthened.[70]

The turning point comes when the question arises of
how to bring up their child. Arthur concludes that the
child must be brought up as a Jew. "His name is Levy,
and the more of a Protestant American he was in his
heart and soul, the more disastrous to him would be the
things which in a Protestant-American civilization are
bound to happen to someone named Levy."[71]

In this novel, the marriage ends in failure. When
Arthur's sister Hazel asks him about Elizabeth, Arthur
replies:

---

70. Ludwig Lewisohn, *The Island Within* (New York: Harper and
Brothers, The Modern Library, 1940), pp. 254–55.
71. *Ibid.,* p. 276.

"I am not sure that Elizabeth and I will go on living together." . . .

Eli looked concerned. "What's wrong?"

"Nothing," Arthur said. He felt a sudden sense of liberation. "Nothing except that she's a Gentile and I'm a Jew. We're fond of each other and we understand each other intellectually, but at the emotional basis of life there is—no, no opposition—there's a divergence. You've heard of the parallel lines that can never meet. It isn't very clear to me yet—the whole thing; I haven't probed it. But I feel as though I'd never been married at all. Maybe I'm wrong and it's just because Elizabeth is a very modern woman and I am, by instincts, an old-fashioned man. . . . She's a splendid woman and I hope she finds her true happiness sooner or later."

When Eli asked: "How about your boy, Arthur?" Arthur lowered his head and felt the corners of his lids burning. "I don't know . . . I don't know."

They gathered about him after that first evening, his sister and his brother and even their child, as though to protect him from the blows of untoward circumstances. Something streamed from them all that was deeper than affection.[72]

The couple finally agree and come to the conclusion that it is best for them to separate. Arthur then goes as psychiatrist on a mission to investigate the possibility of aid to Jews in Roumania.

A different approach, the opposite of Lewisohn's, to the problem of Jewish-Gentile marriage is presented in the novels of Norman Katkov, Jerome Weidman, and Myron S. Kaufman. In Katkov's *Eagle at My Eyes*,[73] the life of Joe—the protagonist, the alienated marginal Jew of the second generation—reflects that of the author, who, like some of his contemporary Jewish novelists of the 1920s and 1930s, is overwhelmed by emotions of hatred of social conditions, of fear of being a Jew, and of self-hatred. Joe is a newspaper reporter in St. Paul, the son of Jewish immigrant parents, who marries Mary,

72. *Ibid.,* p. 271.
73. Norman Katkov, *Eagle at My Eyes* (Garden City, N.Y.: Doubleday and Co., Inc., 1948).

a Gentile girl whom he loves. The marriage is opposed by both families and there is hatred on both sides. The novel, which begins with a story Joe's father tells him about a pogrom in Russia and ends with the line "all right, you bastards, here I come," is characteristic of novels of the 1920s and 1930s, years of poverty and anti-Semitism.

In *In The Enemy Camp*[74] Jerome Weidman portrays a marriage between a Jew and a Gentile. The main character, George Hurst, was raised by his Aunt Tessie, and was brought up to believe that Gentiles are not to be trusted and belong in the enemy camp. George, from the lower East Side of New York, married a rich Gentile girl (Philadelphia Main Line), but because of his distrust of Gentiles, he failed to take his wife in his confidence.

The central main thesis of the novel is Uncle Zisha's advice to him, "Don't make a private Ghetto for yourself and creep into it the way Aunt Tessie did. Do what your heart tells you, not your religion."

The protagonist repeats Uncle Zisha's words, which represent the author's thinking. "It is more important to be a man than a Jew." To be a Jew must one be less than a man? To be a man, must one shed his Jewish identity? Is there a conflict between them? The criticism has been leveled against the novel that it could easily foster a rationalization in the minds of non-Jews: that they don't like Jews because Jews don't like Gentiles, which the novel implies.

The theme of mixed marriage is dealt with in Myron S. Kaufmann's "Remember Me to God."[75] The novel, which like some of the best-sellers is negative in its approach to Jewish life, tells the story of the Amsterdam

---

74. Jerome Weidman, *In the Enemy Camp* (New York: Random House, 1958).
75. (Philadelphia: J. B. Lippincott Co., 1957).

family in Boston. During World War I, Richard Amsterdam, a third-generation American Jew and a student at Harvard, is obsessed by a desire to escape his Jewish family background and shed all signs of a Jewish appearance. He is a vulgar social climber who apes the manners of the Yankee, blue-blooded, Christian clubmen, and dissociates himself from unassimilated Jews. Instead of taking Jeanie, his Jewish girl friend, to the Pudding Club dance, he takes, in order to be more cosmopolitan, a Gentile girl from an aristocratic, Protestant, old-Bostonian family. Finally deciding to break with his family and his people's heritage, he converts to the Christian religion.

Richard alienates himself from his family when his father comes to Harvard to plead with him not to convert, Richard says: "Scram, will you? I'm not coming home." Kaumann's protagonist, thus abandoning his family and his people, is another negative, self-hating Jew—another negative character.

INTERMARRIAGE AND JEWISH SURVIVAL

That there is no easy answer to the problem of intermarriage in a free and open society is now being generally recognized. Intermarriage cannot be viewed as a mere accident, but rather as the inevitable result of strong social factors operating in the free American society. Sociologically, it is pointed out that continuous social-cultural contact, the commingling of men and women of different religious and ethnic groups, renders intermarriage unavoidable. Therefore, so long as young people meet each other in an open society, interdating in the colleges and outside will go on and will naturally lead to intermarriage.

It is important, however, to assert here that the danger for Jewish group survival lies only in mixed marriages, that is, when the non-Jewish partner in marriage is not converted. At the Conference on Intermarriage sponsored by the American Jewish Congress, Reform Rabbi Joseph Klein of Worcester, Massachusetts, sharply criticized Reform rabbis who officiate at mixed marriages, charging them with contributing to the ultimate destruction of Jewish life. However, the mere refraining by rabbis from officiating at a mixed marriage could do little to prevent it, and since intermarriage in a free society is unavoidable, the problem is not so much how to prevent it as how to face and cope with it.

In sum, the Jewish objection to intermarriage arises, not because of any feeling of superiority or sense of group exclusiveness, but mainly because of deep concern for Jewish group survival and of concern for the human happiness and harmony of the family and home.

8
Changes in Religious Life

EFFECTS OF SOCIAL INTERACTION AND
CULTURE CONTACT

The area in which the adjustment of Jews to the American environment is most noticed is that of their religious life, at home and in the synagogue. Because it was the major factor in holding the Jewish people together as a distinct cultural identity, the Jewish religion served as a unifying force in time of trouble, and "without it they doubtless would have lost their main adhesive nature."[1]

Through social interaction and culture contact with Americans of different creeds, Jews, like other minority groups, tend to take over the standards, behavior, and thought patterns of the majority. Thus the customs of the majority group of American Christians also affect the thought and life style of most American Jews, so obviously exemplified in the celebration of the Christmas holidays. Interviews with merchants in the West Side district of Manhattan disclose that 70 percent of the purchasers of Christmas trees in 1945 were Jews.[2]

1. Emory S. Bogardus, *Sociology,* 4th ed. (New York: The Macmillan Company, 1954), p. 294.
2. Abraham Duker, "On Religious Trends in American Jewish Life," in *Yivo Annual of Jewish Social Science,* vol. 4 (New York: Yiddish Scientific Institute—YIVO, 1949), pp. 51–63.

Some effects of social interaction and culture contact are well illustrated in an episode related by Mary Antin in *The Promised Land.* Her friend Miss Hale, daughter of the famous Boston Christian minister, Dr. Edward Hale, wanted a baby for a picture of the Nativity she was doing for her father's church, and "of all babies in Boston, our Celia, our little Jewish Celia was posing for the Christ child." The author further relates that

> my mother, in less than half a dozen years of America, had so far shaken off her ancient superstitions that she feared no evil consequences from letting her child pose for a Christian picture.[3]

The changed environment and social situation weakened the religious attitude of the immigrants, especially of the women. In "Uncle Moses" there is a scene where seventeen-year-old Charlie sits down at table for breakfast with uncovered head and without having prayed or washed. His father, Berl, who has just pronounced a blessing on the food and, therefore, cannot stop to speak before starting to cut a piece of the bread, turns to his son. "Genendel!" he grumbles, indignantly. But his wife answers: "What's the matter. It's all right, you're praying for him. You pray for all of us. No one has time to pray in America."[4]

Berl's brother, Aaron, stares at his sister-in-law; he simply does not recognize her any more. Can this be the pious Jewish wife who recited her prayers in the women's balcony of the synagogue at home, and who had often run into the prayer house? What has happened to her during the short time she has spent in America?

---

3. Mary Antin, *The Promised Land* (Boston and New York: Houghton Mifflin Co., 1912), p. 349.
4. Sholem Asch, "Uncle Moses" (New York: G. P. Putnam's Sons, 1938), p. 21. See Acknowledgments.

RELIGIOUS CHANGE: NEW MOVEMENTS
IN AMERICAN JUDAISM

Reform: The secularization of modern society has
caused changes in the traditional forms of Jewish religious beliefs and practices. Since the Emancipation following the French Revolution in 1791, which admitted
Jews to citizenship and resulted in closer contact with
their Gentile neighbors, it became increasingly difficult
for them to observe all the minutiae of the Jewish religious ritual in the new social situation. Attempts were
made to introduce changes in the religious practices so
that modern Jews would be at home in the contemporary
world.

One such attempt was the Jewish Reform movement
in Germany in the nineteenth century. Its purpose was
the adjustment of Jewish religious practices to modern
thought and economic circumstances. This new movement
found its most fruitful soil in the newly developing Jewish community in America, where changes in Jewish
religious practices began to be manifest in the early part
of the nineteenth century. Although the majority of
Jewish immigrants from Germany were brought up in
the Orthodox tradition, there were a considerable number who realized that conditions in America were different and that adaptation to the new environment was
necessary.

The first changes relating to the externals of worship
in the services were made in the Congregation Beth Elo-
him of Charleston, South Carolina, as early as 1824.
Motivated mainly by a desire to adjust their religious
life to the cultural pattern of the majority, these changes
consisted in greater decorum, omission of superfluous
prayers, elimination of the curtained women's gallery,
addition of an organ or mixed choir, and sermons in
English. In these changes one notes the influence of the

predominant religious patterns of the Christian environment. This, however, did not involve a rejection of Judaism; it was rather an effort to stem the tide of conversion and to hasten the adaptation of Jewish religious patterns to American conditions. The underlying continuity with the past was still there.[5]

Both the Reform movement, and the one formed later, the Conservative group, were based on the fundamental principle that Judaism permits and even requires modification and adjustment so that it may meet the changed situations of the contemporary world. Later, new demands for the "simplification" of dietary laws and of Sabbath prohibitions were heard. In 1885, at Pittsburgh, the Central Conference of American Rabbis (Reform), consisting of fifteen rabbis, asserted the right to change or abolish traditions and religious practices at will. One example of the increased radicalism of the Reform group was the change of the Sabbath services from Saturday to Sunday.

Changing Membership and Ideology of Reform Jews.
Soon, however, a reaction against radical reform set in. With the increased immigration of East European Jews, the Reform Temple began to relax its social rules to admit East European Jews as members. Thus the membership, which had hitherto consisted of prosperous German Jews, changed, and along with this development, the tendency in more recent years was toward more traditional practices and greater sympathy with Jewish nationalism, especially with Zionism. Rabbi Charles E. Shulman observes that some in the Reform ranks sigh for the good old days when the Reform group was not overloaded with Orthodox and Conservative influences. He cites Alfred Segal's observation that if a survey were

5. Oscar Handlin, *Adventure in Freedom* (New York: McGraw-Hill Book Company, 1954), p. 79.

made, it would show that the larger portion of the membership of Reform temples today is of Orthodox parents of East European origin, and that Reform Judaism lives largely by the devotion of Jews who came out of Orthodoxy a few years ago.[6]

Rabbi Shulman further points out that Reform, Conservative, and Orthodox organizations now draw their membership from a single pool—the five and a half million Americanized Jews who rub elbows at the country clubs and at the United Jewish Appeal meetings, who proudly assert their American citizenship and commingle freely in American Jewish communal life.[7]

A further step indicating a return to the more traditional in ritual and beliefs by the Reform wing of American Judaism was evidenced, according to Israel Knox at the sixty-fifth annual convention of the Central Conference of American Rabbis (Reform) held in 1945 at Pike, New Hampshire. He attributes this tendency to the influx of East European Jews in Reform congregations, and to their children entering the Reform rabbinate.[8]

Another Reform rabbi, discussing the changing ideology of Reform Judaism, says:

what has happened in the last decade or two is warming up. Reform has not become more orthodox, but it has become more Jewish. We have corrected some of the errors of the first generation of reformers "who nearly threw the baby out along with the water."[9]

The change to a more positive attitude to traditional-

6. Charles E. Shulman, "Trends in Reform Judaism," *Congress Weekly* 22, no. 28 (Oct. 24, 1955):7.
7. *Ibid.*, p. 8.
8. Israel Knox, "Reform Judaism Re-Appraises Its Way of Life," *Commentary* 18, no. 6 (Dec. 1954):504–11.
9. Richard C. Hertz, "What It Means to Be a Reform Jew," *Bulletin* 28, Temple Beth El, Detroit, Michigan, 28, no. 14 (Dec. 11, 1953):5.

ism and to Zionism is also viewed by many as the cause for the growth of Reform Judaism from 300 affiliated congregations in 1943 to 536 in 1956.[10]

Fifty years after the Pittsburgh meeting, when America became the center of world Jewry and Hitler was in power, and when Zionism became a spiritual and political force, Reform Jews adopted in 1937 the "Columbus Platform," which reflected the changed attitude of the Reform movement. Rabbi Felix A. Levy, outspoken Zionist, presided over the conference, and of the 110 members present only five voted in the negative.[11]

A radical change of attitude toward Israel by the Reform movement is expressed in the recent announcement by the late Dr. Nelson Glueck, President of the Hebrew Union College-Jewish Institute of Religion, that beginning with the academic year 1970-1971, each student will have to spend the entire first year of his rabbinic studies at the Hebrew College-Institute School in Jerusalem. Dr. Glueck stated that "one can not be a rabbi without being deeply immersed in the life and spirit of Israel. . . . That knowledge gained by our future rabbis by intimately living for a full year with the reality of Israel will further enrich and deepen the strong ties between American Reform Judaism and the ideals of Israel.[12]

Ideological Differentiation. In the first decade of the century there were two ideological streams among Jewish immigrants from Eastern Europe. The great majority of them were rooted in the age-old tradition of East European Jewry, while a smaller but significant group was secular in its ideology and under the influence of

---

10. Temple Beth El *Bulletin,* Detroit, Mich., 31, no. 20 (Jan. 11, 1937) :5.

11. W. Gunther Plout, *The Growth of Reform Judaism* (New York: The World Union for Progressive Judaism, Ltd., 1965), p. 100.

12. Quoted in The Temple Israel *Bulletin,* Columbus, O., no. 13 (November 28, 1969).

labor radicalism. With the new immigration wave after 1905 a second group grew in number and influence; they were the creators and ardent followers of the Labor unions, of the Socialist party, and of the Zionist and labor-Zionist movements, whose basic character was secular. As a means of cultural adjustment they created the first Hebrew periodicals, the Yiddish press, the Yiddish theater and a Yiddish literature. A smaller group also created a Hebrew press, and literature in Hebrew.

Changing Orthodoxy. In their efforts to transplant the old religious and communal institutions to American soil, the more orthodox group also had to make their adjustments. Changes in their religious practices were evident in their daily life, as well as in synagogue services.

In a sociological analysis of contemporary American Orthodoxy, Charles S. Liebman, professor at Yeshivah University, observes that the same social processes that took place among Jews a half-century or more ago, which resulted in the Conservative synagogue, are continuing to operate within the Orthodox community and are expressed in the development of "modern Orthodoxy."[13]

Orthodox Judaism in the United States in our generation, says late Orthodox rabbi David De Sola Pool, "no longer mirrors East European life, and is far from being identical with orthodoxy anywhere else. It (Orthodoxy) is adapting itself to the American environment." In the American Orthodox Synagogue, the ladies' gallery may not be blocked off by a curtain or lattice-work, or the reading desk may not be in the center of the Synagogue. American orthodoxy is no longer concerned with the prohibition of shaving, the law forbidding the mixture of materials in one's garments, or hundreds of similar

13. Charles S. Liebman, "A Sociological Analysis of Contemporary Orthodoxy," *Judaism* (a Quarterly) 13, no. 3 (Summer 1964).

Jewish regulations which had been strictly observed by
Orthodox Jews in other ages and lands.[14]

Change in religious practices by East European Jewish
immigrants is sharply portrayed in *The Rise of David
Levinsky*. David Levinsky has begun to feel the impact
of the changed social situation, for he is the butt of ridicule. For some time he has hesitated to shave, honoring
the old Jewish law which forbids shaving one's beard.
But a fellow-peddler's remark causes him to yield.

> Many of the other peddlers made fun of my piety and said
> it could not last long. Very few of the women who passed my
> push-cart wore wigs, and men who did not shave were an
> exception. . . . It was inevitable that, sooner or later, I should
> let a barber shave my sprouting beard. . . .
> What actually decided me to commit so heinous a sin was
> a remark dropped by one of the peddlers that my down-
> covered face made me look like "a green one." It was the most
> cruel thing he could have told me. I took a look at myself as
> soon as I could get near a mirror, and the next day I received
> my first shave. "What would Reb Sender say?" I thought.
> When I came home that evening, I was extremely ill at ease.[15]

In his *Journey to Dawn,* Charles Angoff describes the
experiences of a Jewish immigrant family during the
early years of this century. He tells how Mottel, in introducing American life to his brother-in-law, Moshe,
the new arrival, reveals to him what he should expect. As
far as religion is concerned, Mottel says, "Judaism still
means much to us, though I must tell you also that we are
not as pious as we should be." Mottel looks around the
restaurant and Moshe automatically does likewise, again
noticing how many Jews are eating without their hats on.

14. David de Sola Pool, "Judaism and the Synagogue," in *The
American Jew* (New York, London: Harper and Brothers, 1942), p. 35.
15. Abraham Cahan, *The Rise of David Levinsky* (New York and
London: Harper and Brothers, Publishers, 1917), pp. 110–11.

"You can tell that easily enough," added Mottel, with a slight note of apology in his voice."[16]

Rise of the Conservative Group. An important development in the religious group life of the American Jew was the rise and rapid progress of the Conservative wing in American Judaism, whose ideological center is the Jewish Theological Seminary of America; the Conservative congregations form the United Synagogue of America, and their Rabbis are members of the Rabbinical Assembly of America. Like the Reform movement, this variant in Judaism had its origin in Germany in the middle of the nineteenth century. According to its founder, Zechariah Frankel, head of the Positive-Historical School, Judaism had always been growing and changing, but these changes were made within the framework of Halacha—the system of laws embodied in the Bible, Talmud, and later codes—and were based on the practice of most Jews who adhered to tradition. In contrast to Reform, Conservatism has insisted that for Judaism to survive and continue in America, it must not permit radical change of tradition or religious practices, or drastic adaptation to new environment. Conservatism has tried rather to develop a pattern for balancing tradition and change in Judaism.

The Conservative school of Judaism had its counterpart in America during the latter part of the nineteenth century. Its prominent exponents were Isaac Leeser, Marcus Jastrow, Benjamin Szold, Sabato Morais, and Alexander Kohut. In 1887 the Jewish Theological Seminary of America was opened in New York. However, as a religious movement within American Judaism, the beginning of the Conservative wing may be dated as of 1902, the year of the arrival in the United States of Solomon Schechter, who had given up a prominent aca-

16. Charles Angoff, *Journey to Dawn* (New York: The Beechhurst Press, 1951), p. 69.

demic career in England in order to head the reorganized Jewish Theological Seminary in New York. Schechter set as his task the creation of a viable equilibrium between the poles of change and tradition.[17] The nearest approach to an interpretation of the ideology of Conservative Judaism is the phrase used by its founders, namely, "historical Judaism." This implies, on the one hand, that Judaism is a historical phenomenon, possessed of a rich and valuable past, and that Jews ought to preserve their heritage as it was transmitted to them. On the other hand, it implies that Judaism is a growing, evolving organism, and that, though holding to its past, it must change in conformity with a changing world.[18]

In his discussion of Conservative Judaism, Dr. Simon Greenberg, Vice Chancellor of the Jewish Theological Seminary of America, asserts:

> Protest against the excesses of the Reform Jewish school was the immediate cause which brought it into being. But the founders of historical Judaism were not interested merely in preserving Judaism as they had received it from their immediate fathers. They knew that no living organism can remain static. *Change* leading to growth or decay was inevitable. They believed that no living organism can develop normally if it breaks sharply, completely and suddenly with its own past. Hence, they sought to guide Jewish life in a manner that would effect the necessary change without destroying or impairing the essential continuity of Judaism in all of its phases. They looked upon a knowledge of history as indispensable for the achievement of this continuity within change or change within continuity.[19]

17. Cf. Moshe Davis, *The Emergence of Conservative Judaism* (Philadelphia: The Jewish Publication Society of America, 1963) and Mordecai Waxman, ed., *Tradition and Change* (New York: The Burning Bush Press, 1958), pp. 3 ff.
18. Milton Steinberg, *A Partisan Guide to the Jewish Problem* (Indianapolis, Ind.: The Bobbs-Merrill Co., 1945), p. 165.
19. Simon Greenberg, "Conservative Judaism," in *Living Schools of Religion*, ed. Fern Vergilius, Student Outline Series. (Ames, Iowa: Littlefield, Adams and Co., 1956), pp. 325–28.

A case in point is the recent change introduced by the Rabbinical Assembly of the Conservative Rabbis in the Ketubah (marriage contract) in order to solve the problem of the Agunah (deserted wife), mentioned in the preceding chapter.

The rapid progress of the Conservative group during the last four-and-a-half decades was largely due to the failure of adequate adaptation on the part of the more orthodox. In a period of high social change, such as the mass immigration from the "shtetl" to the industrialized metropolitan city, the strains on the Orthodox synagogue were immense. While Orthodoxy flourished for a time, and functioned as a cultural constant in the life of the disoriented immigrant, a haven in the stormy new environment, it failed to meet the challenge of secularism and of modern thought which characterized the general environment.[20] While in a theological sense Conservative Judaism assumes a midway position between Orthodoxy and Reform, sociologically viewed, it represents the continuing socioeconomic change among American Jews by which many formerly of the labor class entered into the American Jewish middle class. It should be added, however, that in addition to the factor of social mobility in the rise of the Conservative group are the desire and search of the modern American Jew for new forms for the expression of the old religious feelings and traditions of his fathers.

Reconstructionism. An important development in the religious group life of American Jews in the last three decades is the Reconstructionist movement, whose founder and leader is Mordecai M. Kaplan, Professor of Jewish philosophy and homiletics at the Jewish Theological Sem-

---

20. Marshall Sklare, *Conservative Judaism* (Glencoe, Ill.: The Free Press, 1955), p. 43.

inary of America. Reconstructionism, which is regarded by some as the extreme left wing of Conservatism, views Judaism as an "evolving religious civilization," of which religion is the major but not the only component, others being Jewish literature, Hebrew language, music, and art. Reconstructionism firmly believes in, and strongly supports, the Zionist movement.

A basic concept in Reconstruction is "Jewish peoplehood," by which the Jew is able to live in two civilizations, the American and the Jewish. Every people, states Dr. Kaplan, Jewish or non-Jewish, is nowadays confronted with the problem of living in two civilizations—its own historic civilization and that of the country in which it dwells. The Jewish community, with its pragmatic philosophy of Judaism as a dynamic religious civilization, by which the organic Jewish community could secure creative survival of the Jewish people, and by its rationalistic, positive approach to Jewish life and Jewish religion, is to be the social framework which will hold together all Jews interested in the future of Jewish group life.[21] Reconstruction has won many adherents among the Reform group, among the secularists, and among Jewish social workers and educators.[22]

Each of the three main religious wings in American Judaism has its own rabbinical and congregational associations. In 1968 the Reform group reported 224,000 family membership and Conservative congregations reported 231,000. Orthodox congregations had a membership of well over 200,000 families.[23] The Conservative

21. Mordecai M. Kaplan, "The Principles of Reconstructionism," *The Reconstructionist* 21, no. 3 (March 18, 1955) :22.
22. Cf. Bernard Cohen "Dr. Mordecai M. Kaplan," *Bnai Brith Messenger,* Los Angeles, Calif. (April 13, 1951, June 22, 1956, July 4, 1965, and Jan. 15, 1971), also in *Jewish Herald Voice,* Passover Issue (April 1951), Houston, Texas.
23. Morris Fine and Milton Himmelfarb, eds., *The American Jewish Year Book,* vol. 70 (New York and Philadelphia: The Jewish Publication Society of America), p. 147.

and Reform groups report having more than 800 affiliated congregations each.

The changing pattern in the religious life of the contemporary American Jew is manifest in the extent of his observance of the dietary laws, the Jewish Sabbath and Holidays, and those religious rites that are associated with important events in the lifetime of a Jew. Such events are the *Bris* (circumcision), *Bar Mitzvah* (literally, "son of Commandment"), confirmation, wedding ceremony, and funeral.

In *Marjorie Morningstar,* Herman Wouk describes a number of scenes reflecting changing Jewish customs and religious ceremonies. Marjorie is a Jewish girl whose immigrant parents have risen from poverty in the Bronx to the better, more comfortable neighborhood of Central Park, West. Living in an environment devoid of Jewish religious values, Marjorie, like many of the new generation, follows the path of least resistance, the road of vulgar cultural assimilation. She experiences conflict, goes through an inner struggle with her religious traditions, but deviates from the Jewish religious patterns of living when she eats the non-Kosher food of lobster, and eventually eats pork.[24]

Bar Mitzvah. In Jewish religious tradition, when a boy reaches his thirteenth birthday he becomes Bar Mitzvah; he has then reached religious maturity and is expected to assume responsibility for his actions. In the past, up to a generation or two ago, no special preparation was necessary for the Bar Mitzvah rite. The boys would start their Hebrew studies at the age of five or six, and were

---

24. Herman Wouk, *Marjorie Morningstar* (New York: Doubleday & Co., Inc., 1955), pp. 289–90.

well prepared in such studies before their thirteenth birthday, when they were called up in the synagogue to read the Torah and chant the Prophetic portion assigned for the Sabbath of that week. Some of the youngsters would even prepare a Talmudic discourse for the occasion. Today the Bar Mitzvah ceremony has radically changed, and parents, even those who are not observing religious ritual, insist that their sons—and recently also, their daughters—be confirmed. Then they celebrate their Bar Mitzvah or Bas Mitzvah with a big party.

The rite of Bar Mitzvah has of late become so popular among parents that even Reformed Jews, who long ago abolished the traditional Bar Mitzvah, and the secularists, who did not prepare their children for Bar Mitzvah in their schools, were recently moved to include Bar Mitzvah preparation in their school curriculum. Because of its increasing popularity, parents are now incurring great expense in arranging a lavish party, which is usually held outside the Temple, often in a luxurious hotel. An illustration of the changed pattern of Bar Mitzvah celebration, often vulgarized and disgusting, is given in *Marjorie Morningstar,* where Wouk describes a twelve-hundred-dollar Bar Mitzvah extravaganza at Lowenshein's famous hotel.[25]

Wedding Ceremony. Change effected by the impact of the American environment may also be noted in the Jewish wedding ceremony. Such songs as "O Promise Me" and "Because," never before used in Jewish ceremonies, are now being rendered. The wedding described in *Marjorie Morningstar* was a "Lowenshein's Number One, at $6,500."

Marjorie herself saw the scene differently. She saw a tawdry

25. *Ibid.,* p. 86.

mockery of sacred things, a bourgeois riot of expense, with a special touch of vulgar Jewish sentimentality.[26]

Worthy of note is the reaction to such change, regarded as vulgarization, by religious Jewish leadership. An article that appeared some time ago in the *Jewish News,* organ of the Jewish Community Council, presents the view of Rabbi Joachim Prinz of Newark, New Jersey,

> that synagogue weddings have become a rarity, because ceremonies are usually held in hotels or catering establishments. There, he said, the ceremony is "a strange and inorganic interlude between the inevitable hors d'oeuvres and liquor served before . . . and the festivities that follow. . . .
> The music during the ceremony, he said, consists of tunes written "by the rabid anti-Semite, Richard Wagner, and a converted Jew, Felix Mendelssohn-Bartholdy . . . (and) songs selected from the trashiest of popular musical literature."
> At wedding ceremonies held in Temple B'nai Abraham, Dr. Prinz said that "the trashy music is omitted." It is replaced by an arrangement of the Biblical Song of Songs, written by . . . a noted Jewish composer.

Observance of Jewish Festivals. A case illustrating the changed manner of Jewish festival observance, due to environmental influence, is seen in the celebration of Hanukah, the Feast of Lights. This festival, which occurs about the same time as Christmas and commemorates the victory of the ancient Maccabees over the Syrian forces, is traditionally observed by the lighting of the eight-branched candelabra, and by reciting the blessings of thanksgiving and chanting appropriate songs. One notes today, however, some changes in the manner of its observance. While formerly each of the children received Hanukah "gelt," a gift of money in honor of the joyous festival, today the children receive presents rather than money.

---

26. *Ibid.,* p. 556.

Another example of the changing form of the observance is the growing importance attached to the Hanukah
observance. Many parents, desiring their children not to
be jealous of their Christian playmates' Christmas presents, present them with eight different Hanukah gifts,
one for each night of the festival. The special parties
held during the Hanukah week in the religious schools,
in the Jewish Community Centers, and in private homes,
and the gifts and the ceremonial lighting of the Menorah,
give to Hanukah the same psychological values that
many Christian children experience from Christmas. A
further manifestation of the change in the manner of
Jewish holiday observance due to the influence of the
Christian social environment is the joint Christmas-
Hanukah celebrations in the public schools of a number
of cities.

The Passover festival, which continues to be the most
popular Jewish holiday, has acquired new forms differing
from those which prevailed in the European countries.
The tremendous preparation for the holiday which Jews
had to make, the special spring pre-Passover cleaning, the
Passover food preparation, the custom of outfitting the
family with new clothes—all these activities have van-
ished from the American scene. The Passover Seder, the
religious service and the meal, in which every member
of the family participates, has always served as a powerful bond in the family tie, and still retains its great popularity. The Passover Seder may serve as an index to the
extent that tradition is still being retained and observed.

Contemporary American-Jewish novelists have used
the Passover Seder night to depict one of the most important scenes of Jewish family life in their novels. In
The Old Bunch,[27] Meyer Levin describes a Seder celebration by some of the second generation of American

_____

27. Meyer Levin, *The Old Bunch* (New York: The Citadel Press,
1937), p. 479.

Jews. The manner of celebration, devoid of religious, spiritual content, becomes a vulgar and disgusting imitation of the traditional Seder. The Seder celebration is held in the apartment of Ev Goldberg, one of "the bunch." To this Seder is also invited a non-Jewish couple, Mr. and Mrs. Mellwain, "who were dying to see a Jewish Passover ceremony." The Seder celebration begins with "cocktails and little caviar canapes on matzoth."[28] Then

> in the center of the table was a layer cake, topped with a doll in a long flowing robe, with white cotton for a beard pasted to the doll's chin. The place cards were cut-outs of biblical characters, only Ev had fixed devilish little short skirts over the long gowns of the women characters and put derby hats on the men. But the most comical thing she had done was to get pictures of monsters and paste their faces on the biblical figures.[29]

Characteristic of the remarks by members of "the bunch" around the table is the one, "If you can't eat bread, eat cake."[30] For caps, everyone wears party paper hats, generally used at New Year's Eve parties. Hot biscuits are served and the maid brings in "an immense, sugar-baked ham." As the cheap parody and vulgarization of the sacred Passover Seder becomes unbearable, Sam Eisen—who preferred going to his folks' for the Seder but his wife had insisted on going to Ev Goldberg's—got up and moved toward the door—even his wife could not stop him—mumbling in his throat, "This is where I get off, this is where I get off."[30]

The decline of the traditional Jewish mode of living among the second generation as shown in the novel *Marjorie Morningstar* and the vulgarization of the time-

28. *Ibid.,* p. 49.
29. *Ibid.,* p. 481.
30. *Ibid.,* p. 485.

honored religious Bar Mitzvah and wedding ceremonies result from a shallow assimilation of second-generation American Jews who "abandon the best part of their heritage in order to take on the worst aspects of their new environment."[31]

31. Maxwell Geisman, "*Marjorie Morningstar:* a review of the novel by Herman Wouk," *New York Times* Book Review (Sept. 4, 1955), p. 1.

9

Changing Jewish Education

JEWISH EDUCATION OF EARLIER TIMES

Next to the family in its influence upon the molding of the character of the individual and of his social group is the school. Education viewed as a social process is concerned with "the transmission of culture from one generation to the next, and is at bottom social heredity in actual operation."[1] In Jewish group life in various ages and climes, the education of the young was a primary concern. It was part of an integrated social pattern deemed essential for transmitting the Jewish cultural heritage, strengthening Jewish group life, and assuring a satisfying adjustment and creative survival of the group.

Role of Education in Jewish Life. Louis Wirth, discussing the role that education has played in the life of the Jewish people, thinks of education as part of a process by which societies keep themselves alive and renew themselves in the face of changing circumstances. In no phase of Jewish group life, he observes, is the will to survive more convincingly manifested than in the adjustment efforts of Jewish education to changing social situations. He further points out that, from the days of the Jewish

---

1. Clarence M. Case, *Social Process and Human Progress* (New York: Harcourt, Brace and Company, 1931), p. 217.

154

dispersion throughout the world, in the absence of a concentrated settlement in their own politically independent state, it was only through communication among their members in time and in space that the widely separated remnants of Israel ever held together.[2]

Historically, the education of the Jewish child was the prime responsibility of his parents. It was the father's duty to ". . . command his children and his household after him, that they may keep the way of the Lord, to do justice and judgment."[3] The mother also took an active part in the child's training, teaching him prayers and passages from the Torah. After the boy's fifth birthday he came under the care of his father, who was duty-bound to instruct him in the Torah and such portions of the Talmud as were necessary for every Jewish child to know. This duty is proclaimed by the Biblical injunction: "And these words which I command thee this day shall be upon thine heart and thou shalt teach them diligently unto thy children, talking of them when thou sittest in thy house and when thou walkest by the way, when thou liest down and when thou risest up."[4] Thus, both the Jewish family and the Jewish school have molded the character and controlled the attitudes and actions of the children thereby assuming the responsibility for the continuity of the people's life and culture.

Jewish Education a Community Responsibility. Later, in post-Biblical times, elementary education became institutionalized and was the responsibility of the community. Before the fall of the Jewish state, Simon ben Shotah, a president of the Sanhedrin (the Jewish High Court), established schools of advanced studies for young men

---

2. Louis Wirth, "Education for Survival," *The American Journal of Sociology* 48 (1943–43) :682.

3. Genesis 18:19.

4. Deuteronomy 11:19.

in every district of the country. In the same first century, Joshua ben Gamla[5] established elementary schools in every town and village of Palestine. An ordinance required the residents of every town to establish a school which children aged six or seven must attend. Teachers were appointed for all these community-supported schools.

After the dispersion (70 A.D.), Jewish schools for the young were established wherever Jews settled. Thus, free public education was introduced in the Jewish community and, continuing to modern times, the religious education of the child was the responsibility of the entire Jewish community, for this training was considered essential to the existence and welfare of the group.

It was characteristic of the Jewish people's desire for learning that their religious life in the period of their dispersion was not so much connected with a city or a land as with a book. The Torah became—to quote Heinrich Heine—the Jews' "portable fatherland" in exile, and the Talmud served as a fence around the Torah.[6]

Changing Role and Scope of Jewish Education. Education among the Jews, designed to assure the survival of the group's social heritage, was adapted to the changing situation in which Jews found themselves.[7]

A historical review of the Jewish school curriculum reveals two motivating principles: preservation and adjustment. In the Biblical and Talmudic period, the school curriculum in Palestine was a response to the need of the people to live a normal life in their own land. Following the Jews' loss of their political independence and subsequent dispersion, the school and its curriculum served

5. A high priest who was in office in the latter part of the first century (c. 64 B.C.E.).
6. Wirth, pp. 214–24.
7. *Ibid.,* pp. 683–85.

as a means of conservation of solidarity and group consciousness.

The role of the Jewish school, like that of the family, has undergone a great many changes. Social developments brought about a situation in which the roles of the family and the synagogue in educating the young have become less prominent than in previous years.

From the Old Heder to the Heder Metukan. Among Jews of Eastern Europe, the elementary school for children was called a "Heder" (a room), taking its name from the fact that the children usually met in a room of the teacher's home. The lower, elementary Heder served the very young children, who were beginning to read and write Hebrew and to translate sentences from the Pentateuch. The higher Heder prepared the student for more advanced study in the Talmud and for the Yeshivah (a high school of Talmudic study). Under the impact of the Haskalah (Enlightenment), which started in Germany in the latter half of the eighteenth century, the desire for adjustment to new social situations and for greater social interaction with their non-Jewish neighbors resulted in the inclusion of secular studies in the curriculum of the Jewish school. Also, in Russia and in other East European countries, due to the influence of the Haskalah and the Jewish nationalist movement which followed it, a new, more modern Jewish school, called "Heder Metukan" (the improved Heder, improved in method and content), came into being. Its curriculum called for a more intensified study of the Hebrew language and aimed to imbue the child with a love for Hebrew culture and an appreciation of the rising national renaissance movement, Zionism.[8]

---

8. Julius B. Maller, *The Role of Education in Jewish History,* in *The Jews,* ed. Louis Finkelstein, vol. 2 (New York: Harper and Brothers, Publishers, 1949), p. 92.

DEVELOPMENT OF JEWISH EDUCATION
IN THE UNITED STATES

In their efforts at adaptation to the new American environment, Jews regarded the adjustment of their educational system to the changed social situation in America as essential.

In the United States, Jewish education as a community obligation may be traced to the year 1731, following the establishment of the first synagogue on Mill Street, in New York, when the Yeshivat Minhag Areb was organized by the Spanish-Portuguese Jewish community. In the religious school of the Synagogue, as in the American school of the colonial period, Jewish children received both religious and secular instruction. With the increased number of immigrant German Jews in the middle of the nineteenth century, the German-Jewish congregations organized their own complete schools.

Emergence of the Sunday School. After 1860, when the American public school became well established and the principle of separation of church and state was adopted, Jews began to send their children to the public schools, after which, influenced by American practice, the Jewish religious school became merely supplementary to the public school. Gradually the Jewish religious school became a Sunday School on the pattern of the predominantly Protestant American Sunday School.

The first Jewish Sunday School, organized by Rebecca Graetz in Philadelphia in 1838, was associated with the Orthodox Congregation Mikve Israel. With the growth of the Jewish Reform movement, the number of Sunday Schools spread throughout the land and in 1886 a Sabbath School Union was organized. The Sunday School, attended by more than half the Jewish children in the country, evidences the direct influence of the American environment on Jewish education.

The educational achievements of the Sunday School, were of little value, and were unsatisfactory, largely because of the limited one or two hours of instruction per week. However, a new period in Sunday School education began in 1923 when the Union of American Hebrew Congregations (Reform) organized an Educational Department with Dr. Emanuel Gamoran as its director. By introducing new textbooks, modern educational techniques, and better-trained teachers, the situation improved considerably.

From the Old Heder to the Talmud Torah. It was the East European Jew who, in the first mass immigration after 1881, brought along the old forms of Jewish religious education, the Heder and the Talmud Torah. The state of Jewish education in those days is described as follows:

> Jewish education was in a sad state—and not because of lack of teachers. On the contrary, there were too many of them. According to statistics published by the Baron de Hirsch Fund in 1890 there were 251 melamdin [private teachers] on the East Side. Because of this glut, tuition fees were reduced to fifty cents a month. In the case of further reduction in the tuition fees the teachers threatened to give up teaching and go back to their former calling: tailoring, shoe repairing, and the like.[9]

In East European countries the Heder was a private school for children whose parents could afford to pay the necessary tuition, while the Talmud Torah was a community-supported school for fatherless and poor chil-

9. Shlomo Noble, "The Image of the American Jew," *Yivo Annual of Jewish Social Science,* vol. 9 (New York: Yiddish Scientific Institute—YIVO, 1954), pp. 83–108.

dren. In the United States these schools underwent fundamental changes. The Heder, the normal private school in Europe, soon deteriorated because of lack of parental interest. The immigrant father—the Jewish peddler or worker—who worked all day to eke out a living for his family, had no time to attend to the Jewish education of his children. This situation is aply expressed by Morris Rosenfeld in his popular Yiddish poem, "My Son":

> I have a little boy,
> A little son so dear,
> When I but glance at him,
> The whole world seems to be mine!
> But seldom do I see him,
> My lovely one, awake
> I always find him sleeping,
> I see him only at night.
> I leave for work so early
> Returning home so late
> A stranger am I unto myself,
> A stranger to my child.[10]

The Talmud Torah, the community's school for the poor in Europe, then became in the United States the most hopeful form of Jewish schooling during the years of mass immigration from 1880 to 1914.[11]

The Old Heder in American Jewish Novels. The more orthodox Jewish immigrants tried to adjust to the new conditions by transplanting the old Heder. According to Dushkin, there were over 500 Hedorim in New York City in 1917.[12] But, lacking a well-formulated program

10. *Jewish Life* (May 1953), p. 15.
11. Alexander M. Dushkin, "Changing Conception of Community Responsibility in Jewish Education," *Jewish Education* 26, no. 3 (Spring 1956) :11.
12. *Ibid.*, *Jewish Education in New York City* (New York: Bureau of Jewish Education, 1918), p. 68.

and communal supervision, the Heder soon deteriorated and became the happy hunting ground of ill-prepared, maladjusted individuals who brought it into disrepute. However, it should be mentioned here that there were in the first and second decades of the century many self-sacrificing private teachers who established such schools.[13] The children who attended the Heder and were taught by those teachers called "melamdim," were not favorably impressed by their instructors. Most of the teachers were old, weak men who were unable to find other work.

Novelist Henry Roth, who received his education in the public school and in Heder in the afternoon, draws a picture of the Heder in *Call It Sleep*. In this novel, recently rediscovered 35 years after it first appeared, he gives us an insight into the conditions of the old Heder in the first decade of this century, and into the psychological reactions of the child attending the Heder.

> While his mother and the rabbi were discussing the hours and the price and the manner of David's tuition, David scanned his future teacher more closely. He was not at all like the teachers at school, but David had seen rabbis before and knew he wouldn't be. He appeared old and was certainly untidy.
>
> What had been, when he and his mother had entered, a low hum of voices, had now swollen to a roar. It looked as though half of the boys in the room had engaged the other half in some verbal or physical conflict. The rabbi, excusing himself to David's mother, turned toward them, and with a thunderous rap of his fist against the door, uttered a ferocious "Shah!" The noise subsided somewhat. He swept the room with angry glittering eyes, then softening into a smile again returned to David's mother.
>
> "Sit down over there," said the rabbi curtly as soon as his mother had left. "And don't forget," he brought a crooked knuckle to his lips, "In a heder one must be quiet."[14]

13. Simon Greenberg, *The Jews,* ed. Louis Finkelstein, vol. 2 (New York: Harper and Brothers, 1949), p. 929.
14. In *A Golden Treasury of Jewish Literature* (New York: Farrar and Rinehart, 1937), pp. 39–44.

Another bitter criticism of the atmosphere, program, and poor discipline of the Heder was leveled in 1923 by Samuel B. Ornitz in his novel *Haunch, Paunch and Jowl*, in which he describes the life of the Jewish boy on the East Side of New York.

In *A Walker in the City*, Alfred Kazin gives us this picture of his teacher who prepared him for his confirmation:

> For several months before my confirmation at thirteen, I appeared every Wednesday afternoon before a choleric old Melamed, a Hebrew teacher, who would sit across the table eating peas, and with an incredulous scowl on his face listen to me go over and over the necessary prayers and invocations, slapping me sharply on the hands whenever I stammered on a syllable. I had to learn many passages by heart, but never understood most of them, nor was I particularly expected to understand them; it was as if some contract in secret cipher had been drawn up between the Lord of Hosts and Gita Fayge's son Alfred which that Amerikaner idiot, as the melamed called me, could sign with an x. In the "old country" the melamed might possibly have encouraged me to understand the text, might even have discussed it with me. Here it was understood that I would go through the lessons simply for form's sake, because my mother wished to see me confirmed; the melamed expected nothing more of me.[15]

There was little about the Hebrew school that would interest or attract Jewish youngsters to attend after the hours spent in public school while other children were free to play. In one of his novels about the Polonsky family in Boston, Charles Angoff says:

> When David's parents heard about their son's losing interest and misbehaving in Hebrew school, they were rather surprised. In Russia, they recalled, David enjoyed Hebrew school, respected his teachers and was generally a quiet boy. What in heaven's name has happened to him here?

---

15. (New York: Harcourt, Brace and Company, 1951), pp. 45–46.

". . . We all become goyim [non-Jews] here," said Moshe, "and our children are becoming just like their parents, hooligans, ashamed of their Judaism, disrespectful to their teachers and parents, liars, and God alone knows what else they are."[16]

The theme of Hebrew instruction for Jewish children in the first and second decades of this century is similarly treated by Joseph Opatoshu in his Yiddish novel of 1919, *Hebrew*.[17] In his novels he realistically portrays the rough life of the underworld of the immigrants on New York's East Side. Himself a teacher in the afternoon Hebrew School while attending school at Cooper Union, he describes the unscrupulous and intellectually dishonest school principals, who, although they were not religious in the traditional sense, served as teachers in orthodox, religious schools. He depicts the pupils, who disliking the school and their teachers, preferred to spend their afternoon hours after public school in playing ball outdoors.

EMERGENCE OF NEW TYPES OF SCHOOLS

With the greater social stratification, mobility, and ideological differentiation that has taken place since the turn of the century among American Jews, new types of Jewish schools have emerged. While in the period from 1900 to 1920 a majority of the sons of Jewish immigrants, the second generation, received religious education by attending Hedorim, today a very small number attends these schools. The communal weekday school called Talmud Torah (literally, study of the Law), for the last half century the school with the more intensive Jewish educational program, is now gradually giving way to the new congregational weekday school and no longer dominates the scene as it did a generation ago.

16. *In the Morning Light* (New York: The Beechhurst Press, 1952), p. 21.
17. (Wilno: Farlag B. Klezkin, 1920.)

The Congregational School. In the four decades since 1930, Jewish elementary education in the United States has shown a definite tendency to come under congregational auspices. In explaining this new tendency, Simon Greenberg observes that as the wealthier and more Americanized Jewish families moved out of the old congested areas to new neighborhoods, they organized their communal life around the synagogue, of which the school attended by their children was an integral part.[18]

The Secular Yiddish Schools and Changed Ideological Attitudes. In the beginning of the second decade, the number of secular, or labor-minded, "radical" Jewish immigrants increased. Seeing their growing children become alienated from them and from their social ideology and Jewish heritage, this radical immigrant also became aware of the need for his child's Jewish education. In 1911 the first Yiddish School was organized by the National Workers Alliance, an affiliate of the Zionist-Labor group, and was named "National Radical School." The curriculum included Jewish history and the Bible; Hebrew and Yiddish were the languages of instruction. Later, the Workmen Circle members and other socialist and secularist groups, moved by the same motives, opened supplementary schools for their children's Jewish education. The declaration made my the educational committee of the Workmen Circle at their convention in May 1916, states:

> Our children are growing up alien to our language, to the ideals and customs of our people. They look down upon the majority of our people . . . as of an inferior culture. Occasionally their attitude is that of contempt. . . . Our children should be acquainted with the immense treasures of Jewish

18. *The Jews*, p. 930.

culture, old and new . . . that they may be able to continue
to create its culture.[19]

A clear indication that in the labor and socialist classes
those favoring Jewish education had won the argument
against those favoring cultural assimilation was the ten-
cent quarterly school tax placed on the members of the
Workmen Circle in 1922. The need for more advanced
Jewish education grew when the first *mittel shule* (high
school) was opened in New York in 1921.

All-Day Schools. A striking change in Jewish education in
the United States is shown by the rapid development,
in the past decade, of the all-day school. These schools,
in most cases conducted under Orthodox auspices, have
now nearly one-seventh of the reported total enrollment
of children.[20] They provide a complete program of secular and Jewish studies, and assign an average of fifteen
hours of instruction per week to Jewish studies. In evaluating the all-day school, Louis Ruffman, president of the
National Council for Jewish Education, states that "it
can and does provide the thorough and intensive type of
Jewish education capable of producing literate Jews and
reducing the ignorance that prevails among American
Jews."[21]

In advocating the Jewish day school, Jewish educators
maintain that the Sunday School and the afternoon Hebrew School, both the communal Talmud Torah and the
Congregational Weekday School, fail to impart the
knowledge of the Jewish heritage, essential for Jewish
cultural survival. Worthy of mention in this connection

19. Report, Workmen Circle Convention, *Friend,* vol. 2 (June 1916),
quoted by Melech Epstein in *Jewish Labor in U.S.A.* (New York: Trade
Union Sponsoring Committee, 1953), p. 276.
20. Gerald Lang, "Jewish Education," in *American Jewish Year
Book* 69 (New York: The American Jewish Committee, 1968) :371–83.
21. Louis L. Ruffman, *Congress Weekly* 21, no. 12 (1954) :8.

is the point expressed by Trude Weiss Rosmarin that

> unlike the Catholic Parochial School, the Jewish All-Day
> Schools use the textbooks of the public schools. Jewish All-
> Day Schools are not averse to appointing non-Jewish teachers
> for the general subjects. . . . The Jewish All-Day School,
> while giving its students a broad Jewish training, never de-
> viates from the democratic principles that govern American
> public schools.[22]

Bureaus of Jewish Education. In 1910 educators and communal leaders attempted to raise standards and assume responsibility for adjusting Jewish educational efforts to the American environment. The first Bureau of Jewish Education was then organized in New York City with Dr. Samson Benderly as its head, one of its major achievements being the setting of a pattern for central coordinating agencies, and it later became instrumental in changing the Jewish educational process in the United States. Considerable improvement has since been shown in the major areas of education and an increasing number of bureaus or boards of Jewish Education operate today in which many Jewish communities. By interpreting the needs and problems of Jewish education to the communities, the bureaus are receiving considerable allocations for Jewish schools from the local Jewish welfare funds and federations. The efforts of the Bureaus to unite the diverse educational groups within the Jewish community is evidence of the change in community responsibility for Jewish education. All groups, the Orthodox, Conservative, Reform, and Yiddish-secularist, are given representation in the bureaus. Since 1939 the American Association for Jewish Education has effectively served communities on a broad national scale.

---

22. Trude Weiss Rosmarin, "Are Day Schools the Answer?" *Congress Weekly* 15, no. 20 (1948) :6.

Enrollment. Some of the changes that have occurred in the Jewish school situation are shown in the following facts and figures:

According to the latest report by the National Census of Jewish Schools, conducted by the American Association for Jewish Education, there are today 2727 known Jewish schools of all types in the country, serving an estimated 544,468 children. Attendance by type of school shows 13.4 percent in Jewish Day Schools, 42.2 percent in one-day-a-week schools, and 44.4 percent in midweek afternoon schools that are in session from two to five times a week.

Of these, 35.7 percent are in schools under Reform auspices, 34.3 percent in schools under Conservative congregations, and 21.5 percent in schools under Orthodox auspices, 1.0 percent in Yiddish schools, and 0.6 percent in communal or intercongregational schools.[23]

About 92 percent of those enrolled in 1966-1967 were in schools under congregational auspices. Communal schools account for 5 percent of the children of elementary school age who attend Jewish schools (with New York City and Los Angeles below the average). Sixteen percent of the children of secondary-school age attend Jewish schools.[24]

Close to one-seventh of reported Jewish school students received intensive All-Day School education. The vast majority of students attended one- or three-day-a-week schools. High school enrollment substantially increased in the 1962-1966 period. Enrollment in All-Day School, which increased by 19 percent in the 1962-1966 period; under Conservative auspices the Solomon Schechter Day School more than doubled. There is a growing recognition also, among Reform Jews of the need for All-Day Schools under Reform auspices.

23. *American Jewish Yearbook,* 1969, vol. 70, p. 153.
24. Goldfarb, p. 289.

In his call for a Communal Day School, Rabbi David
Polish states:

> Products of Sunday Schools, Bar Mitzvah and even con-
> firmation classes, will not make rabbis, Jewish educators, and
> for that matter, qualified Jewish leaders in any field of lay
> endeavor. Nor will this limited training create a category of
> learned Jews who always existed within the Jewish commu-
> nity and were distinguished for their Jewish wisdom which
> was a value in itself.
>   Once we stop kidding ourselves that the Hebrew School
> child who reads the Four Questions flawlessly at the family
> seder is a scholar, or that the Bar Mitzvah who can read a few
> lines from the Torah is breathing hard down the rabbi's neck,
> we will awaken to the need for developing a small nucleus of
> enlightened Jews. Unless this is done soon, we will find in a
> generation that the blind are leading the blind.
>   I therefore feel that it is urgent that a community-sponsored
> day school be organized for the intensive Jewish training of
> those children who may eventually rise to Jewish leadership
> or who may simply want to master Judaism as others master
> music or the dance.[25]

Leaders in the field of Jewish education feel that events
in Israel and the fate of the Jews in Soviet Russia have
created a greater sense of Jewish identity; and parents
may now be expected to give higher priority to Jewish
education.

CHANGED EMPHASIS IN JEWISH EDUCATION

Worthy of note is the changed motive in emphasizing
the need for Jewish education. In addition to the emphasis on the need of preserving Jewish culture and the Jewish people, the personal adjustment of the Jewish child,
or the mental health value of Jewish education, is now
being stressed. For this purpose the researches by Kurt

Lewin are being utilized. At a conference of Jewish educators Lewin reported on a study made of two groups of young Jews, one a group with a strong sense of Jewish identity and a good Jewish education, the other a group of university students without a strong Jewish identification and with either inadequate Jewish education or none at all. The members of the second group found nothing positive in their Jewishness and felt anti-Semitism keenly, while the members of the group with strong Jewish identification were less troubled by anti-Semitism and found many positive features in their Jewishness.[26]

An illustration that bears out this point is found in *The Naked and the Dead* by Norman Mailer. Two Jews who suffer much in marching with their platoon and fighting on a small island in the Pacific are pictured. One, Goldstein, is conscious of his Jewishness and, although as unhappy a human being as most of Mailer's soldiers, he emerges from the horrible experiences an honorable and brave man. The other, Roth, is an "agnostic" who tries to keep apart from other Jews, but, in spite of his efforts, he is labeled a Jew by his fellow soldiers. He is uncertain of himself, unhappy in his failure to adjust to a Jew-hating world, and he breaks down under the strain.[27]

Sociological Aspects in the Changing Situation. The vast majority of children now attending weekday afternoon schools are enrolled in those conducted by congregations. This changed position of the congregational school, despite the fact that it is still regarded as inferior in educational quality and achievements to the communally sponsored Talmud Torah, may be explained by the steady

---

26. Kurt Lewin, "Psychological Problems in Jewish Education," *Jewish Social Service Quarterly* 23 (March 1947):271.
27. Norman Mailer, *The Naked and the Dead* (New York: Rinehart, Holt, & Winston, Inc., 1948).

and continuing shift of Jewish population from metropolitan areas to the suburbs. Another factor is the quest for identity of the new residents in the suburbs, mostly young people and third-generation Americans, who, in their desire for identification, tend to affiliate with a congregation and synagogue which can provide their children with some religious education.[28] Another sociological explanation for the rapid rise of the congregational school is the fact that in the general American community, diversity of groups on a religious basis is more readily understood and sanctioned than are differences on a linguistic and ethnic basis.

JEWISH CAMPS

A constructive development in Jewish education in recent decades is the rapid growth of the number of camps, some of which are open year round. Sponsored by various religious denominations, Zionist groups, Community Centers, and secular Yiddish Culture organizations, these camps provide a setting and an intensive program of Jewish educational experience. Established camps are sponsored by the United Synagogue (Conservative), the Union of Hebrew Congregations (Reform), the Orthodox Congregation, and secular Yiddishist groups, and are found in various parts of the country.

One notices an important change in the purpose and program of the camps, which were formerly called Fresh Air Societies, or Mothers' and Babes' Camps, and were concerned mainly with getting children and families out of the hot, crowded cities into the fresh air of the country. Today, most Jewish camps combine informal study and play and are designed primarily to instill in the

---

28. Herbert J. Gans, "Progress of a Suburban Jewish Community," *Commentary* 23, no. 2 (February 1957):113 ff.

camper an appreciation of Jewish values and a knowledge
and love of Judaism.

Worthy of special mention is the Brandeis Camp Institute in California, which carries on a most effective
year-round educational program, including seminars and
workshops for high school and college youth, also special
programs for adults.

The Brandeis Institute, located in the Santa Susana
mountains forty miles from Los Angeles, was founded
and organized by Dr. Shlomo Bardin in 1941, on the
advice of the late Justice Louis D. Brandeis. In 1947
the Institute moved to Santa Susana, California. By his
effective teaching method and specially designed program, Brandeis Camp had helped many alienated American-Jewish young people achieve a feeling of a meaningful Jewish identity and an intelligent understanding and
appreciation of Jewish living.

Founded on the principle of a laboratory of living
Judaism, Brandeis Camp is training leaders for the
American Jewish Community who are knowledgeable
and appreciative of their Jewish heritage. The camp for
youngsters, "Alonim" (Young Oaks), under the able
leadership of its director, Benjamin Herson, has had in
the eighteen years of existence about 10,000 children.

High praise for the program and accomplishments of
Brandeis Camp has been expressed by leading educators
and community leaders who have visited it. A survey by
sociologist Gene N. Levine reveals that fully 94 percent
of the alumni considered the exposure to the completely
Jewish environment at Brandeis Camp Institute a good
idea; also that more than half the alumni felt that
Brandeis had a lasting effect on their attitude toward
Israel and on their continued interest in and pursuit of
Jewish studies.

A review of the development of Jewish education in the United States indicates that it is varied and diversified, reflecting the socioeconomic and ideological differentiation in the American Jewish community. It reveals further that the various groups in the Jewish community, though differing in the intensity of their programs of instruction, in the number of hours allotted, and in the emphasis given to certain subjects, are agreed on the common goal of their educational efforts: to provide for Jewish group survival by means of educating and molding the American-born Jew into a person who consciously identifies himself as a loyal member of the Jewish people.

10

Social Movements in
Modern Jewish Life

Social movements having their origin in mass dissatisfaction and social unrest represent an effort to effect social change. They derive their motive power from both dissatisfaction with the current existing conditions and a strong desire for a new system of living.[1] In addition to being a manifestation of change, social movements are also an agency of change.

Conditions of Jewish life in Eastern Europe at the end of the last century made Jews aware of their difficult situation and awakened in them a strong desire for change, which found expression in national and social movements begun in the 1890s. In studying the rise of social movements among Jews in the last nine decades, one notes that the main motivation of most of them was the desire to abolish persecution of Jews and assure their survival as a people. In the ideologies and practical programs of these movements, the aim has been the creation of such conditions as would assure the continued normal existence and creative cultural development of the Jewish people.

---

1. Herbert Blumer, "Collective Behavior," Part IV of *New Outline of the Principles of Sociology*, ed. Alfred McClung Lee (New York: Barnes and Noble, Inc., 1946), p. 199.

The two most important social movements among Jews in the last decade of the nineteenth century were Zionism, the most dynamic Jewish movement of modern times, which strives to change and normalize Jewish life through the establishment of a sovereign Jewish State on the Jew's ancestral soil in Palestine; and Socialism, which aims at changing the present social order for a socialistic, classless society. The sociocultural changes which these movements effected constitute a central theme in modern Jewish literature.

ZIONISM

Appearing in Jewish life as a protest against the people's social position, the Zionist movement soon spread throughout the world and profoundly affected the home, the school, the synagogue, and the total Jewish community. Modern Zionism was launched as a political movement at the first Zionist Congress, called by Theodore Herzl, at Basle, Switzerland, 1897. It then set forth as its goal "the securing of a legally secured, publicly recognized homeland for the Jewish people in Palestine." In his appraisal of the Zionist movement, Hans Kohn states:

> As a movement, Zionism has undoubtedly been the most important factor in modern Jewish history. As the national hope of the Jews during the two thousand years of their dispersion, Zionism has, since the deterioration of their situation in central and Eastern Europe, again become the hope and refuge of many. It has rekindled the fire of Jewish nationalism in the heart of many an assimilated Jew. It has taught the Jews a new pride in their history and a new consciousness of their destiny.[2]

---

2. Hans Kohn, "Zionism," in *Encyclopedia of the Social Sciences,* vol. 15 (New York: The Macmillan Co., 1935), pp. 528-36.

Zionism a Factor of Change. Official interest in the ideal of Zionism among American Jews may be traced to Mordecai Manuel Noah (1785-1851), a descendant of a prominent American family of Portuguese Jews, a playwright and American consul in Tunis. Another early American Zionist was poetess Emma Lazarus of New York City (1849-1887), who wrote in *The Epistle to the Jews* of the need for a "Free Jewish state, a home for the homeless, a nation for the denationalized." Shortly after the first Basle Congress, the first American Zionist convention was held, at which was formed the American Zionist Organization under the leadership of Professor Richard Gottheil of Columbia University as president, and Stephen S. Wise as secretary.

With the new wave of East European immigration, the Zionist movement in America gradually grew and crystallized, as did new groups, the Fraternal Order of Sons of Zion (1907); a youth group, the Young Judea (1909); and a women's division, Hadassah (1912). These groups later became vital influences in the growth of Zionism in America.

A marked advance in American Zionism came during the years 1914-1917, under the new leadership of Louis D. Brandeis, whose authority attracted to the movement individuals of distinction and ability. These played an important role in the negotiations that led to the Balfour Declaration, November 2, 1917.

Changing Role and Function of the Zionist Movement. With the establishment of the State of Israel in 1948, the scope and role of the Zionist movement were radically changed. While, in the pre-State period, the chief activities were, first, to win the support of the Jewish people to the cause of Zionism, and second, to represent the Jewish people in the political negotiations on behalf of the Zionist aim, from 1948 on, these roles and functions were assumed by the government of the newborn state of Israel. Thus American Zionists were freed to assume new roles and functions such as providing economic help through fund raising, encouraging cultural activities through stressing Hebrew culture, and offering moral and political support to the reborn state.

In its early years the Zionist movement caused ideological conflict and cleavage between generations, in America as well as in Europe. Strictly orthodox parents could not accept their children's modern outlook on Zionism that was to take the place of the old traditional belief in the coming of the Messiah. Also, most of the radical Jewish Socialists, the "Bund," opposed Zionism. These ideological conflicts among members of the same family are reflected in several novals dealing with American Jewish life.[3] The home life of many American Jews was also influenced by the Zionist movement's reintroducing and reviving religious ceremonials such as the proper observance of Hanukah and the Passover Seder.

Zionism also effected a change in the educational program of the Jewish school, especially in the establishment of the Heder Metukan (the modernized Hebrew school) in Europe, which marked a radical departure from the old Heder. Intensive study of modern Hebrew and new methods of teaching, with emphasis on the importance of rebuilding Palestine as the land of the Jewish people, were introduced.

In the course of time Zionism brought about a radical change in the new temples and synagogues, particularly those of the Reform wing. This change is especially

---

3. Abraham Cahan, *The Rise of David Levinsky* (New York: Harper and Brothers, Publishers, 1917), pp. 473–74. Also Chaim Potok, *The Chosen* (Greenwich, Conn.: Fawcett Crest Book, 1967), and Charles Angoff, *In the Morning Light* (New York: Beechhurst Press, 1952).

noticed when one compares the anti-Zion resolutions of the American Reform movement at the Pittsburgh Conference in 1885 with the recent pro-Israel resolutions by the Central Conference of American Rabbis. At present there is strong support for Zionism in all Jewish religious groups in America.

Changes in the structure and functions of the organized American Jewish community are largely due to the efforts of the Zionist-oriented toward democratizing Jewish communal life. The founding of the American Jewish Congress in 1918, the attempt to establish the New York Kahilah (community) in 1911, the calling of the American Jewish Conference in 1942, and the growing number of recently formed Jewish community councils in many communities have in large measure come about through the initiative and influence of Zionist leadership. Illustrious leaders of American Zionism who have exerted great influence on Jewry were Justice Louis D. Brandeis, Rabbis Stephen S. Wise, and Hillel Silver, Louis Lipsky, and Henrietta Szold. Development of modern Jewish literature was also stimulated by the Zionist movement. Zionist publications were for many years the source of introduction for Jewish novelists, poets, and artists. Before the establishment of the State of Israel, a few of the novels in English by American Jewish writers dealt with the Zionist theme. Meyer Levin, Ludwig Lewisohn, Maurice Samuel, and others wrote of the Jewish aspiration. and promoted the movement for a Jewish homeland. It was after the establishment of the State of Israel that more writers began to project their work in the Zionist framework.

Outstanding among contemporary novels dealing with Zionism are *Yehuda* and *The Old Bunch* by Meyer Levin; *The Embarkation* by Murray Gitlin; *Quiet Street* by Zelda Popkin; and *The Juggler* and *Behold the Fire* by

Michael Blankfort. The authors reveal themselves as affirmative in their Jewish identity and attitude toward Israel.

Back-to-the-Soil Movement. The basic motive and ideal underlying the movement of Zionism and other Jewish colonization efforts was the striving to normalize the life of the Jew through a "return to nature" and by giving him opportunity to earn his bread as a tiller of the soil. Dissatisfied with the occupations of artisans and merchants to which they had been confined in Russia, and influenced also by the revolutionary movement in Russia, a great many idealistic young Russian Jews dreamed of a life "in the bosom of nature." This ideal found expression first in the "Bilu" movement, an early Jewish effort at colonization in Palestine,[4] and in the *Am Olam* group, founded about the same time, whose aim was to lead a collective life on land in the New World.

Imbued with this spirit and motivated by the ideal of changing both their own personal mode of living and the socioeconomic structure of the Jewish people, some of the young Jewish immigrants left their sewing machines and tenements in New York and Chicago to form into groups that took to farming. A Yiddish song in praise of the natural and carefree life of the farmer was then most popular among many of the newcomers. The song, "The Sokhe," written in Yiddish in the 1890s by the immigrant bard Eliakum Zunser, begins with the words:

> Of plow and soil
> God speeds the toil . . .

---

4. In 1882 a group of Russian Jewish Students at Kharkov University in Russia organized to set sail for Palestine. The title "Bilu" derived from the initial letters of the Biblical verse "Bet Ya'akov, L'chu V'nelcha" (House of Jacob, come let us go up).

These young, intellectual, idealistic immigrants received their first help from the Alliance Israélite Universelle of France; farm colonies were started in various states of the Union, and in the first three decades of the present century the Jewish farm population grew slowly, with new settlements in a number of states. From 1,000 in 1900, this population grew to 100,000 in 1954, with approximately 20,000 farming units.[5] Further stimulus for this movement came from the Baron de Hirsch Fund, established in 1891, which created the Jewish Agricultural Society in 1900. Baron Maurice de Hirsch, public-minded humanitarian, gave close to $10,000,000, and endowed and formed in England the Jewish Colonization Association. In its endeavor to help Jewish farming in the United States, the Baron de Hirsch Fund, in line with the philosophy of its founder, was guided by the principle of self-reliance.[6] A tract of land comprising 5,300 acres in Cape May County, New Jersey, was purchased, and on August 28, 1891, the agricultural and industrial colony known as Woodbine was inaugurated.[7]

A survey by the Jewish Agricultural Society of New York reveals the following interesting facts:

> since its founding in 1900 the Society made available a total of more than $13,000,000 in loans to Jewish farmers in 41 states. In the state of New Jersey the Jewish farmers are a predominating factor in the fast growing poultry and egg industry. Their annual output is close to 75,000,000. While nearly 10 percent of the Jews who came to this country after

5. Rufus Learsi, *The Jews in America: A History* (Cleveland and New York: The World Publishing Co., 1954), pp. 150–51.
6. *Jews in American Agriculture* (The Jewish Agricultural Society, Inc., 1954), p. 6.
7. Philip Reuben Goldstein, "Social Aspects of the Jewish Colonies of South Jersey" (Ph.D. dissertation, University of Pennsylvania, 1921), pp. 20–26.

World War II have gone into farming, farmers constitute
only two percent of the general Jewish population in the
United States.[8]

Significant about the Jewish movement farmward is
the fact that it took place during the very half century
when the general population drift was in the direction
of the city. The adaptation of nonagricultural people to
a new agrarian way of life meant a transformation in
their social and cultural patterns of living.

In a number of Yiddish novels and short stories, the
Jews' changed mode of living as farmers in the New
World is vividly portrayed. Isaac Raboy in *New England*
treats the theme of the Jewish farm families in Chapel
Hill, New England, and their efforts to change their way
of life by becoming rooted in the American soil. Old
Weinbaum, his wife, and their daughter, Esther, who
have been living on the farm for more than thirty years,
are natural farmers. So is the spiritually and physically
strong young David Walden, a native American. The
Jewish farmers maintain friendly relationships with their
Gentile neighbors. Old Bill, one of the latter, expresses
his joy when he finds out that the Jews are building a
new road, and offers his assistance. "That's fine, a
straight and new road. That's what I like. I will help
you. Whatever work you will give me I will gladly do.
I will even carry stones."[9] David Walden marries Esther
Weinbaum because, according to the author, these two
families are best adapted to the difficult kind of life on
the good earth.

In his *Herr Goldenberg*, Raboy portrays Jewish farm
life in the Northwest, far away from New York. Gold-

---

8. Reported in *The Jewish Community Bulletin,* San Francisco (May
20, 1955), p. 8.
9. Isaac Raboy, *New England* (New York: Farlag America, 1918),
p. 192.

enberg had left New York to work as a farmer on the prairie in North Dakota. Here the young boys and girls ride horses and lead a more normal life than the city provides. Goldenberg helps cultivate the West, and his pioneer work and achievements on the prairie, along with his integration into the community as a useful citizen, form the theme of the novel.[10]

In 1910 an attempt was made to establish a cooperative Jewish colony in the state of Utah, Clarion, which existed for about five years. The experiences and struggles of the pioneers at Clarion are depicted by I. Friedland in his book *Roye Erd* (Virgin Soil).[11] Baruch Bender, who was born and raised on a farm in Cherson, South Russia, after spending a few years in New York City working first in a "sweat shop," then as an iceman, and later as a "custom peddlar," decides to go West and realize his dream of acquiring land, tilling its soil, and living among his own people in a Jewish cooperative colony. He joins a group of idealistic young Jewish men from New York and Philadelphia and is chosen as one of the first twelve pioneers who are to settle and prepare the soil. Baruch, by his devotion to his ideal, his selfless effort, and his readiness to do everything necessary at any time, sets the example for the rest of the group at Clarion.

The themes of the aspiration of idealistic young Jewish immigrants to go "back to the soil" and the changed mode of life on farms in the West are also treated by the American Yiddish novelists D. Ignatov, in *In Kesel Grub* (Whirlpool)[12] and I. Schwartz, in *Kentucky*.[13]

---

10. *Ibid., Herr Goldenberg* (New York: Farlag America, 1918).
11. I. Friedland, *Roye Erd* (Los Angeles: Friedland Buch Committee, 1949).
12. David Ignatov, *In Kesel Grub* (New York: Farlag America, 1920).
13. I. Schwartz, *Kentucky* (New York: Verlag M. N. Meisl, 1925).

REGIONALISM IN AMERICAN YIDDISH LITERATURE

Like *In New England* and *In Kesel Grub, Kentucky* represents the novel of "regionalism" in modern Yiddish literature, which introduces the reader to the quaint life of Jews on farms in the West and South, far away from the big Eastern cities. The Jew Josh came to Kentucky as a peddler right after the Civil War; his neighbors, who had never before seen a Jew, help him to establish himself. As time passes, Josh becomes wealthy, his son marries a Gentile girl, and their child attends both the church and the synagogue which grandpa Josh helped build. The relationship between Josh and Negroes is friendly, although Josh's neighbors are whites. But his son Jacob is affected by the anti-Negro prejudice of the white neighbors. Reared in an environment that encourages prejudice, Jacob is not so sensitive to oppression and human suffering as his father. Though he does not actively join the mob in lynching, he nevertheless watches it indifferently. Josh's children grow up in the new environment and fully assimilate; only old Josh feels estranged and lonely, spending his time telling stories with old Sam, the first Negro with whom he had worked years back.[14]

SOCIALISM AND THE JEWISH LABOR MOVEMENT

An important role in the process of adjustment to and acculturation in his new American environment by the Jewish immigrant was played by the Jewish Labor movement, the beginning of which can be traced to the year 1888 when the United Hebrew Trade Union was founded. Through cultural activities, mainly by the medium of the Yiddish press, Jewish labor greatly helped the

---

14. *Ibid.,* p. 148.

Jewish immigrant workers in their adjustment to their new American environment. Unfavorable working conditions in the early period of East European Jewish mass immigration and exploitation of workers among the immigrants caused great dissatisfaction with the social order so that their main cultural activities were devoted to the support and development of socialistic propaganda. In 1890 these groups began publishing the Yiddish periodicals *Arbeiter Zeitun* and *Freie Arbeiter Stimme;* in 1892, the monthly *Zukunft;* in 1894, the *Abend Blatt;* and in 1897, the Jewish daily *Forward.*

The majority of immigrants entered trade unions and even created their own unions. In its beginning, observes Will Herberg, Jewish trade unionism in the United States was built from the top down, under the tutelage of ideological radicals who organized Jewish workers as part of their revolutionary program. In the formative period of the Jewish labor movements, these radicals, who had been trained in the atmosphere of the revolutionary movement in Russia or in the socialist school of the West European countries, became the leaders of the Jewish immigrant workers. Their success was owing to the dreadful anomaly of the early immigrant's life, and his spiritual confusion and insecurity.[15]

A description of the early days of the socialist movement and the strikes by Jewish unions is found in *Uncle Moses.* Asch relates that when Berl's son Charlie grows up, he joins the socialist movement. His aspiration is to organize a strike of the Kusmin tailors and thus break the rule of the "boss," Uncle Moses. Charlie, who belongs to a circle of young Jewish students full of optimistic idealism, is acquainted with active members of the

15. Will Herberg, "The Jewish Labor Movement in the U.S.," *American Jewish Year Book,* vol. 53 (New York: The American Jewish Committee, 1952), pp. 3–74.

Jewish labor group, from whom he has heard much about the revolutionary and labor movements in Russia. He then joins the movement, and devotes himself to it.

Charlie has faith in the ideal of a better, more equitable human society, and when he goes out with Mascha he discusses international affairs, sharing with her his plans to organize a strike in Uncle's factory. His seeming excitement about everything in the world except Mascha as a woman makes her feel that she and all her trivial problems are too unimportant to be discussed at all.[16]

Charlie and several professional agitators of the Union finally succeed in organizing Uncle's workshop secretly, and win over one man after another, until suddenly, to the great surprise of Uncle and his henchmen, a strike is declared. Charlie comes to the Chevra Ansche-Kusmin every evening and talks to the members; he also brings other speakers to address them and confers with the newspapermen. Charlie seems to be their second Moses, come to free the Kusmin countrymen from Uncle Moses, from their own particular Pharaoh of Egypt.[17]

The two largest unions organized by Jewish labor were the International Ladies Garment Workers Union, the women's branch in the apparel industry, founded in 1900, and the Amalgamated Clothing Workers of America, the men's branch of the same industry, founded in 1914.

A strong wing of the Jewish labor movement was the Jewish Fraternal Society, *Arbeter Ring* (Workmen's Circle), established in 1892, for the purpose of providing mutual aid and education for its members. With increasing Jewish immigration, the Workmen's Circle progressed steadily and soon became the strongest Jewish labor fraternal order.

16. Sholem Asch, "Uncle Moses" (New York: G. P. Putnam's Sons, 1938), p. 104. See Acknowledgments.
17. *Ibid.*, p. 105.

Second Generation—Deproletarianization. During the period from 1905 to 1920, which marked immense improvement in the conditions of Jewish labor, Jewish workers began leaving the shops and factories in increasing numbers to go into business or into the professions. Many of them studied in night schools and later became doctors, lawyers, and teachers, most of whom still remained within the movement and became the "aristocracy" of the labor movement.

Most immigrant parents sent their children to college to prepare for a profession and the process of deproletarianization of Jewish labor began. Thus this new period saw not only a shift in occupation and economic status, but also an ideological shift of emphasis from the socialistic theory of class struggle to practical trade unionism, manifested in the tendency toward adaptation to the pattern of organized American labor, which stresses mainly the improvement of the economic life of the worker. The free, open, American social environment thus influenced the Jewish worker to lose the class consciousness that was in vogue among workers in Europe.

An important milestone in the annals of American labor was the successful cloak strike in 1910, which won the issue of the union shop. Thanks to the intervention of Louis D. Brandeis, a settlement was attained, including a fifty-hour week, minimum wage rate, and abolition of subcontracting. An immense achievement in labor-management relations was achieved by providing for a Board of Grievances to deal with disputes arising between workers and employers. Further ideological change, evidenced in the deviation from past practices, took place when in 1933 American labor actively supported President Roosevelt's New Deal policy. Jewish union leaders with socialistic traditions were then, for the first time, calling upon their members and followers to vote for "capitalistic" candidates in political elections.

With the end of immigration in the early 1920s, a significant change was noted. According to Will Herberg, Italian and Slavic membership in Jewish unions began to grow toward the end of the second decade. In 1913 over 80 percent of the men's clothing workers were Jewish, but in 1950 less than 30 percent of the members of the International Ladies Garment Workers Union were, and only about 25 percent of the members of the Amalgamated.[18]

CHANGING ATTITUDE TOWARD JEWISH IDENTIFICATION

In the decade from 1930 to 1940, another significant change in the ideological outlook of Jewish labor was noted. In the earlier periods Jewish labor had been strictly dogmatic in its socialistic outlook and had shown a limited interest in purely Jewish problems. Workers of the generation of Jewish immigrants were largely under radical "internationalist" and "cosmopolitan" influence. Jewish labor leaders would then denounce religion as "reactionary" and "capitalistic," and repudiate any Jewish interest that transcended proletarian class lines. They were bitterly anti-Zionist, and little concerned with the continuity of Jewish culture or of Jewish group survival. Consequently, their attitude toward the Jewish education of their children was essentially negative.

Beginning with the early 1930s, a radical change of attitude came about. The rise of Nazism and the demonic fury of Hitler's racial and anti-Semitic policy brought to most Jews a new sense of "group consciousness" and a deeper concern for the fate and welfare of the Jewish people living in various countries. They also roused a positive interest in Zionism, in the Jewish edu-

18. Herberg, p. 54.

cation of their children and growing youth, and in Jewish philanthropic endeavor.

Worthy of note is the growing interest American Jewish labor has shown since the 1930s in helping the Labor Federation of Israel—the Histadrut. The annual campaigns for the Histadrut, which were first launched by a small group of Jewish labor leaders in 1923-1924 with only the formal approval of the Hebrew Trades Union, really began to be effective in the 1930s, when leaders and workers increasingly entered into all pro-Israel activities. During this same period one could also discern a more positive attitude of Jewish labor toward the religious traditions of Judaism.[19] Joseph Shlossberg, veteran Jewish labor leader, points out that "the more Americanized the Jewish immigrants became, the more Jewish conscious and Jewishly active they became. . . . This is but proof that Jewishness and Americanism are compatible, develop together and mutually strengthen one another."[20]

Since the turn of the century there were also those Jewish workers in America who identified as labor-Zionists. These were the members of the Poale-Zion, known as the Labor Zionist Party, which contributed much to the rebirth of the state of Israel.

Also noteworthy is the role played by, and the influence on American Jewish labor of, Abraham Cahan, veteran labor leader, author of *The Rise of David Levinsky* and editor of the Yiddish daily, *The Forward*. During the almost seventy years of his active life in the United States following his arrival in 1882, Cahan represented the changing patterns and attitudes of the three generations

---

19. C. Bezalel Sherman, "Secularism and Religion in the Jewish Labor Movement," in *Jewish Life in America,* ed. Theodore Friedman and Robert Gordis (New York: Horizon Press, 1955), pp. 109-27.

20. "Two Generations of Jewish Labor in America," *The Future* (*Zukunft*) (May–June 1947), pp. 330-33.

of American Jews. His own former negative attitude toward the Jewish effort in Palestine changed to a positive one after he visited there in 1926 and became deeply impressed by the dynamic democratic force and accomplishments of the Histadruth, the Labor Federation in Israel. As labor leader and editor of the most widely circulated daily, Cahan exerted great influence in favor of Palestine Jewish labor. Since the late 1930s, American Jewish labor has increasingly supported the efforts of the Histadruth and participated actively in all endeavors pertaining to the welfare of the Jewish people everywhere.[21]

---

21. Cf. H. Lang, "50 Years of Trade Unionism," *Yiddisher Kemfer* 37, no. 1 (March 23, 1956) :126–30.

11
Social Welfare and
Community Organization

The internationally changed situation created by World War II, which most tragically affected Jews all over the world, has made American Jews aware of their increased responsibilities and position of leadership in world Jewish affairs, and since the establishment of the State of Israel in 1948, American Jewry has become especially aware of the change in position and status of the Jewish people in the world. With its social welfare program assuming a global character, modifications in regard to concept, structure, and function of its program have taken place.

PHILANTHROPY IN JEWISH TRADITION

True to their historic tradition, American Jews, who constitute the largest Jewish community in the world, have willingly assumed the responsibilities of helping their brethren in need. Since 1939, American Jews have raised, through their networks of Federation and Welfare Funds, the sum of $3.9 billion.[1]

These annual efforts to raise such vast sums constitute

---

1. Reported by Louis J. Fox, President at the 38th General Assembly of the Council of Jewish Federations and Welfare Funds, in Boston, November 1969 (J.T.A. report in the *California Jewish Voice,* November 21, 1969).

the largest philanthropic endeavor ever undertaken by so small a group and is in keeping with the age-long historic tradition of the Jewish people who, throughout the centuries, have been faced with the need of extending help to their brethren in distress. This deep concern for their fellow Jews is rooted in the people's religious traditions and historic experiences, which developed a strong "consciousness of kind" and sense of group solidarity and responsibility.

In the words of a pioneer in the field of American Jewish philanthropy,

> The tie that connects the Jews is not due to a formula of practical reasoning, it lies deep in the emotional nature of humanity which is responsible for the intense feeling for kith and kin.[2]

COMMUNAL SERVICE IN HISTORICAL PERSPECTIVE

The development of Jewish social welfare and community organization in the United States may be divided into the following major stages, which parallel historical periods.

The First Stage corresponds to the time when the Sephardic Jews, from the early days of their immigration to 1820, had hegemony over Jewish communal life. Following the prevalent pattern of sectarian American philanthropy, they administered their charitable work through their synagogue and other congregation channels.

The Second Stage, 1820-1880, corresponds to the time of German Jewish immigration and the early formative period of Jewish group life in the United States. First concern was then for the immigrant who needed shelter. The Hebrew Benevolent Society was founded in 1822 in New York with the primary object of visiting

2. Boris Bogen, *Jewish Philanthropy* (New York: The Macmillan Co., 1917), p. 6.

hospitalized war veterans of the Revolution. This society later became the Jewish Social Service Association of New York.

The Third Stage, 1881-1914, in the development of Jewish social welfare corresponds to the period from the first mass immigration from Russia and other East European countries to the First World War. This period saw the beginning of the widening of the scope of Jewish welfare work, when initial steps were taken to develop a modern social service program. The Hebrew Immigrant Aid Society was formed in 1885 and in 1909 was named the Hebrew Sheltering and Immigrant Aid Society, popularly known by its abbreviated name, HIAS.

To meet the constantly increasing needs during this period of mass migration, and to coordinate the new agencies and their campaigns, a new welfare institution, the First Federation, was formed in 1895 in Boston, marking a step forward in the organization of Jewish communal services.

The Fourth Stage, 1914-1933, corresponds to the period between the First World War and the rise of Nazism in Germany. In the First World War, American Jews moved to unite for lending aid to their brethren overseas; they created the relief organization, The Joint Distribution Committee, which united the old Jewish settlers with the new immigrants, united the orthodox with the labor elements for relief action. This reduced the cleavage between the older and more recent immigrants, and, as American Jewry became more homogeneous because of the growing American-born generations, the cultural and social distance gradually disappeared.

The Jewish Community Center. A further step in widening the scope of welfare activity was the emergence of the Jewish Community Center. The process of acculturation resulted in alienating many of the younger people from Jewish life, as well as from their parents, and also caused problems of family disorganization and personality conflict to arise. The Jewish Community Center then appeared, assuming the important tasks of relating Jewish youth to their cultural heritage, promoting greater harmony between parents and children, and developing among them a greater Jewish consciousness and sense of identification.

In the development of the Jewish Community Center one notes the change in the conception of the Center and of its program. While in its early years the Community Center was primarily concerned with the Americanization of the immigrant Jew, or with providing settlement house facilities for poor youngsters "to keep them off the street," the situation is very different today. Dr. Oscar Janowsky, head of the Jewish Welfare Board Survey Commission states in his recent survey:

> The old conception of the Center as an agency for the underprivileged has all but disappeared. A majority of the agencies affiliated with the Jewish Welfare Board aspire to serve the total Jewish population of their communities or neighborhoods.[3]

The ideological change mentioned in the Janowsky report and acknowledged at the annual meeting of the National Council of Jewish Welfare Boards was also approved by majority vote of the National Association of Jewish Center Workers at their conference in Atlantic City in 1948.

The Fifth Stage, 1933, marked a new era in Jewish Communal Service. Further significant changes occurred in the period beginning with the rise of Hitler's Nazism, a crisis-period in Jewish history which continued from 1933 through the establishment of the State of Israel in

---

3. Quoted by Arthur Frankel, *J.W.B. Circle* (New York: National Jewish Welfare Board, 1947), p. 4.

1948 to the present day. These events helped to create a deep sense of concern and group solidarity among Jews, to an extent unknown before.

To meet the increasing needs and responsibilities for relief overseas, for aid to Israel, and for the newly created local Jewish educational institutions, the Council of Federation and Welfare Funds had to broaden its scope of activities for local and national purposes. (The number of Jewish Welfare Funds has grown from fifty in the early 1930s to over three hundred in 1948). The sociological significance of the widened scope of Jewish Welfare Fund and its campaign for funds lies in the fact that it has become a potent instrument for uniting diverse and conflicting groups for cooperative social action.[4]

CHANGING SCOPE AND CHARACTER OF JEWISH SOCIAL SERVICE

The change in the scope and character of Jewish social service follows recent developments in the American Public Welfare Program, which, since the passage of the Social Security Act in 1935, has assumed responsibility for the overwhelming share of basic relief and consequently has affected Jewish social service by releasing their funds and activities for other services. Also, improved economic conditions and increased income have made possible the raising of larger sums for new communal services, such as Jewish educational and recreational activities.

As was stated in 1955 by Isidore Sobeloff, executive Vice-president of the Jewish Welfare Federation of Detroit, at the fifty-eighth annual conference of Jewish Social Work held in St. Louis, Missouri, defining Jewish

---

4. Bernard Cohen, "Sociological Aspects in the Welfare Activities Among American Jews with Special Reference to Welfare Activities in Los Angeles," Master's thesis, University of Southern California, Los Angeles (January 1949), pp. 52–53.

Communal needs: there are no more needs of an economic nature, but rather needs for wholesome family life, through proper relations between parents and children, and for a rich program of Jewish education, encouraging scholarship, research, and creative activities.[5] The increased number of contributions and workers in American Jewish communities, according to Sobeloff, is a result of a greater sense of identification with Jewish group life.

Greater concern for the totality of Jewish life and for cooperation of all Jewish groups in the community gave rise to the pressing need for a centralized democratic community organization. This need was aptly emphasized by Leo Gallin, Executive Secretary of the Los Angeles Jewish Community Council, who stated:

> For too many years the control of Jewish institutional and community life has been in the hands of a small group of individuals of wealth and influence whose conduct, benevolent and well-intentioned as it frequently was, nevertheless represented a philosophy more feudal than modern and more European than American. . . . In many respects the Jewish community of Los Angeles makes an interesting case study in the carrying out of these new directions in American Jewish Community organizations, although we have not as yet realized the merger of the council, welfare fund and Federation functions into one central instrument.[6]

Jewish Community Council. The next development in Jewish community organization was the Community Council. With the increasing need for help in the years 1933-1948—the period of the rise of Nazism in Germany, of the spread of anti-Semitism in the United States, and of the mobilization for aid to the reborn

5. Isidore Sobeloff, "The Future of Organized Jewish Community Life," *The Day* (April 8, 1955).
6. "Directions in American Jewish Community Organization," paper delivered at the Western Assembly Council of Jewish Federations and Welfare Funds, San Diego, California, March 8, 1947.

state of Israel in 1948—the need for a more representative community instrument was keenly felt. This found its expression in the Community Council, which, composed of all segments of the Jewish population, has broadened the scope of its activities to include all important phases of Jewish communal life. The Community Council also seeks to improve relationships with non-Jewish groups, and to effect a cooperative relationship between the ideologically diverse Jewish groups. There are now about seventy-five councils, fifty of which also serve as welfare federations.

Pertinent in connection with changing forms of Jewish community organization is the view of Dr. Mordecai M. Kaplan, founder of the Reconstructionist movement, that, in order to overcome the present fragmentation of American Jewish group life and to counter the disintegrative forces, it is necessary to form an organic community that would function as the instrument of Jewish life as a whole and would meet all its needs. It would be, in his words, "organized for and around the purpose of transforming Judaism for each and every Jew from a burden to a privilege."[7] He maintains that the social structure of American Jewry must be reconstituted, and that "only a democratically constituted organic Jewish community will enable American Jews to achieve the kind of adjustment that will spell integration into American life and the survival and development of Jewish cultural individuality."[8]

Changing Leadership. Another important change in Jewish leadership is the increasing number of Jewish social welfare agencies led by descendants of East European Jewish families. This becomes more obvious when one

7. *Ibid., The Future of the American Jew* (New York: The Macmillan Co., 1948), p. 118.
8. Mordecai M. Kaplan, *The Greater Judaism in the Making* (New York: The Reconstructionist Press, 1960), pp. 456, 485–86.

considers that only about three decades ago the leadership of Jewish communal institutions was still in the hands of Jews of German descent, who had control of most philanthropic and other communal endeavors in the country. Criticism and challenge of the leadership of the Jewish Federations, so many years in the hands of those possessing little Jewish knowledge and with no commitment to positive Jewish living, are increasingly being voiced.

Eli Ginzberg, on the role of Jewish leadership, observes that

> since American Jewry represents a voluntary community in which no effective religious or legal sanction exists to force the individual to fulfill his responsibilities to the Jewish community, the long standing neglect of thought in favor of action has led to marked atrophy in the intellectual and cultural life of American Jews . . . that the activists long ago usurped positions of prominence and forced those whose contributions lay in the realms of ideas into the background.[9]

Ginzberg believes that it is the lack of knowledge of most American Jews in matters of Jewish interest which explains the rise of the new type of professional leadership; that, preoccupied with earning a living, men tend to look to the leadership in areas where they do not consider themselves competent; and that, consequently, this situation results in a disproportionate degree of responsibility, with control left in the hands of a few.[10]

CHALLENGING YOUTH AND CHANGE OF LEADERSHIP

The leadership of the Jewish Federation was also recently challenged by the younger generation. Speaking for a group called "Concerned Jewish Youth," Rabbi

9. Eli Ginzberg, *Agenda for American Jews* (New York: King's Crown Press, Columbia University, 1950), p. 6.
10. *Ibid.*, p. 19.

Hillel Levin, at the General Assembly of the Council of Jewish Federation and Welfare Funds held in Boston in November, 1969, demanded a reordering of priorities in allocating funds and urged the creation of a Special Foundation for developing a positive educational program designed to strengthen Jewish consciousness. He also called on the Federation leaders to share their decision-making power with "men whose qualifications are Jewish learning and commitment to Jewish life," including rabbis, "Jewish educators who are normally not included in the decision-making body of our Federation."[11]

Claiming that the spiritual malaise and low quality of Jewish life in America is due to lack of Jewish education, "Concerned Jewish Youth" demand that Jewish education on all levels become the first priority in Federation allocation for domestic needs. These Jewish radical youths maintain that American Jewry cannot flourish as a creative, religious-cultural community unless the Federation leaders recognize their own lack of Jewish education. This demand was most graphically demonstrated during the silent vigil, where one student held a sign which asked in Hebrew: "Who among you can read and understand Hebrew?" Indeed, few of the delegates seemed to indicate any understanding of the sign as they filed by.

ALTERED COMMUNITY ATTITUDE TOWARD YOUTH

The attention of those who are concerned with the future of the Jewish community has of late been focused on Jewish youth, particularly those of college age. It is estimated that 5 percent of the overall campus population is Jewish, which rises to 15 percent in the prestige colleges, and that from 85 to 90 percent of Jewish youth

11. *The Jewish Post and Opinion* (Nov. 21, 1969), p. 1.

of college age are on college campuses. Studies of the radical student movements have shown, as Seymour Lipset observed recently, that a predominant number of the radical left-wing students come from Jewish backgrounds.

A number of Jewish students who belong to the "far Left" and the "Third World" definitely oppose those who lend their support to Israel, Zionism, and anti-Jewish propaganda. Though it must be stated that they do not represent the majority of Jewish students, they yet cause deep concern to Jewish leaders who think of the college campuses as the disaster area for the future of Judaism and of Jewish life. This alienated youth arouses grave concern and becomes a source of agony to responsible Jewish leadership.

Estranged, angry youth has most recently led established leaders to recognize the need for a program to bridge the gap and to win youth back to Judaism and to their people. This altered attitude was expressed by Max Fisher, President of the Council of Federation and Welfare Funds who, at the 39th annual meeting of the Council spoke about "facing the frightening possibility that we could lose almost the entire generation of our young people"[12] and called for the creation of a program designed to win back alienated youth.

Recognizing the vexing problem of estranged youth and the need to counteract the corrosive forces of assimilation and disintegration that seriously endanger the continuity of American-Jewish life, two important research projects were recently launched. One, "Task Force for the Future," was set up by the Council of Jewish Federation and Welfare Funds. Another, "Task Force for the Future of the Jewish Community in America," was established by the American Jewish Committee.

12. Quoted in *The Temple Bulletin,* Cleveland, Ohio (Jan. 12, 1969), p. 1.

Both projects indicate a changed attitude and a new trend of American-Jewish leadership in its efforts to strengthen the self-awareness and sense of group identity of American Jewish youth.

CHANGING ROLE OF THE RABBI

The complex growth of the American Jewish community and its social and cultural changes resulted in increasing the number of the functions of, and in a changed role for, the modern rabbi.

"Upon no one else in the Jewish community," says Rabbi Morris Adler, "have the hammer blows of change and mutation fallen as forcefully as upon the American rabbi."[13] The scion of a long tradition and heir of a great faith and culture, the modern American rabbi must now function in the midst of a technological setting in which historic cultural differentiations are obliterated and traditional values and modes are discounted.

Rabbi Adler further observes about the role and position of the American rabbi that

> he is isolated at the very center of the community he "leads" and serves as a spokesman of a group-tradition at a time when the group has become all but traditionless. . . . The issues about which his organized thinking revolves—God, Torah, moral values, social goals, the crisis of faith, theology—are remote to the people to whom he ministers.[14]

The lives and careers of men dedicated to the Jewish ministry, says another American rabbi, are bedeviled and beset by conditions that were not prevalent two generations ago. On the heels of rapid changes in living has come an increase in materialism and vulgarity, deteriora-

---

13. Rabbi Morris Adler, "The Rabbi: 1966," *Jewish Heritage* 8, no. 4, published by B'nai B'rith Adult Jewish Education (Spring 1966):7.
14. *Ibid.*, p. 9.

tion in religious values, and rapid reversals in the emphasis on factors in Jewish survival.[15]

The average rabbi is now expected to serve his congregation as an educator, a scholar, a preacher, a pastor, an organizer and administrator, and an ambassador of good will to the non-Jewish world. He has to address a host of communal organizations, give courses in Christian camps, arrange interfaith meetings, and often sponsor an Institute on Judaism in his own pastorate.

The traditional role of the rabbi as the student of Torah and teacher of Judaism to his people has radically changed. The modern American rabbi, says Rabbi Arthur Hertzberg, has lost his authority; he is no more the leader, but rather a follower, an institutional worker. He points out that the people who are now occupying the pews of the congregation differ from their parents a generation ago, in whose relationship to the rabbi there was the distinct aura of respect for learning. This change, says Rabbi Hertzberg, is even demonstrated in the wording of the announcement of new rabbinic appointments. In the past, the rabbi was usually "called" to be the "spiritual leader"; nowadays he is generally "elected" by the board to "serve" as rabbi.[16]

The changed attitude of the layman to the rabbi, and the rabbi's frustration and grievances against the Temple leadership, were recently expressed by rabbis in their call for a union. In his article in *The Reconstructionist,* Rabbi Sholom A. Singer of Highland Park, Illinois, argues that the traditional parity between the rabbi and the lay community (the board of trustees) has been disrupted and that the remedy is unionization. The editor of *The Reconstructionist* notes in his column that "while this

15. Rabbi Charles E. Shulman, "The Role of the American Rabbi," *Jewish Digest* (Houston, Texas) 1, no. 11 (August 1965) :5.
16. Arthur Hertzberg, "The Changing American Rabbinate," *Midstream* 12, no. 1, published by the Theodor Herzl Foundation (January 1966) :16–29.

(unionization) may seem to some an oversimplification of the solution to a complex problem, it is worth putting on the agenda of public discussion."[17]

A survey of the American rabbinate conducted by the Jewish Statistical Bureau in 1956 revealed that of the 4,257 rabbis in the United States, 945 or 22 percent were engaged in specialized fields of Jewish education and welfare work.[18]

THE RABBI IN CONTEMPORARY FICTION

The rabbi has been the central theme of several contemporary novels. Conceiving of religion as the important moral force molding life and affecting human relations, rabbis feel it is their duty to deal with the vexing problems of life, war, race relations, and civil rights, and to review from their pulpits books dealing with important social problems. This is often the cause of conflict with the leading congregants. His position and changing role in the American Jewish scene have been portrayed in a number of novels. He is the main character in Blankfort's novel *The Strong Hand,* discussed earlier in the chapter on the changing family. In her novel *Awakened,* Margaret Abrams[19] gives a vivid description of the American Jewish small-town community life and of Rabbi Rosen, who dedicates himself to the awakening in the community of moral, ethical, and religious values and responsibilities.

The novels of Harry Kemelman,[20] *Friday the Rabbi Slept Late* and *Saturday the Rabbi Went Hungry,* depict

---

17. *The Jewish Post and Opinion* (Oct. 17, 1969), p. 2.
18. H. S. Linfield, quoted by Boris Smollar in *California Jewish Voice,* Weekly, Los Angeles, California (December 1956), p. 4.
19. Margaret Abrams, *Awakened* (New York: Jewish Publication Society of America, 1956).
20. *Friday the Rabbi Slept Late* (New York: Crown Publishers, Inc., 1964); *Saturday the Rabbi Went Hungry* (New York: Crown Publishers, Inc., 1966).

the interrelationship of a Conservative rabbi with various members of his New England congregation. The protagonist, Rabbi David Small, is trying to help enrich his people's knowledge of Judaism, but he is compelled to devote his time and energy to solving social difficulties. In *Friday the Rabbi Slept Late,* while his name is being considered for renewal of contract, a young girl is found murdered near the synagogue. The rabbi is suspected, for her purse is found in his car. He is in a predicament but he meets with calm the disturbing circumstances of a seeming lack of a suitable alibi and of the possibilities of dismissal from his position and arrest for murder. The rabbi works with the Catholic police chief and, with the help of his Talmudic training, finally finds the killer and solves the mystery.

In *Saturday the Rabbi Went Hungry,* another detective mystery story, Kemelman describes the rabbi's troubles that begin when he is accused of having buried an apparent suicide in the Temple cemetery. He has no way out but to prove that the man did not commit suicide but was murdered, and he must go out to find the murderer. Again it is the rabbi's duty to investigate the cause of death with the help of Talmudic reasoning.

In his third novel of this series of detective stories, *Sunday the Rabbi Stayed Home,* Kemelman again portrays the young Conservative rabbi who solves a murder through Talmudic logic in his congregation in Barnard's Crossing, Massachusetts. This murder mystery involves the problems of youth, especially the use of drugs, as well as race, tension, and the intra-synagogue issues. The divergent views of the rabbi and the Temple officials cause him to change from a Temple position to directorship of Hillel Institution on a college campus.[21]

In his novel *The Rabbi,*[22] Noah Gordon portrays a

21. (New York: G. P. Putnam's Sons, 1969.)
22. (New York: McGraw-Hill, 1965.)

Reform rabbi, Michael Kind, who married a convert, the daughter of a Christian minister, revealing the compromises he is making and his experiences in his Reform congregation. Gordon depicts the contrast between the generations—between Michael's grandfather, the "zaydeh," the observant committed Jew who knows no compromises, and the second generation.

The novel is a chronicle, rich with the rabbi's meaningful experiences. He serves a number of different congregations. He has problems with the members, once-a-year worshipers; with the racial issue in the South; and with the problem of fund-raising up North for the new Temple that must be built.

In the novel *Heaven Help Us*,[23] Herbert Tarr depicts with wit and delightful humor the many serious problems the modern rabbi is facing as the spiritual leader in a suburban community. Young Rabbi Gideon Abel, newly ordained, gets his first rabbinical position in suburban Hillendale Temple. Rabbi Abel is determined to teach and persuade his congregation that if Judaism is to be genuine, it must be practiced. He has very definite ideas of what a rabbi and a congregation should be; he is aware of the importance of learning and of performing Judaism's demand to make this a more Godly world. Because he takes his calling seriously he becomes involved in civil rights, in peace movements, and in anti-poverty work. He even pickets the house of Bill Evans, the slumlord who exploits Negroes and is a member of his congregation.

However, the members of the congregation are more concerned with fashion shows, a Temple musical comedy, and fund-raising for the Temple, so that they have no time for religion. And although the people of Hillendale have a very slight knowledge of Judaism, they have

---

23. (New York: Random House, Inc., 1968.)

very definite ideas of what their rabbi should be. They demand that the rabbi be all things to all people, that he be the preacher, pastor, teacher, administrator, and fund raiser, and also director of the Temple show, *My Fair Sadie*. He objects strongly to the catering house of Stein-gut, with its lavish affairs, to the funeral home run by Goldwyn, and to the vulgar and costly Bar Mitzvah parties of the Evans and Margolin boys. The rabbi insists on maintaining ethical standards for the members.

The above-mentioned novels all reflect the changed role of the rabbi, who in the past was the scholar of Torah, judge, and teacher of Judaism, but whose role in our time has become that of preacher, pastor, administrator, fund-raiser, and community representative. These changes often frustrate the rabbi and produce in him a sense of futility.

12
Trends in the Third and Fourth Generations

SUBURBIA

In the stage of development of American Jewry from 1939 to the 1970s, a radical transformation of Jewish life seems to have taken place. The general trend in recent years to move from city centers to the suburbs, which marks an important social change in American life, has also been followed by some ethnic groups. A recent striking phenomenon in the life of American Jews is their steadily growing move from the cities, a phenomenon that alters their established sociocultural urban patterns to a new suburban style of life. It is estimated that two-thirds of American Jews now live in the suburbs.

Recent community studies indicate a growing self-awareness and desire for group identification among the Jewish residents of new suburban communities, most of whom are of the third and fourth generations.[1] The majority of Jewish suburban residents are young couples who seek in the new location better schooling for their children and also more room for themselves. Feeling the

1. Cf. Marshall Sklare and Joseph Greenblum, "Jewish Identity on the Suburban Frontier," *The Lakeville Studies,* vol. 1 (New York: The Lakeville Studies, Basic Books, 1967).

need for belonging and group identification, they join a Jewish center or synagogue, and often help to organize a religious school for their children's education.[2]

What motivates these young families to move to the suburbs? When these young Jewish families investigate a model home in the suburbs, their primary question is: "How far are we from the Temple?" or "Is this a Jewish community?" The following account is given in *The Reconstructionist:*

> The real estate agent knows how to deal with the question. "The rabbi lives in our colony," he replies. . . .
> "But why the insistence upon a religious community, a synagogue nearby and Hebrew school?" I asked. The answer came in spurts of analysis.
> "They want to be among their own. Then, they feel more comfortable in their own community."
> I wondered. "But," I argued, "they have long ago turned their backs upon religious or Jewish training for their children. In their own lives there is not even a trace, a radio-active trace of Jewish substance . . . and, yet, there is something bothering them. Some atavistic conscience, not completely explainable by social forces, not receptive to classic sociological need. There is a life-driven force, a not too spelled out character working through them, unknowingly, demanding that their suburbia have opportunities for a good and creative Jewish life, if only marginal for themselves, then maximal for their children."[3]

The general trend in the last three decades of mobility from the cities to the suburbs included a considerable number of young Jewish families of the average age-range of 25 to 45 and of the lower-middle or middle-class third- or fourth-generation American Jews. After moving to the suburbs, they enroll their children in the Temple's religious school and affiliate with the local synagogue,

---

2. Herbert J. Gans, "Progress of a Suburban Jewish Community," *Commentary* 23, no. 2 (February 1957) :113–22.

3. Bertram Rosenberg, "Go to Suburbia, Young Man," *The Reconstructionist* 22, no. 3 (March 23, 1956) :11.

although when they lived in the city they had not affiliated with the synagogue. However, to this changed pattern and style of life, it seems, the Jewish suburbanite must conform, because suburbia holds nothing but isolation and loneliness for those who do not.

In her observations on suburbia based on her repeated visits as lecturer to many suburban communities, Dr. Weiss Rosmarin says that suburbia imposes conformity; that the Jewish resident must join the synagogue, which is the symbol of a sense of community for Jewish suburbanites, analogous to the role of the church in the lives of the Christian suburbanites.

She further notes that in suburbia there is more extensive and intensive Jewish education for children and adults and that Jews in suburbia feel strongly toward Israel and are proud of it. Thus, the third- and fourth-generation American Jews, although they may have a Jewishness that is not always authentic, do have a strong sense of self-acceptance and Jewish identity.[4]

GROUP IDENTIFICATION IN THE THIRD GENERATION

According to Marcus L. Hansen, who has studied the processes of adjustment and changing patterns of life among the Scandanavians in America and formulated the theory that "what the son wishes to forget, the grandson wishes to remember," the third generation of an ethnic group, secure in its American-ness, wishes to remember what the second generation had been so eager to forget.[5] This theory applies especially to the third and fourth generation of American Jews. The first, and

4. Trude Weiss Rosmarin, "Jewish Suburbia: Pattern of Conformity," *Congress Weekly* 24, no. 29 (Nov. 18, 1957):5-7.
5. Marcus L. Hansen, *The Problem of the Third Generation Immigrant* (Rock Island, Ill.: Augustona Historical Society, 1939), p. 7, quoted by Will Herberg in *Protestant, Catholic, Jew* (New York: Doubleday, 1955), p. 55.

especially the second generation, like their neighbors, the Italian and Polish groups in America, followed the pattern of making an anxious effort to adjust economically, and to shed their foreignness to become more "American." However, with regard to the third generation, the situation seems to be different. One can readily observe that instead of somehow discarding their heritage, as was the case with other ethnic minorities, the third generation of American Jews is beginning to manifest a desire to return to the heritage their parents discarded and to reassert their group consciousness.

Charles Bezalel Sherman observes that, unlike other minority groups in America—which in the course of time lost their group identity and for which emergence of the third generation regularly meant the approaching dissolution of the ethnic group—Jews retain their group consciousness and identity much longer, as is evidenced by the fact that positions of leadership within the group are assumed by those of the second and third generation of American Jews.[6]

Signs are increasing that the third generation, grandchildren of Jewish immigrants, are turning from the rejection and alienation of their fathers to the road leading to group identification. This tendency is illustrated in some measure in contemporary *belles-lettres*.

In Pinski's *The Generations of Noah Edon*, Noah's grandson, Norman, visiting his grandparents on a Friday evening, suddenly asks, "Grandpa, teach me religion."

"If you want to learn it, you already have it," answered Grandpa Noah. "What is wrong with you, sonny, let me know?"

Grandson Norman opened his heart and said:

---

6. *Yidden un Andere Etnishe Grupes in die Fareinigte Shtaten* [Jews and Other Ethnic Groups in the United States] (New York: Undzer Weg, 1948), p. 424.

There is an emptiness in me. Often I am seized with despair. I don't know why I am living in this world. . . . This emptiness and uselessness will lead me to bad habits, to weakness and dissipation. I thought perhaps religion might help me. Grandpa said: "This confession speaks well of you my son."[7]

This family pattern and situation described by Pinski's novel finds a parallel in many a Jewish home in America. Many of the grandchildren of Jewish immigrants, raised during the late 1920s and 1930s in homes detached from the ideals and values of the faith of their fathers, were assimilated to a shallow Americanism which resulted in a feeling of "emptiness" and "marginality." There are indications, however, that during the period beginning in the late 1930s and continuing up to the present, a change of attitude toward the group's cultural heritage has gradually come about.

CHANGING ATTITUDE TOWARD GROUP IDENTIFICATION

Will Herberg points out that the third generation of American Jews does not seem to share the enthusiastic hope of the "melting pot" approach to America of the first and, especially of the second, generation.[8] The third generation, although it realizes that integration into American life implies many cultural changes in the process of adjustment, does not accept the idea of complete assimilation. This ideological change, a shift from the anxieties and insecurities of the "marginal," alienated, generation is reflected in works and in the publicly expressed attitudes of second-generation Jewish writers themselves. An examination of a number of the works

7. David Pinski, *The Generations of Noah Edon* (New York: The Macaulay Co., 1931), p. 287.
8. Pp. 286–226.

of American Jewish novelists reveals a profound change in attitude from one of total assimilation to those of self-awareness and Jewish survival.

One may readily note a world of difference between Mary Antin's attitude, as expressed in *The Promised Land,* written more than half a century ago, and Charles Angoff's in his series of novels, *A Journey to Dawn, The Morning Light,* and *The Sun at Noon.* Both Antin and Angoff lived in the same city of Boston and wrote on the same themes, but what a great difference in attitude and approach between them!

Overwhelmed by the freedom and opportunity of her new land, Mary Antin expresses enthusiastic praise and sings in ecstasy: "I am the youngest of America's children and into my hand is given her priceless heritage." But, along with her enthusiasm for America, after attending public school and struggling to adapt herself, in her passionate love for the New World there is her willingness to reject her own Jewish past. She says:

> It is painful to be conscious of two worlds. The Wandering Jew in me seeks forgetfulness. I am not afraid to live on and on, if only I do not have to remember too much. A long past vividly remembered is like a heavy garment that clings to your limbs when you would run. And I have thought of a charm that should release me from the folds of my clinging past. I take the hint from the Ancient Mariner, who told his tale in order to be rid of it. I, too, will tell my tale, for once, and never hark back any more. I will write a bold "FINIS" at the end and shut the book with a bang.[9]

In sharp contrast to this will toward total assimilation is the attitude of Charles Angoff more than half a century later. In his current novels on American Jewish life, he shows a deep desire for folk identification and writes with a profound sense of group consciousness and loyalty.

---

9. *The Promised Land* (Boston and New York: Houghton Mifflin Co.; The Riverside Press, Cambridge, 1912), p. xv.

In explaining the reasons for dipping so generously into his Jewish past in his series on the Polonsky family, Angoff says:

> The people and the themes of *Journey into Dawn,* and *In the Morning Light,* selected the writer far more readily than he selected them. My distant past . . . is becoming more "real" to me than my immediate past or the present—and it was a past steeped in Jewishness.[10]

Edna Ferber is another recognized American novelist who, feeling more secure in her Americanness, gradually manifests a longing for group identification. In *Fanny Herself,* published in 1917, Miss Ferber presents a picture of a Jewish family living in a small community in the Middle West. She describes the adolescence and womanhood of an American-born Jewish girl in Wisconsin, away from the immigrant world of New York's East Side. In her small Wisconsin town, the Jews "were of a type to be found in every small town, prosperous, conservative, constructive citizens, clannish, but not so much as their city cousins, mingling socially with their Gentile neighbors, living well, spending their money freely, taking a vast pride in the education of their children."[11] One does not find in *Fannie Herself* the ecstatic approach and enthusiastic mood of Mary Antin. Fannie becomes aware of being Jewish and meditates on the Jewish problem: "Antagonism here isn't religion; it's personal almost. . . . They don't object to us as a sect, or as a race, but as a type."[12] A further stage in Edna Ferber's approach to her Jewish heritage is revealed twenty years later in her autobiography, *A Peculiar Treasure.* This work, published in

---

10. *Congress Weekly* (Nov. 26, 1951), p. 9.
11. Edna Ferber, *Fannie Herself* (New York: The Literary Guild, 1917), p. 11.
12. *Ibid.,* p. 107.

1939, marks the beginning of the new third-generation stage in the adjustment process of the American Jew to the American scene.

In *Fannie Herself,* Fannie thought of her heritage as merely a hindrance, about which "she made up her mind that she would admit no handicap, race, religion, training, natural impulse—she would discard them all if they stood in her way." In *A Peculiar Treasure,* however, Edna Ferber shows a definite sense of identification and a proud affirmation of her Jewish heritage as a source of spiritual strength and as a special privilege.[13]

Of interest is the similar reaction of Mary Antin reflecting her altered, more affirmative attitude and identification under the impact of the Hitler regime. In 1941 she wrote the following:

> At the present moment, under the shocks of Hitlerian object-lesson on the fruits of intolerance, we are all doing a job of reviewing our attitudes and practices. I find myself grateful that social conditions in my early years in America allowed me to follow freely an inborn drive for religious exploration without a hindering concern for the people who gave me birth—who endowed me with my basic traits—on the ground that they were in trouble. For decades I lived cut off from Jewish life and thought, heart-free and mind-free to weave other bonds. There was nothing intentional or self-conscious in this divorcement. It was simply that my path in life ran far from the currents of Jewish experience. Today I find myself pulled by old forgotten ties, through the violent projection of an immensely magnified Jewish problem. It is one thing to go your separate way, leaving friends and comrades behind in peace and prosperity; it is another thing to fail to remember them when the world is casting them out.[14]

From Novels of Protest and Rejection to Novels of Affirmation. In the 1940s, the period of World War II and

13. *A Peculiar Treasure* (New York: Doubleday Doran & Co., Inc., 1939), p. 9.
14. Mary Antin, *Common Ground* (Spring 1941), p. 41.

the years of the holocaust, one notes a changing attitude in a number of literary works as well as in their authors. The social radicalism and "left" inclinations of the late 1920s and 1930s are being supplanted by a growing interest in, and adherence to, Jewish group life. The novels of social protest and rejection of the preceding decades are increasingly replaced by novels of affirmation. Typical of this development is the novelist Albert Halper, who stated that at the beginning of his career as a writer, he would have said "Hell—I want to become a good American writer—what has being a Jew got to do with it?" But after the rise of Hitlerism he felt differently. His later novel, *The Golden Watch* (written in 1953)— unlike his earlier *Union Square, The Foundry,* and *The Shute* of the proletarian era of the 1930s—reveals great tenderness, love, and Jewish consciousness.

The long apologia by Budd Schulberg, written for the 1952 Modern Library edition of his book *What Makes Sammy Run?* is characteristic of the tendency toward identification. Schulberg argues that it is a good pro-Jewish book:

> While admitting the fear that bigots might be able to turn my book against my own people and the democratic ideal, I said this only could be done "by wrenching characters out of their cultural sockets and paragraphs out of their continuity."[15]

Then Schulberg refers to Franz Alexander who, in his *The Age of Unreason,* finds the ultra-aggressive, self-centered type rather common among second-generation Americans of impoverished immigrant families, and writes:

> I am impressed by the accuracy with which Schulberg has described this type, a victim of cultural conditions and how

15. *What Makes Sammy Run?* (New York: The Modern Library, 1952), p. xi.

well he has portrayed his hero, Sammy Glick, the "frantic marathoner" of life, "sprinting out of his mother's womb, turning life into a race in which the rules are right for the rail and elbow on the turn, and the only finish-line is death.[16]

Author Schulberg further says about Sammy:

he has been told he must find a new set of values to fill the moral vacuum in which he throve and strove. In throwing over the ways of his father without learning any sense of obligation to the Judeo-Christian-democratic pattern, he had nothing except naked self-interest by which to guide himself. . . . We are dizzy with change. We are Sunday Christians, and summer democrats. No wonder Sammy Glick (including all the Sammy Glicks who would never allow him into their clubs) has found the moral atmosphere so suitable and the underfooting so conducive to his kind of climbing. Yes, Sammy is still running and the question is, How do we slow him down? Perhaps the answer involves even a bigger question: How do we slow down the whole culture he threatens to run away with and that threatens to run away with us?[17]

In more recent American-Jewish novels one discerns the type of the more balanced American Jew of the third and fourth generation, who is less radical and more secure, is conservative in his social views, and tends to identify himself with his Jewish group. Among these are the novels by Herman Wouk, which reveal a tendency to conservatism and conformity. In *Caine Mutiny*, Barney Greenwald, although basically a liberal, is presented as spokesman for conservatism and conformity. He speaks for the Navy and defends the principle of submission to authority. In *Marjorie Morningstar*, Marjorie wrestles with the problem of rejecting her Jewish heritage and the social code of her middle-class parents to become an actress and the wife of Noel Airman, an uprooted Bohemian songwriter. At last she rejects her lover and

16. Franz Alexander, quoted by Schulberg, p. xiii.
17. Schulberg, p. xiii.

moves into a respectable middle-class family, finding her group identification in "belonging" and becoming active in the suburban Jewish community. Marjorie may thus be regarded as representative of the steadily growing number of third-generation American Jews.

One finds in contemporary American Jewish novelists signs of liberation from the neurotic tensions exhibited by the earlier, the alienated or lost second-generation, writers. Among these novelists is Michael Blankfort, once a Marxist, who after visiting Israel wrote a novel about the new state, *The Juggler,* which was later made into a motion picture. In his twenties, Blankfort became a teacher of psychology and "his views and values were a compound of behaviorism, pragmatism, Freudism." For him God was superstition and Judaism a backward religion; only Marxism seemed to him to be the true faith. In the 1940s, becoming disillusioned with Marxism, he admitted, "It seems to me now that even during those years I had never entirely lost what was pervasive and lasting in my Jewish heritage." In pronouncing his credo Blankfort declares, "In the communism of Judaism, the identification with my people, my active affection for the land of Israel, my faltering efforts to live by the precepts of the prophets, I have found a peace of the spirit."[18]

CHANGING VIEWS IN THE DECADE 1945-1955

A characteristic illustration of the changing views of American Jewish literary men and women in the decade from 1945 to 1955 after World War II and the establishment of the State of Israel, appears in the following expressed opinions and public statements. In 1944, *Contemporary Jewish Record* conducted a symposium entitled "Under Forty," in which the following eleven writers—

18. Quoted by Harold U. Ribalow, "American Jewish Writers and Their Judaism," *Judaism* 3, no. 4 (Fall 1954) :423.

novelists, poets, and literary critics of Jewish birth—
stated their reaction and attitude toward their Jewish
heritage: Muriel Rukeyser, Alfred Kazin, Delmore
Schwartz, Lionel Trilling, Ben Field, Louis Kronenberg,
Albert Halper, Howard Fast, David Daiches, Clement
Greenberg, and Isaac Rosenfeld.

Poet Muriel Rukeyser, in her response to the editor of
the symposium, said:

> There was no mark of Judaism in my childhood home except
> for a silver ceremonial goblet. . . . There was not a trace of
> Jewish culture that I could feel—no stories, no songs, no spe-
> cial food, but then there was not any cultural background that
> could make itself felt.
> I grew up among a group of Jews who wished, more than
> anything else, I think, to be invisible. . . . I was brought up
> without any reason to be proud of being Jewish and then was
> told to be proud; without any reason for shame, and then saw
> that people were ashamed.[19]

To Delmore Schwartz the "fact of Jewishness has been
nothing but an ever-growing good, and it seems to me
that it can be, at least for me, nothing but a fruitful and
inexhaustible inheritance."[20] Since writing this, Delmore
Schwartz has published a number of Jewish short stories.

Alfred Kazin, literary critic and novelist, said in the
1944 symposium, that

> I have never seen much of what I admire in American Jewish
> culture, or among Jewish writers in America generally. . . .
> I think it is about time we stopped confusing the experience
> of being an immigrant or an immigrant's son with the expe-
> rience of being Jewish.

And he ends his statement by saying:

> I learned long ago to accept the fact that I was Jewish

19. *Contemporary Jewish Record* 7, no. 1 (1944) :5.
20. *Ibid.,* p. 10.

without being a part of any meaningful Jewish life or culture.[21]

However, in his book *A Walker in the City,* published seven years later, he wrote:

> We had always to be together, believer and non-believer, we were a people, I was of that people. . . . We had all of us lived together so long that we would not have known how to separate even if we had wanted to. The most terrible word was "aleyn"—alone.[22]

Clement Greenberg, who has since the symposium become an editor of the Anglo-Jewish monthly *Commentary,* asserted in 1944 that "the writer has no more of a conscious position toward his Jewish heritage than the average American Jew—which is to say hardly any."[23]

Of the eleven writers only three seemed to find some values in Judaism as well as in Americanism. However, most of these literary men have since written novels and short stories revealing an affirmative attitude to Jewish life. Interesting is the contrast evidenced in the answers given by nine Jewish novelists seven years later, in 1951, when asked why they chose to write a novel or short story on Jews or Jewish themes. Their replies, published in the *Congress Weekly,* reveal their new attitude on their self-awareness as Jews. Zelda Popkin, author of *Quiet Street,* stated:

> I am not a Johnny-come-lately in discovering my Jewishness and it has never been a source of conflict, self-hatred or even minor trouble to me. I was reared in Orthodoxy and I liked it. The festive spirit of the Holy days and the Shabbat are part of the richness of my childhood. I went to Cheder; I wrote Purim and Chanukah plays and childish poems of religious content . . . and I have personally never known the frustrations and cruelties of anti-Semitism.[24]

---

21. *Ibid.,* p. 13.
22. (New York: Harcourt, Brace, and Company, 1951), p. 60.
23. *Contemporary Jewish Record* 7, no. 1 (1944) :33.
24. *Congress Weekly* (Nov. 26, 1951), p. 19.

218 Sociocultural Changes in American Jewish Life

Ethel Rosenberg, author of *Go Fight City Hall,* said:

> It seemed to me that there was room for a book to present the Jews without problems, other than the everyday garden variety, and with their capacity for joy and humor and warmth shown, in other words, one more side of the picture that we don't get to see often enough.[25]

Herman Wouk, author of *The Caine Mutiny* and *Marjorie Morningstar* said: "As Jewish characters and themes occur to me I will certainly use them. I know of no reason to avoid them."[26]

Yuri Suhl, author of *One Foot in America and Cowboy on a Wooden Horse,* said that

> the process of my Americanization was not accompanied (as so frequently happens) by a process of alienation from my cultural heritage of the past and the American Jewish community. Quite the contrary. It was here in America, that I came to know the secular face of this heritage . . . the dual process is still going on with me and I do not find it in any way contradictory or conflicting. . . . I consider a work of fiction on the Jewish theme as integral a part of the broad stream of American literature as the American Jewish community is of the American scene generally.[27]

Writers' Changed Attitude toward Israel. A significant change in the attitude of American Jewish writers is seen in relation to Israel. In the 1920s and 1930s the majority of those writers were either indifferent to or entirely unaware of their people's efforts to restore Israel. However, since the 1940s, in the third- and fourth-generation era, novels and short stories on Israel and on its war of liberation in 1948 have steadily increased. Among those showing interest and a favorable attitude are the following noted novelists and poets.

---

25. *Ibid.,* p. 20.
26. *Ibid.,* p. 22.
27. *Ibid.,* p. 20.

Ben Hecht, who in years past wrote a bitter, anti-Jewish diatribe, *A Jew in Love,* became involved during Israel's struggle against the British anti-Jewish administration in 1948 as an active propagandist and worker for the extreme terrorist group in Palestine, the IRGUN.

He realized during the rise of Hitlerism that he could not escape his Jewishness. He became an ardent follower of the extreme Zionist-revisionist group, the IRGUN. In an article, "My Tribe Is Called Israel," Hecht called upon all who had ever thought of themselves as Jews to rise up in defense of Jewish rights and Jewish values. He raised large sums of money for them, and wrote short stories of positive Jewish character.

Michael Blankfort's novel *Behold the Fire* dramatizes the heroism and sacrifices of a small group of Palestinian Jews—The NILI—in liberating the land from the Turks during World War I, thus laying the foundations of present-day Israel.[28] His earlier novel, *The Juggler,* dealing with Israel, was made into a film.

The poet Karl Shapiro, who had been estranged from Jewish life, wrote a stirring poem on the birth of Israel, and even Norman Katkov, whose novels were written in a negative vein about Judaism, described, in a short story published in *The Saturday Evening Post,* the problems of the American-Jewish G.I. who decides to go to Israel and join the Haganah.

NOVELS AND WRITERS IN THE 50S AND 60S

In much of American contemporary prose fiction of the 1950s and 1960s, the depiction of American-Jewish life is a dominant theme. Much space in the literary magazines is devoted to reviews of books dealing with the life of American Jews, a number of which were on

28. Michael Blankfort, *Behold the Fire* (An-Nal World Book, published by the New American Library, 1965).

the best-seller lists. Included among these authors are Herman Wouk, Leon Uris, Arthur Miller, Meyer Levin, Charles Angoff, Bernard Malamud, Saul Bellow, Isaac Bashevis-Singer, Edward Louis Wallant, and Philip Roth, all now well known as American-Jewish writers. However, it must be added that they are not all Jewish in the same sense or in quite the same way. Some of them, alienated intellectuals, defiantly reject Jewishness with all its ethical ideals, moral values, and traditions. Some of them, lacking the knowledge of their heritage and culture, write about Jewish life as if it were entirely strange and foreign to them. Some seem to have an ambivalent attitude, others a more affirmative approach to their people and their heritage. A brief review of the attitudes reflected in the works of some of the above-named novelists is pertinent to this discussion. One of the most recently acclaimed popular novelists is Saul Bellow.

Saul Bellow. Though Bellow's major themes are not explicitly Jewish, his protagonists are recognizably Jewish in tone and feeling, as is obvious from their references to themselves and their use of Yiddish phrases. The basic ideas in Bellow's writings are akin to the basic principles of Judaism—the affirmation of man, the defense of human dignity, and the values of brotherhood and community. His dominant note of joyful living and acceptance of life suggests the Hassidic approach and teachings.

In *The Dangling Man*[29] Bellow depicts Joseph, an intellectual of the young generation who is awaiting his draft call, as the alienated Jew who has nothing but contempt and disgust for the people around him. A basic theme in his *The Victim*[30] is anti-Semitism. Asa Leven-

---

29. (New York: The Viking Press, Inc., 1947.)
30. (New York: Signet, New American Library, 1947.)

thal, a Jew, accepts his moral responsibilities despite suffering from illness and the treachery and malice of the Gentile Kirbee Allbee. Like Joseph in *The Dangling Man* he is struggling desperately merely to survive. The friends of the protagonists of *The Dangling Man* and *The Victim* are assimilated, decultured, and de-Judaized Jews. The old Yiddish Journalist, Schlossberg, represents the secular Yiddishist and mirrors the contribution of the Jewish immigrant to America.

The Jewish aspect of Bellow's characters is even more sharply delineated in his novel *Seize the Day*.[31] Tommy Wilhelm, jobless and estranged from a materialistic wife, is persuaded to seize the day by gambling his last $700 in the stock market. He employs Yiddish phrases and jokes, and is searching for his identity; he asks "What is a Jew?"

In *Seize the Day*, Bellow uses three names for Wilhelm to symbolize the Jew: Tommy (the modern Jew who assimilates), Wilkie (whose heritage is inescapable), and Velvel (whose heritage is loved). Tommy Wilhelm remembers that his grandfather called him *"Velvel,"* the name which connotes the cozy affection of his heritage, and he chooses to *be* Velvel, for more and more he comes to think in Jewish terms. By using the name Velvel he identifies himself with his heritage and his people.

The protagonist in *Seize the Day* expresses a direct acceptance of his heritage. Unlike other contemporary Jewish novelists, Saul Bellow is aware of himself as an American Jew of East European Yiddish background. A definite Jewish tone and feeling are evident in his frequent use of Hebrew and Yiddish phrases, and in his recalling bits of the Holiday liturgy, which includes prayers for mercy and forgiveness. He has also edited a collection of Yiddish short stories and translated Bashevis-

---

31. (New York: The Viking Press, Inc., 1956.)

Singer's *Gimpel the Fool* from the Yiddish.

In his popularly acclaimed novel *Herzog*,[32] where Bellow uses his Jewish material more liberally, he reveals his own affirmation of the modern Jewish intellectual in search of identity and of a meaningful existence.

Bernard Malamud. Bernard Malamud, unlike some of his contemporaries, is not concerned with the negative, vulgar types portrayed by Budd Shulberg, Jerome Weidman, Philip Roth, and others. True to the basic Jewish principle of the sacredness of human life, Malamud shows a profound concern for human existence, human responsibility, and human suffering. This concern is reflected in the character of the hard-working Jewish immigrant in *The First Seven Years.* Malamud here, and also in *The Assistant,* fills his work with positive content.

The increasingly controversial theme of the relationship between Blacks and Jews is reflected in his short story "Black Is My Favorite Color" (1963). Nat Lime, a Jewish bachelor who owns a liquor store in Harlem and wants to be friendly with the Black people, is discouraged. He is not permitted to share life with people of his "favorite color." When Nat takes the Black girl Anita to the movies, they are attacked by three Negroes. Bitter words are exchanged. Nat realizes that his "Jewish heart" has nothing to do with how Negroes feel about white men, especially Jews. To Blacks, Nat will always be a successful white man, a Jewish landlord and merchant, a part of the social and economic structure that keeps Negroes in their ghettos, and thus he cannot expect to earn their love. Anita asks her brother to tell Nat that she appreciates his intentions but that she does not think their friendship will work out.

Malamud's attitude toward Jewish survival or assim-

---

32. (New York: The Viking Press, Inc., 1964.)

ilation is best illustrated by his symbolic story entitled "The Jew Bird,"[33] in which he portrays the contrast between two types of Jews. Harry Cohen is a frozen-food salesman into whose home a black crow-like bird flies. It is a talking bird, and it informs the family that its name is "Schwartz" and that it is a "Jew Bird," running away from "anti-Semmeets." Schwartz, "the Jew Bird" prays with passion, and arouses the sympathy of the young son, Maurie, who asks his parents to allow Schwartz to stay. Despite Harry Cohen's disapproval, the Jew Bird settles down for a long stay, helps Maurie in his lessons, and tells him about his experiences as a Jew. Notwithstanding Schwartz's attempts to be helpful, Cohen resents his presence and begins to harass him.

Cohen is interested only in getting Maurie into an Ivy League college. Schwartz, who eats only traditional Jewish foods, gently keeps Maurie working at the violin and at his studies, in keeping with the traditional Jewish love of scholarship. While Schwartz is religious, praying "without book or tallith, but with passion," Cohen doesn't even bow his head during the prayer.

Assimilationist Cohen keeps urging Schwartz to migrate to the north, to the Bronx, or south to Miami Beach. He hates Schwartz because he represents the traditional Jewish way of life, which he, Cohen, has tried to discard and forget. The climax occurs one winter evening when he finally throws the Jew Bird into the street and the dead bird is later discovered by Maurie, "a dead black bird in a small lot near the river, his two wings broken, neck twisted, and both bird eyes plucked clean." The boy weeps and asks, "Who did it to you, Mr. Schwartz?" His mother knew. She answered: "anti-Semeets."

In this symbolic story the author subtly suggests that

33. "The Jew Bird," in *Idiots First* (New York: Farrar, Straus and Co., 1963), p. 113.

when the modern Jew rejects his Judaism and its tradition, he himself becomes an outsider, a destructive "anti-Semeet."

Philip Roth. In his novels and short stories, set in the milieu of the suburban life of the younger Jewish generation, Philip Roth presents what many term caricatures rather than realistic typical characters of Jews. In *Goodbye Columbus,*[34] a collection of short stories which describes a suburban Jewish generation and tells of a frustrated love affair, Roth presents through the romance of Brenda, the daughter of a businessman, Ben Patimkin, and the poor young librarian Neil Klugman, the shallow values and emptiness of suburban middle-class life. In portraying the middle-class Patimkin family, made comfortably wealthy by Ben's business of selling kitchen and bathroom sinks, the women are depicted as sensual, the men as knowledgeable and ruthless, if not unscrupulous, in their conduct of business. They seek social status through affiliation with the local Temple and the Jewish organizations in which they hold offices. Ben, the father, is the typical fictional "all rightnic" who professes "dog eat dog" as his business ethic and whose attitude toward life is dominated by his business ideal. Similar negative and vulgar types of Jews are portrayed in Roth's short stories "Epstein" and "The Conversion of Jews." In still another short story, "The Defender of the Faith," he depicts a Jewish army private who uses his religion unscrupulously to obtain special favors.

Roth's recent novel, *Portnoy's Complaint,*[35] highly controversial as to its literary merit but nevertheless a best seller, presents a cruelly caricatured image of Jewish parents, particularly in its treatment of the protagonist, the Jewish mother.

---

34. (New York: Random House, Inc., 1959.)
35. (New York: Random House, Inc., 1967.)

Alexander Portnoy loathes and denigrates his Jewish parents, whose only guilt is that they love him too much. He hates to hear the word "Jew" and can speak only contemptuously of his parents. A generation ago, it is said, a self-respecting author in America would have been ashamed to include such scenes as one finds in abundance in *Portnoy's Complaint*. But today, when few believe in restraint as a tasteful requisite of the arts, *Portnoy's Complaint* has been defended by some as sophisticated literature.

Some critics, in praise of the book, point out that Portnoy transcends religious and ethnic limitations and that Roth has presented not merely a sick boy, but the psychoerotic schizophrenia of contemporary man torn between traditions, morality, and the new sexual permissiveness. However, many of the Jewish literary world have denounced the book as repulsive and offensive to the feelings of the reader, Jewish or otherwise, because of its vulgar expressions and its degradation of human emotions.

Many a Jewish reader of these stories feels that there is very little artistic truth in them and that Roth's greatest harm lies in his potential for provoking hatred among Jewish youngsters toward their parents, and in his propaganda against Jewishness in general, which can feed the smoldering coals of anti-Semitism among non-Jews.

Roth's negative portrayal of Jewish life reflects his ignorance of Jewish tradition and history, and his own personal alienation, obsessions, and self-hatred.

There are, to be sure, such negative types among all minority groups, including the Jewish; however, the question being asked by many is why Roth has selected for characterization only vulgar, self-satisfied, egotistical Jews.

Trude Weiss Rosmarin anticipates that for years to come

Portnoy's Complaint will be quoted as a documentation of the Jewish self-hatred of some American Jewish intellectuals. She further observes that Philip Roth speaks only for a certain segment of alienated Jewishly ignorant Jews who write and teach, for "he is not more typical of American Jewish intellectuals than Alfred Kazin whose 'A Walker in the City' is a loving evocation of Jewish Brownsville and of his immigrant parents."[36]

In his evaluation of Roth's novel, Robert Kirsh, Book Editor of the Los Angeles *Times,* says: "If Philip Roth's new novel, *Portnoy's Complaint,* is destined to be the best seller of the year, the reflection is on the taste of American book buyers, for it is unquestionably the sickest book of the year, or perhaps of the decade, a masturbatory fantasy, undistinguished by anything except a morbid self-concern."[37]

Charles Angoff. In sharp contrast to some of the abovementioned prose fiction are the literary works by Charles Angoff who, with sympathetic understanding and fine insight, presents a comprehensive picture of the life of a Jewish family in America. Beginning with his first novel, *Journey to the Dawn* (1951) on through his seventh, *Memory of Autumn* (1968), Angoff gives a detailed picture of the life of the Polonsky family in America, from their beginnings as immigrants to the present day. In *Journey to the Dawn* we are introduced to this family, who emigrated from Russia at the turn of the century and came to Boston. In *Journey* and the succeeding novel, *In the Morning Light* (1952), the story continues through World War I, describing their efforts and struggles as they strive to adjust themselves to the new life in the New World. The various characters are delineated with sympathy: Moshe and Nechomah Polon-

---

36. *Jewish Spectator* (April 1969), p. 31.
37. *Los Angeles Times-Calendar* (February 16, 1969), p. 34.

sky; Mottel, the businessman; Chashel, the confused intellectual; the wise Alte Bobe, who exerts influence and authority on the family; and young David Polonsky. Here we note the already-appearing ideological conflict, discussions about the rising social movements of Zionism and Socialism. When their economic situation improves, the Polonskys move to a better neighborhood, and with their growing acculturation, changes in their mode of living occur; their Orthodox religious observances begin to weaken and family tension increases. David's jobs require him to work on the Sabbath, and he begins to associate with non-Jewish playmates.

In his third novel, *The Sun at Noon* (1955), we follow David, the leading character, through the years between 1919 and 1922, during his studies at Harvard. It is a crucial period of transition in the Polonsky family. Chashel, the socialist-minded shopgirl, after her romance, marries Shlomo, the former Yeshivah student. Mottel, once the most prosperous member of the family, loses his business and his health, which deeply affects the family. David faces the problem of choosing a career, and instead of choosing one of the more lucrative professions, such as medicine or law, because of his characteristic Jewish trait of thirst for learning, he finally decides to study philosophy and psychology. Affected and molded by his American education and his social and cultural contacts, he feels the widening distance between himself and his immigrant parents. The various scenes and episodes in the novel contain many discussions and debates on attitudes toward religion, socialism, and social issues.

Angoff's fourth volume, *Between Day and Dark* (1959), set in the mid-1920s, is rich with many fresh moments: changing events in the family, the breakup of the marriages described in his earlier volumes, and David's new work as a journalist in Boston.

In *The Bitter Spring* (1961), we see David accepting

an invitation from Harry P. Brandt (H. L. Mencken) to go to New York and work as assistant of the *American World* (*American Mercury*), a magazine for sophisticated intellectuals. David is unable to adjust to the new cynical crowd and finds himself a stranger, lost and disappointed. He longs for his old parental, traditional, religious home in Boston. He meets Jewish youths, graduated students, who are alienated and estranged from their parents and unidentified with Jewish life. After many discussions with these members of the "lost generation," he inspires them and they are aroused to self-awareness and their Jewish identity.

The period of the 1930s—of the New Deal, during the Franklin Roosevelt era and the years of Hitler's rise in Germany—are dealt with in *Summer Storm* (1963), the sixth volume in the series. We see David, sensitive and morally minded, leaving his boss, Editor-in-Chief Brand, who defended Hitler. While some of his young Jewish friends are estranged from their people, David remains anchored in his Jewish heritage. He leaves his friend Phil, and Alice, his girl friend from his Hebrew schooldays, because they have turned away from their Jewish heritage and their people's interests and problems. He marries Sylvia, who personifies to him the ideal of Jewish womanhood.

The years of the 1940s are dealt with in Angoff's recent, seventh, novel in the saga of the Polonsky family, *Memory of Autumn* (1968). David, the protagonist of all the volumes in the series, is now editor for the liberal *Globe* and is encountering the anti-Jewish bias of one of the editors and of one woman who follows the Soviet line. He is disappointed with such magazines as *The Nation* and *The New Republic,* and with highly praised authors Hemingway and Faulkner, with playwrights Kaufman and Behrman, and with much of the intellectual life of the times which seems to have become vulgarized, profaned, and dehumanized. In depressed spirits he goes to synagogues and Temples, where he finds comfort, where "the recollection of the longsuffering and endurance of the Jewish people gave him some hope and kept him from sinking into complete despair."[38] David sees some of his friends drifting away from their Jewish sources, some falling in with Communism. This tragic period of Hitler's rule and power in Germany strengthens David's loyalties to the ideals and values of Judaism and sharpens his attachment to his Jewish people. With rich insight and understanding, Angoff has depicted on a vast canvas an epic story of a typical family, from their early beginnings as immigrants to the present. This series of novels truly mirrors the experiences and trials in the changing life of generations of American Jews.

Meyer Levin. Novelist Meyer Levin presents in his life, as in all of his writings, an exception on the American Jewish literary scene. From his first novel, *Yehuda,* in 1931 to his latest, *The Stronghold,* he is preoccupied with the search for truth and justice and with the problem of Jewish identity or assimilation. The problem of the Jew's full adjustment to the American environment and his retention of his Jewish heritage is Levin's deep concern and the central theme of his literary works.

His novel *The Old Bunch,* considered by many a classic, gives an honest portrayal of the Jewish American-born-and-reared generation. It artistically mirrors the experiences and changing life-style of the American Jew. Levin wrote *The Old Bunch* in the 1930s, while spending a year in Palestine working in a Kibbutz near Haifa.

As a war correspondent in Germany in World War II, Levin had rushed in his jeep ahead of the first tanks and entered the concentration camps to identify and talk to

---

38. *Memory of Autumn* (New York: Thomas Yoseloff, 1968), p. 23.

the survivors. When the war ended he went to Palestine, became active in the Haganah underground, and filmed the entire illegal operation of smuggling Jews from Poland across Europe to the Palestine shore. This later became the historic documentary film, *The Illegals.*

In his novel *The Fanatic* (1963), the central theme is the struggle of a writer to preserve the Jewish content of a book. Maury Finkelstein, a young American and former Reform rabbi who as a U.S. Army Chaplain witnessed the Nazi horrors, writes a play that accentuates the inhuman torture endured by Jews in the Nazi extermination camps. Though branded a "fanatic," he will fight alone and against all odds for what he believes is right. His search and struggle for justice are not limited to man on earth; he also raises the question of God's justice and struggles for an understanding of the horror of the six million Jews, martyrs in the Nazi concentration camps.

Levin's work *Compulsion* deals with the Leopold-Loeb murder case in Chicago, in which he discerned an expression of Jewish self-hatred. The same qualities of Jewish life and character are present in his latest book, *"The Stronghold,"*[39] which appeared on his sixtieth birthday.

In *The Stronghold,* one Jew, an ex-Premier of an occupied country, is now held a hostage by the Nazis in order to force absolution from their war crimes. Kraus, Hitler's associate and baron of the castle, make numerous false charges against the Jews. This novel further contains a dialogue between Judaism and Christianity, and the contrast in their attitudes toward the brutality and callousness of a world that permitted the rise of Hitler and the holocaust.

All Meyer Levin's writings are imbued with a deep Jewish consciousness and a dedication to the moral ideals

---

39. (New York: Simon and Schuster, 1965.)

of his Jewish heritage. Unlike most of his contemporaries of the 1950s and 1960s, in whose novels Zionism and modern Israel are ignored, Levin's works are "oriented toward an organic view of Jewish life in which America, Europe and Israel have their place."[40] His dedication to Zionism and to Israel can be traced to his first visit to Palestine in 1925, and it is evident even in his first novel, *Yehuda*, which appeared in 1931 and early revealed his love and attachment to Israel and the Jewish people.

Marjorie Duhan Adler. Illuminating the search for identity of the new generation is the recent novel *A Sign Upon My Hand by* Marjorie Duhan Adler. The author, herself brought up in an assimilated, de-Judaized family, portrays a young American-Jewish woman who is alienated and ashamed of being Jewish. Experiencing unhappiness in her married life, she searches for true identity and self-awareness and finally finds appreciation and sustaining strength in returning to her people's heritage.

The author's change of attitude to the affirmative and her appreciation of Judaism are shown both in the Biblical title she has chosen for her novel and in her acknowledging "deep gratitude to Rabbi Charles E. Shulman who brought to me the God of my fathers at the time I most needed Him."[41]

Isaac Bashevis-Singer. The literary works of Isaac Bashevis-Singer, who came to the United States in 1935 from Warsaw, Poland, were all written in Yiddish and translated into English. Though the setting of Singer's most highly acclaimed novels is East Europe, *The Little Shoemaker* is set in both Eastern Europe and an American suburb. In *Gimpel the Fool,* reminiscent of Y. L. Peretz's

---

40. Quoted in *Congress Bi-Weekly* (Nov. 27, 1965), p. 14.
41. Marjorie Duhan Adler, *A Sign Upon My Hand* (Garden City, N.Y.: Doubleday & Co., Inc., 1964), p. vii.

Bontsche Schweig, he portrays a pious, humble, simple-minded Jew who emigrates to America, is exploited by his fellows, and later becomes a shoe manufacturer.

Gimpel the Fool, made popular in the English translation of Saul Bellow, depicts the contrast between life in Eastern Europe and that in the United States, and specifically the adjustment of Gimpel from the traditional Jewish life of the Old Country to modern life in the American milieu. Within Bashevis-Singer's several novels, much use is made of Jewish folklore, magic, the supernatural, and the mystical.

POSITIVE PROSE IN YIDDISH

Although the present study deals primarily with American Jewish life as reflected in selected fiction written in English, some of the important works portraying the American-Jewish scene written by distinguished Yiddish writers must also be mentioned. The Yiddish novels reflecting the experiences of the immigrant generation and of their children, which were discussed in preceding chapters, included those by Sholem Asch, Leon Kobrin, Morris Rosenfeld, David Pinski, Sholem Aleichem, Joseph Opatoshu, H. Leivik, Isaac Raboy, David Ingatev, I. J. Schwartz, and I. Friedland.

In addition to these must be added the literary works of the noted dramatist and novelist Peretz Hirschbein; the sketches and short stories of Z. Libin; the short stories of Abraham Reisin, acclaimed as "the People's Poet"; the novels of Lamed Shapiro; those of Isaac Raboy, especially *A Jew Came to America,*[42] and the works of Jacob Glatstein, noted poet, essayist, and author of the trilogy *When Yash Went Away,*[43] *When*

---

42. I. Bashevis-Singer, *Gimpel the Fool,* trans. Saul Bellow. In *A Treasury of Yiddish Stories,* edited by Irving Howe and Eliezer Greenberg (New York: The Viking Press, Inc., 1954).

43. (Vilno: B. Klatzkin Farlag, 1929.)

Yash Arrived,[44] and *Emil and Carl,*[45] as well as the works of Menachem Boraisha and H. Rosenblatt.

Also to be noted are the novels in Yiddish of Baruch Glazman, Shin Miller, Pinchos Rudoy, and Jacob Singer, novels which dwell on the psychology of the lonely and maladjusted, and depict the disintegration of the American-Jewish family.

Important literary works on the Holocaust during the Nazi period, and on the rebirth of the State of Israel and on their effects on American Jews, were written by the Yiddish poets and novelists H. Leivick, Chaim Grade, Aaron Zeitlin, Kadia Molodovsky, I. Bashevis-Singer, and Eli Wiessl. Author and lecturer Maurice Samuel has contributed richly to an understanding of the Jewish heritage, particularly as he has made the classic works of Peretz and Sholem Aleichem popular with the English-reading public.

Characteristic of American Yiddish and Hebrew writers is that, unlike some who write on Jewish themes in English, they portray Jewish life without ridicule or contempt. Their approach is positive, with a sense of identification with, and understanding of, the people whom they describe.

Through the masterful evaluations and translations by noted authors and literary critics such as Maurice Samuel, Sol Liptzin, A. A. Roback, Alfred Kazin, Saul Bellow, and Irving Howe, modern Yiddish literature has become popular and has won considerable appreciation from the general public.

---

44. (New York: Yikuf Publishing House, 1944.)
45. (New York: M. Sklarsky Farlag, 1940.)

13

Integration and Survival

Closely related to the changing attitude toward Jewishness in the third and fourth generation is the all-pervading problem of the survival of Jews as a minority group in the free and assimilating American society. This matter is also of deep concern to all ethnic minority groups wishing to preserve their social and cultural heritage within the larger American society. Central to the survival of ethnic and religious groups is the ability to establish their own institutions, such as churches, conducting services in their native language; their own press; the theater; national societies; and schools for their children.

FROM THE MELTING-POT THEORY TO
CULTURAL PLURALISM

It is a far cry from the old popular conception of Americanization, known as the melting-pot theory, to present ideas of Americanization. The idea of America as a "melting pot" comes from Zangwill's popular play by that name (1908). America was viewed as a cauldron into which all racial and cultural strains of immigrants were to be poured and blended to form a new nation. This conception of Americanization was the basis of the efforts to assimilate the immigrant, to make him "an American." He was induced by American society to take on the external forms of American life, with very little consideration being given to the deeper cultural and spiritual values which he brought with him. It was thought that immigrants had only to jump into that pot, go through the cooking process, and emerge from the crucible as full "undifferentiated" Americans. All doors would then open for them, and all opportunities would be theirs.

The serious fallacy of the melting-pot theory was the idea that all groups who come to the new world must divest themselves of former traditions, cultures, and heritages in order to boil down into one indistinguishable stew. This idea is no longer acceptable, for it is being increasingly realized that America does not demand uniformity. Rather, the thought is accepted by many that all people have a right to be different, and that diversity is a source of the nation's strength, for it encourages cultural creativity and provides variety and colorfulness.

The American philosopher William James and his disciple Horace Kallen, in evaluating the melting-pot concept, suggested long ago that America ought rather to be viewed as an orchestra of diverse cultures, each of which might appropriately preserve its uniqueness to give its own tonal quality in order to produce the total harmonious symphony. For each group can represent a new contribution to the variety and richness of American society and culture.

Views of noted social thinkers. Eminent sociologists William I. Thomas and Florian Znaniecki, discussing the parochial school in the Polish-American community and its role in the adjustment of the immigrants, state:

> Good or bad, the parochial school is a social product of the immigrant group and satisfies important needs of the latter. The most essential point is neither the religious character of the parochial school, nor even the fact that it serves to preserve

in the young generation the language and cultural traditions of the old country; it is the function of the parochial school as a factor of the social unity of the immigrant colony and of its continuity through successive generations. . . . But even more important than this unification of the old generation is the bond which the parish school creates between the old and the young generation. Whereas children who go to the public school become completely estranged from their parents, if these are immigrants, the parish school, in spite of the fact that its program of studies is in many respects similar to that of the public school, in a large measure prevents the estrangement, not only because it makes the children acquainted with their parents' religion, language and national history, but also because it inculcates respect for these traditional values and for the nation from which they came.[1]

Similar views on this problem have been expressed by the contemporary sociological thinkers Emory S. Bogardus, Kimball Young, Robert E. Park, John Dewey, Horace M. Kallen, Constantin. Panunzio, and others. Bogardus defined Americanization as:

the educational process of unifying both native-born and foreign-born Americans in perfect support of the principles of liberty, union, democracy and brotherhood,

and he succinctly interprets it as follows:

Americanization means giving the immigrant the best America has to offer and retaining for America the best in the immigrant.[2]

Other noted American social thinkers also questioned the value of the melting-pot concept and pointed out that ethnic cultural minority groups could serve the American society and its culture more effectively if they retained

1. W. I. Thomas and Florian Znaniecki, *The Polish Peasant in Europe and America,* vol. 5 (New York: Alfred A. Knopf, 1917):50–51.
2. Emory S. Bogardus, *Essentials of Americanization* (Los Angeles: University of Southern California Press, 1919), p. 11.

their identity and enriched the culture of the whole with their own unique contribution. Horace M. Kallen's analogy to the orchestra has its proponents in William James, John Dewey, Charles Elliot, and Louis Adamic, who term it variously "cultural democracy" or "cultural pluralism." The concept of cultural pluralism recognizes the ethnic diversity of the American people and that all diverse ethnic and religious minority groups have significant contributions to make toward the enrichment of American culture.

The noted Norwegian-American novelist O. R. Rolvaag, addressing himself to his Scandinavian kinsmen in America, wrote in his novel *Their Father's God:*

> If we're to accomplish anything worth while, anything at all, we must do it as Norwegians. Otherwise we may meet the same fate as corn in too strong a sun. Look at the Jews, for example: take away the contribution they have made to the world's civilization and you'd have a tremendous gap that time will never be able to fill. Did they make their contribution by selling their birthright and turning into Germans, Russians, and Poles: Or did they achieve greatly because they stubbornly refused to be de-Jewed? See what they have done in America! Are they as citizens inferior to us? Do they love this country less? Are they trying to establish a nation of their own? Empty nonsense! But they haven't ceased being Jews simply because they live here in America, and because they have adopted this country's language and become its citizens. Do you think their children will become less worthy Americans because they are being fostered in Jewish traits and traditions? Quite the contrary! If they, as individuals or as a group, owe any debt to America, the payment can only be made by their remaining Jews, and the same holds true for all nationalities that have come here. One thing I see clearly: if this process of levelling down, of making everybody alike by blotting out all racial traits, is allowed to continue, America is doomed to become the most impoverished land spiritually on the face of the earth; out of the highly praised melting pot will come a dull smug complacency, barren of all creative thought and effort. Soon we will have reached the perfect democracy of

barrenness. Gone will be the distinguishing traits given us by God; dead will be the hidden life of the heart which is nourished by tradition, the idiom of language, and our attitude to life. It is out of these elements that our character grows. I ask again, what will we have left?[3]

In fairness to Zangwill it must be said that he himself never believed in the melting-pot theory, a stereotyped sameness, as an American ideal. He fully realized that "dislike of the unlike" is a superstition, the source of all intolerance, and would have subscribed to the picture of the American ideal as an orchestra, for David Quixano, the main character in his drama, is a musician expressing this very idea of the melting pot through a symphonic composition.[4]

Zangwill was one of the first active supporters of the Zionist idea of a Jewish State in Palestine. Eight years after the opening of *The Melting Pot* he wrote:

It was vain for Paul to declare that there should be neither Jew nor Greek. Nature will return if driven out with a pitchfork, still more if driven out with a dogma.[5]

With regard to the problem of continuity of Jewish group life in America, Zangwill would have shared the viewpoint of Israel Friedlander, who has pictured the position of the Jewish community in America as follows:

We perceive a community . . . actively participating in the civic, social and economic progress of the country, fully sharing and increasing its spiritual possessions and acquisitions, doubling its joys, halving its sorrows; yet deeply rooted in the soil of Judaism, true to its traditions, faithful to its aspirations; men with straight backs and raised heads, with no emotion stifled,

3. O. R. Rolvaag, *Their Fathers' God* (New York: Harper and Brothers, 1931), p. 9.
4. Israel Zangwill, *The Melting Pot* (New York: The Macmillan Co., 1909), pp. 37–38.
5. Joseph Leftwich, *Israel Zangwill* (New York: Thomas Yoseloff, 1957), p. 255.

with souls harmoniously developed, not yielding like wax to
every impress from the outside, but blending the best they
possess with the best they encounter; not a horde of individuals, but a set of individualities, adding a new note to the
richness of American life, leading a new current into the
stream of American civilization.[6]

Assimilation and Survival. Those who believe in and
work for the group survival of American Jewry repudiate the idea of assimilation in the sense of abandoning
one's group identity and cultural heritage. They believe
that fostering one's cultural heritage, over and above
the shared American civilization, is not only thoroughly
consistent with the law and spirit of American democracy, but also a distinct contribution to it. In his sociological analysis of the Jewish minority problem, Kurt
Lewin says: "Not the belongingness to many groups is
the cause of the difficulty, but the uncertainty of belongingness."[7] In this connection Lewin recalled the famed
statement of Justice Louis D. Brandeis, that "double
loyalty does not lead to ambiguity" and that "every individual belongs to many overlapping groups: to his family,
his friends, his professional and business group, and
so on."

As for the Zionist program, as he summed it up for
himself, Brandeis said: "My approach to Zionism was
through Americanism," for "it became clear to me that
to be good Americans, we must be better Jews, and to be
better Jews, we must become Zionists."[8]

In similar vein, Morris Raphael Cohen states:

The idea that all immigrants should wipe out their past and

6. Israel Friedlander, quoted in *Sabbath and Festival Prayer Book*
(New York: Rabbinical Assembly of America, 1952), p. 296.
7. Kurt Lewin, *Resolving Social Conflict,* ed. Gertrude Weiss Lewin
(New York: Harper and Brothers, 1948), p. 179.
8. Louis D. Brandeis, *The Jewish Problem—How to Solve It.* Noted
in Ludwig Lewisohn, ed., *Rebirth* (New York: Harper and Brothers,
1936), p. 13.

become simple imitations of the existing type is neither possible nor desirable. The past cannot be wiped out. And we make ourselves ridiculous in the effort to do so. . . . All great civilizations have been the result of the contributions of many peoples, and a richer American culture can come only if the Jews, like other elements, are given a chance to develop under favorable conditions their peculiar genius.[9]

Rabbi Joshua Loth Liebman says:

We shall be a minority group, distinctive in our spiritual and social outlook—made distinctive in fact, by our conscious loyalty to a four-thousand-year-old heritage. Perhaps in the new world of the future, a world of genuine good will and of brotherhood, there may be some who would feel that the Jewish community should cease to exist. Our answer, then, as now, should be that only when biology and life cease to treasure differences and seek absolute uniformity, should the Jew disappear from the stage of time.[10]

Integration by Accommodation. Those who believe in the broader conception of Americanization maintain that democratic America is big enough for differences, and has a place for those who are rooted in their faith and culture and can make their significant contribution to American civilization in terms of their historic heritage.

Pertinent and significant are the words spoken on this subject by Chief Justice Earl Warren, in an address delivered in Washington, D.C.:

Our concept of loyalty is different from that insisted upon by totalitarian regimes, for our understanding of freedom is different. Autocratic countries forbid or discourage diversities in religion and culture. They fear these things as dangerous to their nationalism. We do not demand such a sacrifice of freedom. If a man is free to be only what his neighbor wishes he

---

9. Morris Raphael Cohen, *Reflections of a Wandering Jew* (Glencoe, Ill.: The Free Press, 1950), p. 33.

10. Joshua Loth Liebman "Twenty-Five Years of Jewish Community Life in America," *The Jewish Center* 20 (15 June, 1942).

is not truly free. American patriotism requires political allegiance but not uniformity in faith, in culture, or in sentiment. Unity does not involve uniformity.

Here individuals and groups are not merely tolerated but they are encouraged in the free exercise of their different religions, their distinctive ancestral traditions, their diverse social and philanthropic interests. We see in these things not weakness but strength. They are esteemed as facets of freedom, and I firmly believe that, far from setting up conflicting loyalties, they add richness and color and vitality to the fiber of our national life.

The Chief Justice concluded:

In my native California, they have experimented extensively to achieve new forms in horticulture. As each new plant and fruit and flower is cultivated, it is counted as a gain. So in a nation of many ancestral stocks let us not undervalue the vast benefits that may possibly accrue to our nation from the diffusion and interplay of the precious stores of the cultures they brought to our land.[11]

In his June 1964 appeal to strengthen Jewish identity, made at the 50th anniversary of the National Jewish Welfare Board, Arthur J. Goldberg said:

To me, like Justice Brandeis, the true test of an American is this: that he does not conceal but affirms his origin; he is proud of whatever it may be; he wears his difference not as a cause of offense to others but as a contribution to the wonderful richness of American life. In the plurality and mutual tolerance of American culture lies the secret of our strength and of the freedom which we so proudly profess to the rest of the world.[12]

That American democracy provides the opportunity for the Jew to retain his group life within the general

---

11. Given before the B'nai B'rith Society, Washington, D.C., December 29, 1954, quoted in *The Day* (December 29, 1954), p. 1.
12. "Let Us Strengthen Jewish Identity in America," *JWB Circle* (June 1964), p. 14.

American society is pointed out by Mordecai M. Kaplan in his book *The Future of the American Jew:*

> It is generally recognized that all men need to be rooted in a religious tradition and that it is to the various historic religions, older than America itself, that the American nation looks for the strengthening of its own morale. It looks to Judaism, and rightly so, to accomplish this for its Jewish citizens. That expectation is an unequalled opportunity for us Jews not only to retain our group life in this country, but also to achieve a religious orientation that might prove of great value to the religiously starved mankind of our day.[13]

Also worthy of mention is that, at the two-day Tercentenary Conference on American Jewish Sociology, the following findings of research projects were made public by a group of social scientists.

> 1. Increased interest in the Jewish religion goes hand in hand with the degree of Americanization. Jews tend to observe those religious customs and ceremonies which are in line and acceptable to American standards.
> 2. The great majority of Jews have a favorable attitude toward Israel. However, they have little, if any, desire to live there.
> 3. Jews are continuing their traditional practice of supporting philanthropies, contributing liberally to both Jewish and non-sectarian causes. Membership in and activity with Jewish organizations helps the Jew to identify himself and gives him a sense of belonging.[14]

RESOLVING THE DILEMMA

These views expressed by eminent social thinkers on integration and Jewish group survival in the free, pluralistic American society are also held by a number of American Jewish intellectuals and novelists, whose fiction

---

13. Mordecai Kaplan, *The Future of the American Jew* (New York: The Macmillan Co., 1949), p. 57.
14. Quoted from the *Temple Bulletin* no. 10 (Rodef Shalom Congregation, Pittsburgh, Pa.) (December 8, 1954), p. 6.

reflects the life of contemporary American Jewry. These include Ludwig Lewisohn, Maurice Samuel, Irving Fineman, Meyer Levin, Charles Angoff, Michael Blankfort, Bernard Malamud, Chaim Potok, and others whose novels have been discussed in preceding chapters. Worthy of special mention are those whose recent novels, as well as the authors themselves, present an example of positive Jewish identity, concern, and involvement in their people's life and culture: Meyer Levin, Charles Angoff, and Chaim Potok.

Meyer Levin. In his autobiography, *In Search,* Meyer Levin depicts the inner struggle and conflicts experienced by the young American Jew of his generation. In this self-analysis, Levin tells of the experiences he has known as he, the son of a Jewish immigrant family, emerged into the world of Chicago.

The author relates his sad experience of visiting, along with the United States Army, the crematoria of Europe. It served to link him with his whole Jewish past. As war correspondent, he brought out the first survivor list from Buchenwald and other concentration camps. Shortly after the war Levin went to Palestine to cover the fighting and terrorist activities. He also did his documentary film "The Illegals," about the Jewish underground in Palestine. In the course of these experiences, Levin tells that he began to get an inkling of the Jewish future and that this was the meaning for which he had been searching. He says further: "I believe that in following out the sometimes conflicting elements of the Jewish question within itself, I may have served as a testing agent for my own generation, and particularly for the American born."[15]

After his long and honest search, he comes to the con-

---

15. Meyer Levin, *In Search* (Paris: Author's Press, 1950), p. 9.

clusion that his Jewish heritage and American democracy
are not in conflict but can be harmonized to complement
and supplement each other, and thus bring him true personality fulfillment and self-expression. He says in addition:

> I do not, for instance, feel that I am in an issueless dilemma
> as an American and as a Jew, and that I must renounce one
> culture or the other. I recognize that some individuals may
> feel, and for themselves rightly feel, that they have to do this.
> But we also know that there can be successful bicultural and
> multicultural personalities, and I do not see why the modern
> Jew shouldn't strive for such a realization, if it gives the best
> expression to all that is in him. No one argues against bilingual
> or multilingual people, indeed, we feel they are richer and
> more useful for such accomplishment.[16]

Levin's passionate search ends in his reaffirmation of
his group identification and his self-acceptance as an
American Jew. He expresses this clearly in these words:

> There are some ways in which we are unique, and in our souls
> we know and are proud of this uniqueness. Why not then de-
> clare it, since the world knows it, too, instead of apologizing
> for it and pretending that it does not exist. Let us rather seek
> to understand our special compound, so that we may live as
> what we are.[17]

Charles Angoff. An affirmative attitude to Jewishness and
to a meaningful Jewish future is also expressed by the
novelist Charles Angoff, whose nine volumes on the Polonsky family give a true picture of the adjustment
experiences and the transformations of three generations
of the American-Jewish family.

Unlike those American-Jewish novelists who out of
sheer ignorance of Jewishness, or because of alienation
from their people, wrote novels portraying neurotics and

16. *Ibid.,* p. 514.
17. *Ibid.,* pp. 517–18.

self-hating Jews, Charles Angoff, himself well-versed in Jewish lore, depicts his characters with sympathetic understanding and warmth. His novels delineate important issues of Jewish existence and describe various groups in the Zionist, the Jewish socialist and labor movements, and the inner conflicts and struggle of the protagonist, David, over his Jewish identity and concern for Jewish continuity in America. Angoff often uses the Yiddish phrase "dos Pintele Yid" (a latent spark of Jewish kinship), and in his essay on the works of the Yiddish classic writers, Mendele and Peretz, entitled "How to Write About Jews?" he asks the alienated, intellectual Jewish writers who pretend to write perceptively about American life: "Is it narrow-minded and parochial to write about Jews, Jewishly as well as universally?" Angoff concludes the essay by quoting the following words from Peretz's essay, "What Is Missing in Our Literature?": "I am not talking of shutting ourselves up in a spiritual ghetto. We want to get out of the ghetto but with our own spirit, our own spiritual treasure, and exchange—give and take, not beg."[18]

In his address, "The Mission of a Jewish Writer," delivered on May 4, 1969, upon receiving a prize from the Jewish Book Council of America, Angoff emphasized his belief that a Jewish writer must possess a knowledge of Jewish history and religion, and should portray the life of the people with sympathetic understanding and love even when he is criticizing and castigating them. In this, Angoff is following in the grand literary tradition of his revered predecessors, whose works are classics of modern Jewish literature: Mendele, Sholom Aleichem, and Peretz.

Chaim Potok. In *The Chosen,*[19] Chaim Potok portrays

---

18. *Congress Bi-Weekly* (June 26, 1941), p. 40.
19. (New York: Simon and Schuster, 1967.)

the life of the Hassidim, an ultra-religious group, in their compact settlement in Williamsburg, Brooklyn, in the 1950s. This novel is unique in contemporary Jewish fiction. *The Chosen* is not a story of violence or brutality and it contains no sensationalism or obscenity, and therefore it is a refreshing exception to the temper and style of many current novels of American-Jewish life. This novel does not deal with self-hatred, but with true friendship between two teen-age, serious-minded, Jewish boys, Reuben and Danny, who are concerned with the deeper intellectual, and ethical aspects of life. Both boys confront difficult moral problems in their chosen vocations. While the novel portrays the difference between the Hassidim—who emphasize emotionalism, joyous exaltation, and mysticism—and their ideological opponents, the "Mithnagdim"—with their rationalistic approach and emphasis on logic and study—it also reflects the thoughts and the generation gap in the lives of even orthodox Hassidic families, portraying their ideological differences, the tensions between generations, and their society, science, and ethics. The novel also mirrors the two historical events that the present Jewish generation has had to face, the Holocaust and the rebirth of Israel. It is with warm and sympathetic understanding that Potok has written of the Hassidim and the problems of serious-minded Jewish youth in their quest for meaningful fulfillment in their adjustment as Jews in the American environment.

The Promise,[20] a sequel to *The Chosen*, introduces a group of Hassidim who emigrated to the United States after World War II and settled in the Hassidic neighborhood of Williamsburg. Both Danny and Reuben, now in their twenties, continue their studies, Reuben studying for the Rabbinate at an Orthodox Seminary and Danny, now modernized, enrolled in Columbia University's Department of Psychology.

---

20. (New York: Alfred A. Knopf, Inc., 1970.)

WHAT OF THE FUTURE? NEW VOICES AND
AWAKENED YOUTH

Because of the current alienation among Jewish intellectuals and youth and the weakening of Jewish traditions, concerned Jewish leaders are apprehensive about
the future and are asking the question: Can American
Jews survive as a distinct minority group in the free, open
American society? Is there a future for American Jewry?

The optimists, speaking in terms of new creative
forces and trends, are confident of a golden future of
American Jewry, somewhat similar to the Jewries of
Babylonia and Spain in their golden ages. The pessimists,
on the other hand, see only signs of disintegration and
assimilation into American society, similar to what took
place in Western Europe.

In view of the strong assimilative forces at work in
America, it is not easy to predict the future, but there
seems to be reasons for hope in an American-Jewish
future. To be sure, one can hardly discern a general cultural return to vital Jewishness on a large scale. Since
many of the younger generation lack knowledge and
understanding of their Jewish heritage, and, being mis-
guided, may discard their heritage to follow other allure-
ments and ideals, it is realistic to recognize that a number
will fall by the wayside.

New Voices of Awakening Youth. There are also fresh
indications of a desire to return to the source, to search
for meaningful Jewish identification and involvement.
The voices of the young generation, heard of late, reflect a change of attitude from apathy and indifference
to one of participation and commitment to Judaism and
Jewish life, and can only be interpreted as hopeful
sounds. Further encouragement can be derived from the
report of a recent study conducted by Bnai Brith Hillel

Foundation of Jewish college activities on campuses. Growing numbers of Jewish students, this study reveals, define themselves as "radical Jews" and as "anti-establishment," meaning by these terms that they strongly oppose the anti-Israel and anti-Jewish postures of the "Far Left" and the "Third World" movements.

Dr. Sara Feinstein, of the American Jewish Committee, writing in the Winter issue of *Dimensions,* asserts that "a new Jewish voice is beginning to resound on campus."[21] She declares that many new campus newspapers in the United States are expressing attitudes of repugnance to self-effacement by Jewish radicals, and are encouraging a deep concern for the future of Jewry and the security of Israel. Such examples illustrate that the new generation is more eager for Jewish knowledge, self-awareness, and identification than their parents ever were!

Discussing the future of the American-Jewish community, social historian Salo W. Baron states that no one in his senses will have the temerity to predict the type of Judaism and Jewish community likely to emerge from the great turmoil of our present world, but one thing, says Baron, may confidently be asserted:

> If American Jewry turns from quantity to quality, if it builds its communal coexistence less upon the quantitative criteria of financial success, statistically measurable memberships or school attendance, and costly and outwardly impressive buildings and institutions, and devotes more attention to the cultivation of the genuinely creative personality and of the substantive and enduring values in religion and culture, the new type of American Jewry will be a cause of pride and satisfaction. If only our present generation and its successors can become fully cognizant of their heritage, if only they will delve even deeper into the mysteries of their people's past and

---

21. *Dimensions in American Judaism,* 4, no. 2. Publication of the Union of American Hebrew Congregations (Winter 1970) :4.

present, they will not only make certain of that people's creative survival, but also significantly help in charting mankind's path toward its ultimate, let us hope Messianic, goals.[22]

Impact of Israel. A most important factor which strengthens the hope for a continued future of Jewish life in America is the reborn State of Israel. Deeply moved by the fulfillment of the age-old dream of Zion redeemed, American Jews gave tremendous support to the State of Israel, which has brought to Jews all over the globe a sense of pride in their new status and in Israel's achievements. A strong sense of group consciousness began to be awakened, even among those who had heretofore been indifferent to Jewish life and to Israel. The rebirth of Israel and its new form of social organization, based on the Jewish ideals of justice, stimulated the spiritual and cultural life of Jews the world over and increased interest in the study of Jewish history, of Jewish culture, and of Hebrew as a living language.

It is the influence of Israel, particularly the miraculous, heroic event of the Six Day War that explains the most significant phenomenon, the recent remarkable awakening of Jews in Soviet Russia, where thousands of young Jews, although oppressed by the Communist regime and deprived of the opportunity to study Judaism, have in the face of being imprisoned, nevertheless demonstrated their determination to emigrate to Israel. American Jewish youth, too, are now visiting Israel in steadily increasing numbers, attending its universities and working in Kibutzim on farms. This new quest for identity on the part of young people, who are seeking self-awareness and are inspired by Israel's continuing growth

---

22. "The Modern Age," in *Great Ages and Ideas of the Jewish People,* ed. Leo W. Schwartz (New York: Random House, Inc., 1956), p. 483.

and achievement, provides hope and reassurance for a continued Jewish life in the pluralistic, free American society.

On this question can we definitely predict the future of American Jews? Dr. Mordecai M. Kaplan says that "the future that awaits us American Jews is unpredictable. It depends largely on how we shall meet the challenge of the present and avail ourselves of its opportunities."[23]

As one ponders the future of American Jewry, perturbed by the sad conditions of large numbers of its alienated, estranged youth, the analogy of the ancient Prophet Isaiah comes to mind: that Israel is like an oak tree in the autumn season, from which thousands of leaves may fall away, but the trunk of the tree endures.[24] It is the "Sheor Yoshuv," the saving remnant, that will assure continuity of Judaism and of the Jewish people.

There is firm belief and hope in the continuity of Judaism and Jewish life in the United States in accordance with the basic American principle of "diversity within unity," which provides the possibility of a creative, meaningful survival for the Jewish community, integrated into the free, pluralistic American society and contributing in a large measure to the welfare of mankind.

CONCLUSIONS

In examining the life of American Jews during the past nine decades there has been evident a process of transformation in their social and cultural life. Observing the important changes that have taken place in vital areas of Jewish life and their bearing on the all-pervad-

23. Mordecai M. Kaplan, *The Future of the American Jew* (New York: The Macmillan Co., 1948), p. 536.
24. Isaiah 6:13.

ing problem of survival and integration of the Jewish minority into the larger American society, we arrive at these findings and conclusions:

1. The first generation of Jewish immigrants from East European countries nine decades ago found a cultural and social environment radically different from that which they had left. The new urban mode of life in the American industrial cities and the altered social conditions tended to weaken the religious authority and control in their lives. It also involved difficulties such as the shift to the hard proletarian existence, loss of status, disharmony between parents and their American-born or American-reared children. These experiences were depicted in the novels written in that period.

2. Among the second generation, the American-born or American-reared, the tendency was to move into the ranks of the middle classes and the professions. These of the second generation had no less a problem of adjustment than their parents had had. They had encountered the difficulty of psychological and spiritual maladjustment, and problems of culture conflict, marginality, and alienation. This marginality found expression in rootlessness, which at times has led some of them to experience self-hatred and hatred of their people. These experiences, delineated in the prose fiction of the 1920s and the 1930s, also reveal the sense of alienation and self-contempt of the authors in their novels of protest and rejection.

3. The changed environment and factors of social change have affected and altered the structure and functions of the American Jewish family. Much of the general American pattern of dating, courting, mate-choosing and wedding ceremony has become accepted by American Jews. The stability of the traditional Jewish family life has declined, due to the weakening of parental and religious authority and the social distance between children and their parents. Intermarriage, which in the im-

migrant generation was a rare occurrence, has become frequent in the second generation, as a result of social interaction and closer culture contact with other religious and ethnic groups within the free American society. While in the past opposition to mixed marriage was based primarily on religious grounds, at present it is being opposed more on the basis of its threat to the survival of the Jewish people and because of concern for marital happiness and harmony in the home.

4. Changes in religious observances and ritual have taken place within all religious groupings of American Judaism. The influence of patterns of the dominating Christian majority is evident in some of the ceremonials and new forms of festival observances.

5. In the development of Jewish education in the United States are evident the ideological and social differentiations of the community. In the past, Jewish Sunday Schools followed the pattern of the dominant Protestant American Sunday School, but in later years the quality and educational standard changed and improved considerably. Because of social and cultural changes, new types of Jewish schools emerged. As a result of spatial and social mobility, the communal Hebrew school, the Talmud Torah, has been gradually replaced by the Congregational school. In shift of emphasis by some Jewish educators on the reason for giving children Jewish instruction, there is now greater stress on mental hygiene and group identity.

6. Dissatisfaction with the social conditions of the Jewish people and the desire to change their social position gave birth to the Zionist and Jewish socialist movements. Since World War II, the former negative attitude of the Jewish socialists toward Zionism changed to an affirmative one, and they are now giving their full support to the Histadruth, the Labor Organization of Israel, and to other national Jewish causes.

7. Certain American-Jewish writers revealed a sense of alienation and self-contempt in their novels of protest and rejection in which Jews were often depicted negatively as caricatured characters. There are, on the other hand, some novelists who, under the impact of the rise of Nazism, the near annihilation of European Jewry and, later, the miraculous rebirth of the State of Israel, have shown an affirmative attitude toward Jewishness and to the problem of Jewish survival in America. Their literary works reflect the change from a mood of protest and rejection to one of affirmation and identification. There is also evident a change in the third generation, from the anxieties and insecurities of the alienated second generation "of a wasteland," to new tendencies toward Jewish self-awareness and identification.

8. The sociological factors and changed social situations of the past several decades have radically altered the demographic complexion of the American-Jewish population and have resulted in a changed, broadened conception—and a wider scope and function—of welfare activities, and in new forms and directions of Jewish community organization. Following the second World War and the establishment of the State of Israel, in order to meet the need that arose for greater centralization and the mobilization of all groups for help, the United Jewish Welfare Funds and the Community Council were founded. This marked a shift of emphasis, from helping only the economically dependent part of the community to assisting the community as a whole, a shift from the physical and material to the cultural and spiritual, as is shown in the larger sums allocated by the welfare funds for Jewish education and for Jewish youth programs.

It has been noted that the old theory of the melting-pot—that all ethnic groups must divest themselves of their former cultural traditions and become assimilated into the majority group—has been challenged by leading American educators and social scientists. The new idea of cultural or religious pluralism recognizes the right of all people to be different and that all ethnic and religious minority groups have significant contributions to make to American society and culture. This idea is the American democratic principle of diversity in unity.

A new tendency has emerged in the third and fourth generations of American Jews, to assert their group identity and repudiate the idea of assimilation in the sense of abandoning their cultural heritage, and to accept the principle of accommodation as the process which enables American Jews to survive as a culturally creative group integrated into the free American society.

In conclusion, it is hoped that these observations and conclusions growing out of a study of one ethnic group may be applied to other minority groups facing similar problems, and that they also may indicate possibilities for further research into the processes of change and accommodation in other religious or ethnic groups in **America.**

Bibliography

I. PRIMARY SOURCES

A. Novels and Short Stories

Abrams, Margaret. *Awakened*. Philadelphia: Jewish Publication Society of America, 1955.

Adler, Marjorie Duhan. *A Sign Upon My Hand*. New York: Garden City: Doubleday and Co., Inc., 1964.

Angoff, Charles. *Journey to the Dawn*. New York: The Beechhurst Press, 1951.

———. *The Morning Light*. New York: The Beechhurst Press, 1952.

———. *The Sun at Noon*. New York: The Beechhurst Press, 1955.

———. *Between Day and Dark*. New York: Thomas Yoseloff, Ltd., A. S. Barnes and Company, 1959.

———. *The Bitter Spring*. London, New York: Thomas Yoseloff Ltd., A. S. Barnes and Company, 1961.

———. *Memory of Autumn*. New York, London: Thomas Yoseloff Ltd., 1968.

Antin, Mary. *The Promised Land*. Boston and New York: Houghton Mifflin Company, 1912.

Bellow, Saul. *The Dangling Man*. New York: The Vanguard Press, Inc., 1944.

———. *The Victim*. New York: The Vanguard Press, Inc., 1947.

———. *Seize the Day*. New York: Viking Press, 1956.

255

Blankfort, Michael. *The Strong Hand*. Boston: Little, Brown and Company, 1956.

————. *The Juggler*. Boston: Little, Brown and Company, 1952.

————. *Behold the Fire*. New York: An-Nal World Book, published by the New American Library, 1965.

Brinig, Myron. *Singermann*. New York: Farrar and Rinehart, 1929.

————. *This Man Is My Brother*. New York: Farrar and Rinehart, 1932.

Cahan, Abraham. *The Rise of David Levinsky*. New York: Harper and Brothers, 1917.

Denker, Henry. *My Son the Lawyer*. New York: Thomas W. Crowell, 1950.

Ferber, Edna. *A Peculiar Treasure*. New York: Doubleday, Doran and Co., 1939.

————. *Fannie Herself*. New York: The Literary Guild, 1917.

Gold, Michael. *Jews Without Money*. New York: H. Liveright, 1930.

Halper, Albert. *The Golden Watch*. New York: Henry Holt and Company, 1953.

————. *Sons of the Fathers*. New York: Harper's Publisher, 1940.

Hecht, Ben. *A Jew in Love*. New York: Grosset and Dunlap, 1931.

Katkov, Norman. *Eagle at My Eye*. Garden City, New York: Doubleday and Co., Inc., 1948.

Kaufmann, Myron S. *Remember Me to God*. New York: J. B. Lippincott Co., 1957.

Kazin, Alfred. *A Walker in the City*. New York: Harcourt, Brace and Company, 1951.

Kemelman, Harry. *Friday the Rabbi Slept Late*. New York: Crown Publishers, 1964.

————. *Saturday the Rabbi Went Hungry*. New York: Crown Publishers, 1966.

————. *Sunday the Rabbi Stayed Home.* New York: G. P. Putnam's Sons, 1969.

Levenson, Sam. *Everything But Money.* New York: Simon and Schuster, 1966.

Levin, Meyer. *The Old Bunch.* New York: Citadel Press, 1937.

————. *In Search.* Paris: Author's Press, 1950. (An Autobiography)

————. *The Stronghold.* New York: Simon and Schuster, 1965.

————. *The Fanatic.* New York: Simon and Schuster, 1963.

Lewisohn, Ludwig. *The Island Within.* New York: Harper and Brothers, The Modern Library, 1940.

————. *Upstream.* New York: Barney, Boni and Liveright, 1922.

Mailer, Norman. *The Naked and the Dead.* New York: Rinehart and Co., 1948.

Malamud, Bernard. *The First Seven Years.* In *Malamud Reder.* (Collected Stories). New York: Farrar, Straus Co., 1967.

————. *The Jew Bird.* In *Malamud Reder* (Collected Stories). New York: Farrar, Straus Co., 1967.

Ornitz, Samuel B. *Haunch, Paunch and Jowl.* New York: Boni and Liveright, 1923.

Potok, Chaim. *The Chosen.* New York: Simon and Schuster, 1967.

————. *The Promise.* New York: Knopf, 1969.

Roth, Henry. *Call It Sleep.* In *A Golden Treasury of Jewish Literature,* edited by Leo W. Schwarz. New York: Rinehart & Company, Inc., 1937.

Roth, Philip. *Goodbye Columbus.* Boston: Houghton Mifflin, 1959.

————. *Portnoy's Complaint.* New York: Random House, 1967.

Rosenberg, Ethel. *Go Fight City Hall.* New York: Simon and Schuster, 1949.

Schulberg, Budd. *What Makes Sammy Run?* New York: The Modern Library, 1952.

Sinclair, Joe. *Wasteland.* New York: Harper and Brothers, 1946.

Suhl, Yuri. *One Foot in America.* New York: The Macmillan Co., 1950.

———. *Cowboy on a Modern Horse.* New York: The Macmillan Co., 1953.

Tarr, Herbert. *Heaven Help Us.* New York: Random House, Inc., 1968.

Weidman, Jerome. *In The Enemy Camp.* New York: Random House, Inc., 1958.

Wouk, Herman. *The Caine Mutiny.* Garden City, New York: Doubleday, 1951.

———. *Marjorie Morningstar.* New York: Doubleday, 1955.

Zunser, Miriam Shomer. *Yesterday.* New York: Stackpole Sons, Publishers, 1939.

B.   *Novels and Short Stories in Yiddish*

Asch, Sholem. "Chaim Lederer's Return." In *Three Novels.* Translated by Elsa Krauch. New York: G. P. Putnam's Sons, 1938.

———. *East River.* New York: G. P. Putnam's Sons, 1938.

———. *The Mother.* Translated by Elsa Krauch. New York: G. P. Putnam's Sons, 1937.

———. "Uncle Moses." In *Three Novels.* Translated by Elsa Krauch. New York: G. P. Putnam's Sons, 1938.

Friedland, I. *Roye Erd* (Virgin Soil). Los Angeles: Friedland Buch Committee, 1949.

Ignatov, David. In *Kessel-Grub.* New York: Farlag America, 1920.

Kobrin, Leon. *Ore die Bord.* New York: Forward Association, 1918.

Leivick, H. *Shmates* (Rags). Vilno: B. Klezkin, 1928. (A Play.)

Mendele, Mocher Sforim. *The Nag.* Translated by Moshe Spiegel. New York: Beechhurst Press, 1955.

Opatoshu, Joseph. *Di Tenzerin* (The Dancer). Wilno: Farlag fun B. Klezkin, 1938.

———. "Lynching." In *Lynching and Other Stories.* Wilno: Farlag B. Klezkin, 1927.

————. *Hebrew*. Wilno: Farlag B. Klezkin, 1920.

Peretz, Y. L. *Four Generations—Four Wills*. Translated and edited by Sol Liptzin. New York: Yivo, 1947.

————. In *Mein Vinkele*. Collected Works of Y. L. Peretz. vol. 13. New York: Farlag "Yiddish," 1920.

Pinski, David. *The Generations of Noah Edon*. New York: The Macaulay Company, 1931.

Raboy, Isaac. *Herr Goldenberg*. New York: Farlag America, 1918.

————. *New England*. New York: Farlag America, 1918.

Rosenfeld, Morris. "My Son" (a poem). In *Jewish Life* (May 1953), p. 15.

Schwartz, I. J. *Kentucky*. New York: Verlag M. N. Meisel, 1925.

Sholom Aleichem. *Adventures of Mottel Peisy, the Cantor's Son*. Translated by Tamara Kohana. New York: Henry Schuman, 1953.

C. Hebrew Novels and Short Stories

Halkin, Simon. *Yechiel Ha-hagri*. New York: Hebrew Publishing Co., 1913.

————. *Ad Mashber*. New York: Hebrew Publishing Co., 1929.

Isaacs, Bernard. *Bein Shnei Olomot* (Between Two Worlds). New York: Ogen. Published by Histradruth Ivrith of America, 1949.

————. "Haye-Mehager Echod" (The Life of One Immigrant). *Hed Ha-Kvutzah*. (Hebrew) Detroit: Kvutzah Ivrith, 1949.

Wallenrod, Reuben. *B'ein Dor* (A Lost Generation). Tel Aviv: Am Oved Publishing Co., 1954.

————. Ki *Panah Yom* (The Day's Decline). In *Bein Homot New York*. Jerusalem: Bialik Institute, 1953.

II. SECONDARY SOURCES

A. Books

Barnes, Harry Elmer. *Society in Transition*. 2nd. ed. New York: Prentice Hall, Inc., 1952.

Baron, Salo W. "The Modern Age." In *Great Ages and Ideas of the Jewish People,* edited by Leo W. Schwartz. New York: Random House, Inc., 1965.

Bialik, H. N. "The City of Slaughter" (translated from Hebrew). In Abraham M. Klein's *Complete Poetic Works of Hayim Nachman Bialik*. New York: The Histradruth Ivrith of America, Inc., 1948, pp. 129 f.

Birmingham, Stephan. *Our Crowd*. New York: Harper and Row, 1967.

Brandeis, Louis D. *Brandeis on Zionism*. A Collection of Addresses. Washington, D. C.: The Zionist Organization of America, 1942.

Cahnman, Werner J. *Intermarriage and Jewish Life in America*. A Symposium. New York: Herzl Press and Jewish Reconstruction Press, 1963.

Davis, Moshe. *The Emergence of Conservative Judaism*. Philadelphia: The Jewish Publication Society of America, 1963–5723.

———. *Darkel Ha-yahaduth B'America* (Jewish Religious Life and Institutions in America). Tel Aviv: Masadah Publishing House, 1963. In Hebrew.

Eisenstadt, T. S. N. *The Absorption of Immigrants*. Glencoe, Ill.: The Free Press, 1955.

Erikson, Erik H. "The Problems of Ego Identity." In *Identity and Anxiety*. Edited by S. Vidich and Maurice Stein. Glencoe Ill.: The Free Press, 1960.

Friedlander, Israel. Quoted in *Sabbath and Festival Prayer Book*. New York: New York Rabbinical Assembly of America, 1946.

Finkelstein, Louis. *The Jews: Their History, Culture and Religion*. New York: Harper and Brothers, 1950.

Friedman, Theodore, and Gordis, Robert, eds. *Jewish Life in America*. New York: Horizon Press, 1955.

Ginzberg, Eli. *Agenda for American Jews*. New York: King's Crown Press, Columbia University, 1950.

Goldberg, Marie Waife. *My Father, Sholom Aleichem*. New York: Simon and Schuster, 1968.

Goldstein, Sidney, and Goldschneider, Calvin. *Jewish Americans: Three Generations in a Jewish Community*. Englewood Cliffs, N.J.: Prentice Hall, Inc., 1968.

Goldstein, Phillip R. *Centers in My Life* (on the Jewish Center Movement). New York: Bloch Publishing Co., Inc., 1964.

Gordis, Robert. *The Jew Faces a New World*. New York: Behrman's Book House, 1941.

———. *Judaism for the Modern Age*. New York: Farrar, Strauss and Cudahy, 1955.

Gordon, Albert. *Jews in Transition*. Minneapolis: University of Minneapolis Press, 1949.

———. *Intermarriage: Interfaith, Interracial, Inter-Ethnic*. Boston: Beacon Press, 1964.

Hansen, Marcus L. *The Problems of the Third Generation Immigrant*. Rock Island, Ill.: Augustana Historical Society, 1955.

Herberg, Will. *Protestant, Catholic, Jew*. New York: Doubleday, 1955.

Hertz, Richard C. *The American Jew in Search of Himself*. New York: Bloch Publishing Co., 1962.

Hoffman, B. *Fifty Years of the Cloakmakers Union*. New York: Laub Publishing Co., 1948.

Janowsky, Oscar I. *The JWB Survey*. New York: The Dial Press, 1948.

———. *The American Jew*. Philadelphia: The Jewish Publication Society, 1964.

Kaplan, Mordecai M. *Judaism as a Civilization*. New York: The Macmillan Co., 1934.

————. *Judaism in Transition.* New York: Behrman's Jewish Book House, 1941.

————. *The Future of the American Jew.* New York: The Macmillan Co., 1948.

Karpf, Maurice J. *Jewish Community Organization in the United States.* New York: The Bloch Publishing Co.

Lazarus, Emma. "The New Colossus." In *A Second Treasury of the Familiar.* New York: The Macmillan Co., 1950.

Lewin, Kurt. *Resolving Social Conflict.* Edited by Gertrude Weiss Lewin. New York: Harper and Brothers, 1948.

Liptzin, Sol. *Y. L. Peretz.* New York: Yivo, 1947.

————. *Generations of Decision.* New York: Block Publishing Co., 1958.

————. *The Maturing of Yiddish Literature.* New York: Jonathan David Publishers, 1970.

Mace, David R. *Hebrew Marriage.* New York: Philosophical Library, 1953.

Niger-Charney, Samuel. *Derzeilers un romanisten* (Novelists and Romancers). New York: Bicher Varlag, Central Yiddish Culture Organization, 1946.

Park, Robert E. *The Immigrant Press and Its Control.* New York, London: Harper and Brothers, Publishers, 1922.

Pilch, Judah. *Fate and Faith.* New York: Published for the American Association for Jewish Education by Bloch Publishing Co., 1963.

Poll, Solomon. *The Hasidic Community of Williamsburg.* New York: Schocken Books, 1969.

Raisin, Jacob S. *Haskalah Movement in Russia.* Philadelphia: The Jewish Publication Society of America, 1913.

Ribalow, Harold U. *This Land, These People.* New York: The Beechhurst Press, 1950.

Rogoff, Harry. *An East Side Epic.* New York: The Vanguard Press, 1930.

Rolvaag, O. R. *Their Fathers' God.* New York: Harper and Brothers, 1931.

Ruppin, Arthur. *The Jewish Fate and Future.* London: The Macmillan Co. Ltd., 1940.

——. *The Jews in the Modern World.* New York: The Macmillan Co., 1934.

Samuel, Maurice. *The Prince of the Ghetto.* New York: P. Knopf, 1948.

——. *The World of Sholom Aleichem.* New York: P. Knopf, 1943.

——. *In Praise of Yiddish.* New York: Cowles Book Co., Inc., 1971.

Schulman, Elias. *Gesshichte Fun der Yiddisher Literatur in America, 1800–1870.* New York: Biderman, 1943.

Sherman, Charles B. *The Jew Within American Society.* Detroit: Wayne State University Press, 1961.

Sklare, Marshall, ed. *The Jews: Social Patterns of an American Group.* Glencoe, Ill.: The Free Press, 1958.

Sklare, Marshall, and Greenblum, Joseph. *Jewish Identity on the Suburban Frontier.* vol. 1. New York: Basic Books, Inc., 1967.

Shulman, Charles E. *What It Means to be a Jew.* New York: Crown Publishers, Inc., 1960.

Stern, Harry Joshua. *Martyrdom and Miracle.* New York: Bloch Publishing Co., 1950.

Steinberg, Milton. *A Partisan Guide to the Jewish Problem.* New York: Bobbs, Merrill Co., 1945.

Stonequist, Everett. *The Marginal Man—A Study in Personality and Culture Conflict.* New York: Charles Scribner and Sons, 1937.

Waxman, Mordecai. *Tradition and Change: The Development of Conservative Judaism.* New York: The Burning Book Press, 1958.

Waxman, Meyer. *History of Jewish Literature.* 5 vols. New York: Thomas Yoseloff, 1960.

Wirth, Louis. *The Ghetto.* Chicago: The University of Chicago Press, 1929.

————. *Round Table.* University of Chicago (Jan. 28, 1940), p. 5.

Wischnitzer, Mark. *To Dwell in Safety.* Philadelphia: The Jewish Publication Society of America, 1948.

Zangvill, Israel. *The Melting Pot.* New York: The Macmillan Co., 1907.

B. Encyclopedias, Year Books, Newspapers, and Periodicals

Ackerman, Walter I. "Jewish Education: For What?" *American Jewish Year Book.* vol. 70. New York: The American Jewish Committee; Phila.: The Jewish Publication Society, 1969, p. 40.

Adler, Rabbi Morris. "The Rabbi." *Jewish Heritage.* vol. 8, no. 4. Published by B'nai B'rith Adult Jewish Education (Spring 1966), p. 7.

Barron, M. L. "The Incidence of Jewish Intermarriage in Europe and America." *American Sociological Review* (Feb. 1946).

Blankfort, Michael. (Quoted by Harold U. Ribalow). "American Jewish Writers and their Judaism." *Judaism* (Fall 1954): p. 423.

Bloom, Solomon F. "The Saga of America's Russian Jews." *Commentary* (Feb. 1956), p. 5.

Bogardus, Emory S. "Social Distance in Poetry." *Sociology and Social Research* 36 (Sept.-Oct. 1951): 40–47.

————. "Cultural Pluralism and Acculturation." *Sociology and Social Research* 34 (Dec. 1949): 126.

Bokser, Ben Zion. "The Ketubah." *The Jewish Frontier* (Dec. 1954).

Chenkin, Alvin, ed. *The American Jewish Year Book.* vol. 70. New York: The American Jewish Committee; Philadelphia: The Jewish Publication Society of America, 1969, p. 260.

Chipkin, Israel S. *Jewish Education* 27, no. 1 (Fall 1956): 15.

Cohen, Bernard. "Jewish Welfare Institutions." *B'nai Brith Messenger.* (Dec. 3, Dec. 10, Dec. 27, 1965).

————. "The Big Three." 1. "Mendele." *B'nai Brith Messenger* (Jan. 7, 1966).

————. 2. "Sholom Aleichem." *B'nai Brith Messenger* (Jan. 14, 1966).

————. 3. "Yitzhok Leibush Peretz." *B'nai Brith Messenger* (Jan. 21, 1966).

————. "Intermarriage and Conversion." *B'nai Brith Messenger* (April 28, 1967).

Cooley, Charles H. "The Roots of Social Knowledge." *American Journal of Sociology.* vol. 32 (1926–27) : 60.

Duker, Abraham. "On Religious Trends in American Jewish Life." In *Yivo Annual of Jewish Social Science."* New York: Yiddish Scientific Institute, 1940.

————. "Achievements of the Yiddish Press." In *The Day* (Dec. 25, 1949).

Dushkin, Alexander M. "Changing Conception of Community Responsibility in Jewish Education." *Jewish Education,* 26, no. 3 (Spring 1956) : 11.

Fairchild, Henry Pratt. "Accommodation." *Dictionary of Sociology.* Ames, Iowa: Little, Adams and Co., 1955.

Glazer, Nathan. "Social Characteristics of American Jews." *American Jewish Year Book.* vol. 56. Philadelphia: Jewish Publication Society of America, 1955.

————. "The Alienation of Modern Man." *Commentary* 3, no. 4 (April 1947).

Greenberg, Simon. "Conservative Judaism." *Living Schools of Religion,* edited by Fern Vergilius. Student Outline Series. Ames, Iowa: Littlefield, Adams and Co., 1956.

Greenfield, Judith. "Jews in the Clothing Industry." *Yivo Annual of Jewish Social Science* (1947–48).

Hansen, Marcus. "The Problem of the Third Generation Immigrant." *Commentary* 14 (1952) : 492.

Herberg, Will. "The Jewish Labor Movement in the U.S." *American Jewish Yearbook.* vol. 53. New York: The Jewish Publication Society of America, 1952.

Hertzberg, Arthur. "The Changing American Rabbinate." *Mid-*

stream 12, no. 1 published by the Theodor Herzl Foundation (Jan. 1966), pp. 16–29.

Inglis, Ruth A. "An Objective Approach to the Relationship between Fiction and Society." *American Sociological Review* 3 (Aug. 1938) : 526–33.

Gans, Herbert J. "Progress of a Suburban Jewish community." *Commentary* 23, no. 2 (Feb. 1957) : 113–22.

Kaplan, Mordecai M. "When Will American Judaism Be Born?" *The Reconstructionist* 14 (Nov. 26, 1948) : 15.

———. "The Principles of Reconstructionism," *The Reconstructionist* 21, no. 3 (March 18, 1955), p. 22.

Knox, Israel. "Reform Judaism Re-Appraises Its Way of Life." *Commentary* 18, no. 6 (Dec. 1954) : 504–11.

Kohn, Hans. "Zionism." *Encyclopedia of the Social Sciences.* vol. 15. New York: The Macmillan Co., 1935.

Lang, Harry. "50 Years of Trade Unionism." *Yiddisher Kemfer* 37, no. 1 (March 23, 1956) : 126–30.

Lestchinsky, Jacob. "The Socio-economic Physiognomy of Jewish Immigration to the United States." *Yivo Annual of Jewish Social Science,* vol. 9. Edited by Koppel S. Pinson. New York: Yivo, 1954, p. 377.

———. "Economic and Social Development of American Jewry." *Jewish Past and Present.* vol. 4. New York: Jewish Encyclopedia Handbook, Inc., 1955, p. 56.

Lewin, Kurt. "Psychological Problems in Jewish Education." New York: *Jewish Social Service Quarterly* 23 (March 1947) : 271

Liebman, Charles S. "A Sociological Analysis of Contemporary Orthodoxy." *Judaism.* vol. 13, no. 3 (Summer 1964).

Liptzin, Sol. "News and Views" (Guest Column). *The Day-Journal* (Oct. 15, 1952), p. 1.

Maller, Julius B. "The Role of Education in Jewish History." *The Jews.* vol. 2. Edited by Louis Finkelstein. New York: Harper and Brothers, Publishers, 1949.

Niger, S. "Yitzhok Leibush Peretz." *American Jewish Yearbook,* 1953.

Noble, Shlomo. "The Image of the American Jew." *Yivo Annual of Jewish Social Science.* vol. 9 New York: Yiddish Scientific Institute, 1954.

Park, Robert E. "Human Migration and the Marginal Man." *American Journal of Sociology* 33 (May 1928) : 881–92.

Polish, Rabbi David. "A Communal Day School." *Beth Emet-the Free Synagogue.* In *Bulletin* 20, no. 9. Evanston, Ill. (Dec. 30, 1968) : 1.

Rosenthal, Erich. "Studies of Intermarriage in the United States." *American Jewish Yearbook.* vol. 64 New York: American Jewish Committee; Philadelphia: Jewish Publication Society, 1963.

Rosmarin, Trude Weiss. "Are Day Schools the Answer?" *Congress Weekly* 15, no. 20 (May 28, 1948) : 6–9.

Rosenberg, Bertram. "Go to Suburbia, Young Man." *The Reconstructionist* 22, no. 3 (March 23, 1956) : 6–9.

Ruffman, Louis L. "Trends in Elementary Education." *Congress Weekly* 21, no. 12 (1954).

———. "The Survey of Jewish Education in New York City." *Jewish Education* 27, no. 1 (Fall 1956) : 15.

Schlossberg, Joseph. "Two Generations of Jewish Labor in America." *Zukunft* 5 (May-June 1947) : 330–33.

Sherman, Bezalel. "Secularism and Religion in the Jewish Labor Movement." In *Jewish Life in America,* edited by Theodore Friedman and Robert Gordis. New York: Horizon Press, 1955), pp. 109–27.

Shulman, Charles E. "Trends in Reform Judaism." *Congress Weekly* 22, no. 28 (Oct. 24, 1955).

———. "The Role of the American Rabbi." *Jewish Digest* (Houston, Texas) 1, no. 11 (Aug. 1956) : 5.

Sklare, Marshall. "Intermarriage and Jewish Survival." *Commentary* (March 1970).

Smolar, Boris. "Between You and Me." *California Jewish Voice* (Sept. 23, 1955), p. 4.

Soboloff, Isadore. "The Future of Organized Jewish Community Life." *The Day,* April 8, 1955, p. 8.

Starkman, Moshe. "70 Year Jubilee of the Yiddish Daily Press." *Jewish Book Annual, 1951–1952.* vol 10. New York: Jewish Book Council of America, 1952.

Syrkin, Marie. "The Cultural Scene: Literary Expression." In *The American Jew,* edited by Oscar L. Janowsky. New York, London: Harper and Brothers, Publishers, 1942.

———. "Jewish Awareness in American Literature." In *The American Jew: A Reappraisal,* edited by Oscar J. I. Janowsky. Philadelphia: The Jewish Publication Society of America, 1964, pp. 211–33.

Wessel, Bessie Bloom. "Ethnic Family Patterns; The American Jewish Family." *The American Journal of Sociology* 53 (May 1948).

Wirth, Louis. "Urbanism as a Way of Life." *American Journal of Sociology* (July 1938), pp. 1–24.

———. "Education for Survival." *American Journal of Sociology* 48 (May 1943): 682 f.

C. Selected Related Studies

Barron, Milton L. *People Who Intermarry.* Syracuse: Syracuse University Press, 1946.

Blumenfield, Samuel M. *Chevrah V'chinuch B'yahaduth* (Society and Education in Jewry). Jerusalem: (Hebrew) M. Newman, 1966.

Blumer, Herbert. "Collective Behavior"—Part IV of New Outline of the *Principles of Sociology.* Edited by Alfred McClung Lee. New York: Barnes and Noble, Inc., 1946.

Bogardus, Emory S. *Contemporary Sociology.* Los Angeles: University of Southern California Press, 1931.

———. *Sociology.* New York: Macmillan Co., 1943.

———. *Essentials of Americanization.* Los Angeles: University of Southern California Press, 1919.

Bogen, Boris. *Jewish Philanthropy.* New York: The Macmillan Co., 1917.

Burgess, Ernest, and Locke, Harvey. The Family: *From Institu-*

tion to Companionship. New York: The American Book Co., 1945.

Case, Clarence M. *Social Process and Human Progress.* New York: Harcourt, Brace and Company, 1931.

Cohen, Morris Raphael. *Reflection of a Wandering Jew.* Glencoe, Ill.: The Free Press, 1950.

Cohen, Israel. *Jewish Life in Modern Times.* New York: Dodd, Mead and Company, 1914.

Cohon, Samuel S. *Judaism, A Way of Life.* Cincinnati: The Union of American Hebrew Congregations, 1948.

Commager, Henry S. *The American Mind.* New Haven: Yale University Press, 1950.

Daiches, David. *Literature and Society.* London: Victor Gollancz, 1938.

Dushkin, Alexander M. *Jewish Education in New York City.* New York: Bureau of Jewish Education, 1918.

Glazer, Nathan, and Moynihan, Daniel Patrick. *Beyond the Melting Pot.* Cambridge, Mass.: The M. I. I. Press, 1963.

Goodsell, Willystin. *A History of the Family as a Social and Educational Institution.* New York: The Macmillan Co., 1927.

Gordon, Milton M. *Assimilation in American Life.* New York: Oxford University Press, 1950.

Handlin, Oscar. *Adventure in Freedom.* New York: McGraw-Hill Book Co., 1954.

Jones, Marshall E. *Basic Sociological Principles.* Boston: Ginn and Company, 1949.

Kramer and Leventman. *Children of the Guilded Ghetto.* New Haven: Yale University Press, 1961.

Learsi, Rufus. *The Jews in America: A History.* Cleveland and New York: The World Publishing Co., 1954.

Leftwich, Joseph. *Israel Zangwill.* New York: Thomas Yoseloff, 1957.

Lurie, Harry L. *A Heritage Affirmed: The Jewish Federation Movement in America.* Philadelphia: The Jewish Publication Society of America, 1961.

Marcus, Jacob Reader. *Early American Jewry*. Philadelphia: The Jewish Publication Society, 1951.

McDonagh, Edward C., and Richards, Eugene S. *Ethnic Relations in the United States*. New York: Appleton-Century-Crofts, Inc., 1953.

Merril, Frances E. *Social Disorganization*. New York: Harper & Brothers, 1950.

Moore, George Foote. *Judaism*. vol. 11. Cambridge: Harvard University Press, 1927.

Newmeyer, Martin H. *Social Problems and the Changing Society*. New York: D. Van Nostrand Co., Inc., 1953.

Nordskog, John Eric; McDonagh, Edward C.; and Vincent, Melvin J. *Analyzing Social Problems*. New York: The Dryden Press, 1950.

Ogburn, William F., and Nimkoff, M. F. *Technology and the Changing Family*. Boston, New York: Houghton, Mifflin Co., 1955.

Plaut, W. Gunther. *The Growth of Reform Judaism*. New York: The World Union for Progressive Judaism, Ltd., 1965.

Ross, Edward Alsworth. *Social Control*. New York: Macmillan Co., 1912.

Shriver, W. P. "Immigrant Forces" in Dr. Mordecai Soltes, *The Yiddish Press, An Americanization Agency*. New York: Teacher's College, Columbia University, 1925.

Thomas, W. I., and Znaniecki, Florian. *The Polish Peasant in Europe and America*. New York: Alfred Knopf, 1917.

Vincent, Melvin. *Social Aspects of Fiction and Drama*. Syllabus. Los Angeles: University of Southern California, 1953.

Weber, Max. *Ancient Judaism*. Glencoe, Ill.: The Free Press, 1952.

Young, Pauline V. *The Pilgrims of Russian Town*. Chicago: The University of Chicago Press, 1932.

Znaniecki, Florian. *The Method of Sociology*. New York: Farrar and Rinehart, Inc., 1934.

D. *Unpublished Materials*

Bressler, M. "Jewish Behavior Patterns as Exemplified in Wm. I. Thomas's Unfinished Study of the *Bintel Brief*. Ph.D. dissertation, University of Pennsylvania, 1952.

Chen, Wen-Hui Chung. "Changing Socio-Cultural Patterns of the Chinese Community in Los Angeles." Ph.D. dissertation, University of Southern California, Los Angeles, 1952.

Cohen, Bernard. "Sociological Aspects in the Welfare Activities Among American Jews with Special Reference to Welfare Activities in Los Angeles." Master's thesis, University of Southern California, Los Angeles, 1949.

Goldstein, Philip Reuben. "Social Aspects of the Jewish Colonies of South Jersey." Ph.D. dissertation, University of Pennsylvania, 1921.

Larsen, Cecil Evva. "Attitudes toward Social Problems in Norwegian Fiction and Drama from 1870 to 1940." Ph.D. dissertation, University of Southern California, 1948.

E. *Sacred Literature*

The Holy Scriptures According to the Masoretic Text. A New Translation. Philadelphia: The Jewish Publication Society of America, 1956–5716.

The Talmud. New York: Pardes Publishing House, Inc., n.d.
Tractat Shabbath. Tom 2.
Tractat Yebamoth. Tom 10.
Tractat Ketubath. Tom 11.
Tractat Nedarim. Tom 12.
Tractat Gittin. Tom 13.
Tractat Hulin. Tom 25.
Tractat Kidushin. Tom 14.
Tractat Abada Zarah. Tom 20.

The Codes of Jewish Law: Eben Haezer. New York: Pardes Publishing House, Inc., n.d.

Index

273

Rosenfeld, Isaac, 216
Rosenfeld, Morris, 160, 232
Rosenthal, Erich, 126
Rosmarin, Trude Weiss, 166, 207, 225
Ross, Edward Alsworth, 27–28
Roth, Henry, 102, 161–62
Roth, Philip, 103, 220, 224–26
Roye Erd, 181
Rudoy, Pinchos, 233
Ruffman, Louis L., 209
Rukeyser, Muriel, 216
Ruppin, Arthur, 53, 124
Russia: the immigrants from, 50; pogroms in, 82; revolution in, 55
Ruth, Book of, 106

Sabbath, 112
Sabbath and Festival Prayer Book, 239
Samuel, Maurice, 43n., 177, 233, 243
Sanhedrin (the Jewish High Court), 155
Sarahson, K. Zevi, 71
Saturday the Rabbi Went Hungry, 201
Schechter, Solomon, 144–45
Schneider, Isidor, 102
Schools: types of Jewish, 163; Talmud Torah, 163; Congregational School, 164; Yiddish secular schools, 164–65; all-day schools, 165–66
Schulberg, Budd, 103, 213–14
Schwarts, Arnold, 127
Schwartz, Delmore, 216
Schwartz, I. J., 181, 232
Seize the Day, 221
Self-hatred, 220
Septuaginta, 35
Sex: Judaism's attitude toward, 108
Sex in Civilization, 108
Shammai (school of Shammai), 120

Shapiro, Karl, 219
Shapiro, Lamed, 232
Sherman, Charles Bezalel, 208
Shift to working class, 63. *See also* Occupational change
Shlossberg, Joseph, 187
Shmates, 119
Sholem Aleichem, 45, 57, 232–33, 245
Shulman, Rabbi Charles E., 139, 140, 231
Sign upon My Hand, A, 231
Silver, Abba Hillel Rabbi, 177
Simon ben Shotah, 155
Sinclair, Joe, 97
Sinclair, Upton, 29
Singer, Isaac Bashevis, 231–33
Singer, Jacob, 233
Singermann, 77–78, 93
Singer, Rabbi Sholom A., 200
Sklare, Marshall, 126–27
Smith, William Carlson, 69
Smolenskin, Peretz, 37
Sobeloff, Isidore, 193
Social Change, 33
Social change, 18; meaning of, 18; contrasted with cultural change and social mobility, 18; process of, 19; and literature, 27
Social distance: in poetry, 32
Social institutions: function of, 20, 21
Socialism, 174; and Jewish Labor movement, 182–83
Social mobility, 78–79
Social movement, 21; effects social change, 173
Soltes, Mordecai, 72
Sons of Zion: fraternal order of, 175
Sorokin, Pitrim A., 19, 32
Source material for study, 15; primary, 17; secondary, 18
Status, loss of, 63, 66
Steinbeck, John, 30
Steinberg, Milton, 101